What the reviewers said of the first edition of *The Plains of Camdeboo*:

'Every now and then a book comes out of the mass of written material poured out by thousands of writers which makes one pause, read, reflect and read again with renewed pleasure. Eve Palmer . . . has given to South Africa something of a shot in its literary arm.' *The Star*

'Here is a book which is a unique combination of history, natural history, autobiography and research in many fields . . . it is a celebration of the beauty of the Karoo.' *Sunday Times*

'This book, read in a wet Cape winter, made me almost intolerably homesick for the dry places of my country.' *Cape Times*

'Mens se grootste wens is dat daar stadigaan vir elke streek van ons land so 'n boek die lig sal sien, om die bekoring van lore en legende, van plant, dier en mens vir die toekoms te bewaar.' André Brink, *Rapport*

'Her unexaggerated clarity enhances her recording of the desert's wildness, chanciness, and danger, as well as her account of the fixing-up-the-landscape process . . . Because her work is devoted to what is particular and unique, any summary, or even description, of it is a bit of a misrepresentation.' *The New Yorker*

'*The Plains of Camdeboo* not only presents much of the age-old pageant of nature in a storied land, but exudes the triumph of the human spirit.' *Sydney Morning Herald*

'Eve Palmer writes about everything she observes with sympathy and humour . . . Her book is filled with the joy of life . . .

bones of dragons which vanished from the earth tens of millions of years ago and with tools used by Stone Age men, a world where one might come on a cave painting, a new genus of spider, a plant unknown to botany, or the missing link itself.' *Irish Times*

'*The Plains of Camdeboo* is like one of those delightful campfire conversations which drag late into the night but which, regrettably, are over too soon.' *Sunday Tribune*

'Her sense of wonder and her affectionate respect for both living and extinct creatures show how deeply white South Africans can be involved with the land in a life-enriching, non-political way.' William Plomer, *Sunday Telegraph*

THE PLAINS OF CAMDEBOO

THE PLAINS OF CAMDEBOO

Eve Palmer

Jonathan Ball Publishers
Johannesburg

First published in the United Kingdom in 1966 by
Collins, St James Place, London

Reprinted 1986 by
Lowry Publishers cc Johannesburg

This edition published in 1990 by
Jonathan Ball Publishers (Pty) Ltd
P O Box 33977
Jeppestown 2043

Reprinted 1993, 1997, 2001

ISBN 0 947464 31 X

Cover design by Michael Barnett, Johannesburg
Cover reproduction by RT Sparhams, Johannesburg

Typesetting and reproduction by NBD,
Drukkery Street, Goodwood, Western Cape

Contents

Foreword   xi
 1 Karoo   1
 2 Bushmen of the Sea   7
 3 The Yellow and the Brown   25
 4 The Forgotten Highway   40
 5 The Bushmen of the Veld   62
 6 The Beginning   80
 7 Stilettos and Almond Stones   102
 8 Vanished Kings   122
 9 They Drink the Wind   141
10 Twilight Souls   154
11 Cranemere's Bird   175
12 Birds of the Veld   186
13 Consider the Cobras   207
14 The Red Men   221
15 Evolution's Darlings   230
16 'Masters of Thirst'   242
17 The Galgenbosch   261
18 The Greatest of All   282
References   296
Index   305

List of illustrations

1. Map of the Plains of Camdeboo
2. Detailed map of Cranemere
3. Cranemere house today
4. Shearing time on Cranemere
5. Sowing oats in the cracks of the dam (*Author*)
6. Cranemere dam when full
7. The two Davids measuring thorns (*Author*)
8. Bread-baking on the farm (*Geoffrey Jenkins*)
9. William Burchell (*Africana Museum, Johannesburg*)
10. Interior of Burchell's wagon (*Gubbins Library, University of the Witwatersrand*)
11. Robert and Mary Moffat (*from* Robert Moffat: Pioneer in Africa *by Cecil Northcott*)
12. An ox-wagon of the plains (*Africana Museum, Johannesburg*)
13. William Cornwallis Harris (*Africana Museum, Johannesburg*)
14. Cornwallis Harris's painting of gemsbok (*Africana Museum, Johannesburg*)
15. A Bushman (*Africana Museum, Johannesburg*)
16. David in a Bushman's house (*Author*)
17. Cave painting—Bushman's dance (*traced by Dick Findlay*)
18. Bushman painting of a bushbuck (*Dick Findlay*)
19. Dr Robert Broom (*J. P. Vorster*)
20. Dr Rubidge with the skull of Platycyclops (*David Jenkins*)
21. Fossil skeleton of Dicynodon (*Geoffrey Jenkins*)
22. Dr Rubidge with the skull of *Milleretta rubidgei* (*Geoffrey Jenkins*)
23. James Kitching and the bone stiletto (*Geoffrey Jenkins*)
24. The Mountain Dig (*Author*)
25. The skull of *Milleretta rubidgei;* the hand of *Leavachia duvenhagei;* Primitive Man's pestle and mortar; Early Stone Age hand-axe (*from paintings by Dick Findlay*)
26. Black wildebeest (*from a painting by Dick Findlay*)

27. Cape lion (*Dick Findlay*)
28. Mountain zebra
29. Quagga (*Africana Museum, Johannesburg*)
30. Kudu (SATOUR)
31. Herd of springbuck (SATOUR)
32. Baboon and baby (SATOUR)
33. Vervet monkey and baby (*S.A. Dept. of Information*)
34. Lynx (*Dick Wolff*)
35. Meerkats (*Dick Wolff*)
36. Ground squirrels (*S.A. Dept. of Information*)
37. Elephant shrew (*John Visser*)
38. Black-backed jackal (*National Zoological Gardens*)
39. Maanhaarjakkals (*Dick Wolff*)
40. Karoo porcupine (*Herbert Lang, by courtesy of the National Zoological Gardens*)
41. Ant-bear (*Dr R. Bigalke, by courtesy of the National Zoological Gardens*)
42. Cape eagle owl (*Transvaal Museum Library*); Wattled starling (*Transvaal Museum Library*); Cape pelican (*Transvaal Museum Library*)
43. Blue crane (*National Parks Board*)
44. Ostrich chick (*National Parks Board*)
45. Spoonbills
46. Secretary bird (*Dr C. J. Uys*)
47. Mountain tortoise (*Transvaal Museum*)
48. Water tortoise (*Transvaal Museum*)
49. Cape skink (*Transvaal Museum*)
50. Rock leguaan (*Chris Pisart*)
51. Blinkogie (*Transvaal Museum*)
52. Bull-frog (*Transvaal Museum*)
53. Cape cobra (*John Visser*)
54. Brown locust (*J. C. Faure*)
55. Solpuga female (*from a drawing by Dr R. F. Lawrence*)
56. David measuring the stem of a pachypodium (*J. H. de la Rey*)
57. Sita examining a euphorbia (*Author*)
58. The Galgenbosch

Foreword

The Plains of Camdeboo is not the story of the Palmer family, although they impinge upon it at times.

It is the story of Cranemere, a farm – to some a ranch – twenty thousand acres in area, on a great plain towards the southern tip of Africa. This is a countryside either completely overlooked or greatly slandered: few people visit it and none has ever written of it.

The Palmers have now been here for one hundred and six years.

This book was planned when I was a child. It crystallized years ago when a prominent scientist said of our piece of the Karoo, 'It is beyond anybody's orbit', and stung me into action.

It is twenty years since the book was first published.

Since that time many people have asked me two questions about Cranemere. Are the Palmers still there and is it still a happy farm? The answer to both is yes.

Maurice and Sita, who ran Cranemere when the book was written, are no longer there permanently. When Alex, their son, married they moved to their mountain farm, The Fountains, nearby, and later to Graaff-Reinet, but they visit Cranemere often, and when Alex and his wife are away Maurice and Sita come back to run things, to look after the children, and to enjoy the abundant pleasures. Perhaps for them drought has lost a little of its sting.

Certainly the biggest events in the life of Cranemere for this twenty years have been Alex's marriage and Maurice and Sita's departure. Alex, at the University of Cape Town, met (on a blind date) a student from Stellenbosch University, Marianne Linde, daughter of an Afrikaans-speaking Free State farmer. I do not know with what language Alex courted, but the result was entirely satisfactory. (When Marianne's father heard they were engaged, he cried out, 'Die Karoo. My arme kind! But you will starve!') – words which will go down through Cranemere history.

All the Palmer wives have brought their own thing to Crane-mere. Marianne, besides the solid virtues necessary to a farmer's wife, has brought her own brand of charisma and sparkle which the family adores.

As for the other young people of the Cranemere of 1966, Mary, Alex's sister, married John Roberts and they live in Cape Town. David 'Pretoria', our son, married Denise Henderson and they now live in Natal. Patrick Carfax, Sita's nephew, married Amelia de Stefano, and they are off to Australia.

There is now a new crop of Cranemere children. They are Lindelize, Bernadette and Elizabeth Sita, Alex and Marianne's children; Jacqueline, Deborah and Linda, who are Mary and John's; and Dylan, Taryn and Hayley, who belong to David and Denise. Sometimes they converge on the farm and holiday together. Last time David Konos and his wife were there from Port Elizabeth with their brood of comely children – one looked at me with the glint of mischief his father had had twenty-five years before when the two Davids were like 'two peas in one pod'.

Konos and his sister, Tingy, and some of their children and grandchildren are still on Cranemere. They are among the pleasures of returning to the farm.

Iris, who was in Australia when the book was written, is now living in South Africa with her husband Cyril Knight.

Sita made a new museum before she left Cranemere, and it is now housed in the rondavel in which she and Maurice lived when they were newly married. This is more than a family rec-ord, but houses treasures, fossil and others, from the country around, and is now one of the district's sights. It was blessed by the Bishop of London!

A time for Maurice and Sita of burning interest and excite-ment was the search for oil on Cranemere from the years 1966 to 1969 – when the Karoo was a hunting ground for oil – and the coming of the Oil Rig. Sita's letters overflowed with the drama of it all.

In February and March 1967 the Soekor Testing Teams arrived on Cranemere, and a year later their markers, little orange ribbons, were flying in the south-easter from bushes, fences, trees, gates; and there was the perpetual sound of churning wheels, and the sight of dust rising from lorries moving in line across the veld. Soon white stone cairns marked likely drilling spots: the one on which the Oil Rig eventually drilled was on the part of the farm known as the Black Dam, on the great plain west of Honey Mountain.

The Rig itself (everyone spoke of it in capital letters) arrived in 1968. Maurice and Sita remember that the roaring and booming of wheels were heard for two solid weeks and that the largest single piece of equipment weighed 80 tons and came on a trailer with forty-eight wheels. A town arose among the karoo bushes – South African, French, German, what-you-will – overshadowed by the huge tower of The Rig. The Rig itself was the largest and most modern in the country and had newly arrived from the Sahara. Drilling started on Maurice's birthday, but both he and Sita were in bed with Asian flu, and instead of their attending the 'spud in', there were four or five strange men milling about their sickroom, asking questions or permission for this and that, and the chief engineer, a German, with a click of heels presenting Sita with a bouquet of flowers into which she wept influenza tears.

In October they struck gas. It was the first strike in South Africa of any significance, and as it burned it lit up the world, and the countryside was beside itself with anticipation of what could follow. Would oil be the next? Maurice and Sita were caught up in the excitement of it all; but in Pretoria I used to pray, 'Lord, I know we need oil, but let it be somewhere else!' I doubt if my plea counted for anything, but there *was* no oil, and in the end The Rig did go on its way, with its assorted crew, including those who had become fast friends, and this fantastic, bizarre chapter came to an end. But Pearston will never be quite the same again.

What did the men and women who lived in that strange, short-lived Wild West town on the Plains of Camdeboo think of it all and of Cranemere? In a different context, I know at least what one visitor from long ago remembered, and it makes a Cranemere story. In 1942, in the middle of the Second World War, three warships called at Port Elizabeth to refuel, and the crews were distributed through the countryside for a few days' holiday. Sita and I were alone on the farm, and we welcomed three sailors, who stayed four days enjoying ostrich eggs, plum puddings and soft beds. They were called Bunny, George and John and in that terrible year, with Tobruk only two months behind us and the men of the neighbourhood still posted as missing, they came with cheerfulness and jokes, and their wives' and sweethearts' photographs in their pockets, and their normality and niceness were healing. We did not hear from them after they left South Africa, but I always thought of them as 'Cranemere's sailors'.

Two years ago, William Collins and Sons, who publishes Jenks's books, sent us a letter from London signed by a Wilfred Ransom, saying that he had read on the jacket of Jenks's latest book that he had married a Palmer, and that during the war he had stayed on an ostrich farm owned by Palmers, and was this Eve Palmer the same? I wrote back to say if he was Bunny, George or John then I was the right Eve Palmer, and back came a letter saying he was Bunny, and a photograph that gave us immense pleasure.

Back from the war, Wilfred, then a security clerk in Barclays Bank – who cannot play or read music but loves listening to it – founded a famous music club, the Mill Hill Toc H Music Club, which has now run for well over thirty years. (He launched it by asking a Polish musician, whose bank account was badly overdrawn, to give a recital and wipe off his overdraft!) The photograph was of him, with his wife on his arm, and his daughters, preparing to go to Buckingham Palace to receive the M.B.E. for his work with the music club. Cranemere has many bridges with the outside world, and one of the most enchanting is Wilfred, the Cranemere sailor, in his grey top hat off to the Palace to see the Queen.

Cranemere's animals are still much the same as in 1966, except that Angora goats are now of more importance than sheep, and that there are fewer cobras around the house – Marianne feels uneasy with them.

James – now Dr James Kitching – still hunts fossils. We had a telegram once from Sita saying that he was pulling fossil skulls out of the ground like carrots and purring. Sita and I ourselves some years ago found the fossilized jaw and head of a fish outlined on a sandstone boulder in a stream bed. It was identified as *Namaichthys digitata*, and it brought the fossil fish expert Professor Rex Jubb to Cranemere. It was, in its way, a small bit of history. A hundred years before, Dr Atherstone – the same adventuring doctor who had identified the first diamond in South Africa and who had told the story of the crew of the Ark with such glee – presented a fossil fish of this species to the British Museum as coming from the Graaff-Reinet district. Never again had a specimen been collected in that area, and scientists believed that Atherstone's locality had been incorrect. But here now was our fish to prove him right, for in the old days this countryside had been included in the district of Graaff-Reinet. Our link with Atherstone was pure romance.

Dr Sidney Rubidge died in July 1970 at the age of eighty-three. Richard, his son, is now the 'caretaker' of the unique museum on Wellwood: those who are genuinely interested can telephone him and visit the museum by appointment with him. His telephone number is Graaff-Reinet 22016, and that of his son, Robert, who also lives on Wellwood, is 22017.

Richard's eldest son, Bruce, is a palaeontologist at the National Museum, Bloemfontein, and is at present working on the earliest levels of Karoo mammal-like reptiles. He is a young man of great enthusiasm. It is extraordinarily satisfying to those who remember his grandfather handling his Karoo fossils, glowing and filled with ardour, to think that the wheel has turned full circle.

Weather still shapes the story of the farm. Since the book was first written, Cranemere has ridden out two of its worst droughts; the last after four years ended only months ago, and the dam overflowed for more than a month, the longest period in Maurice's memory. Lindelize, who is ten years old, saw it overflow for the first time in her life.

Pretoria, 1986

Acknowledgements

The story of Cranemere is the story not only of the people but of the creatures and plants living upon it. In describing some of them – and other pleasures of Cranemere – I had the help of a number of people, all my family, old and young, and particularly of my sister-in-law, Sita, whose lively accounts of humans and insects, bones and stones, coloured much I wrote; of Rob, our old manager, and his wife, Hannie, and of various old friends and servants.

The scientific details of the book were to a great extent made possible by a number of specialists in their own fields who gave me detailed and generous help – the kinder in that some of these suspected 'popular' science as only a true-blue scientist can! In particular I still thank most warmly Dr R. F. Lawrence, in 1965, at the time *The Plains of Camdeboo* was written, of the Pietermartizburg Museum; the staff of the Transvaal Museum, and in particular the Director at the time, Dr V. Fitzsimons; Dr John Robinson, then on the Museum staff; and the present Director, Dr C. K. Brain, who all helped fill in background for me; Dr R. Bigalke, then of the Nature Conservation Branch of the Transvaal; Mr A. Lea, chief locust research officer for South Africa, now retired; Dr C. J. Skead, at the time field research officer for the Percy FitzPatrick Institute of African Ornithology; the staff of the Bernard Price Institute of Palaeontology – especially Dr James Kitching, through whom we had many thrills; Mr and Mrs Hilary Deacon, then archaeologists at the Albany Museum, and Dr Michael Wells, botanist; Dr N. J. van Warmelo, at the time ethnologist to the Department of Bantu Administration and Development.

A specially warm tribute goes to the memory of Dr Sidney Rubidge, who first showed me something of the fascinations of prehistory.

The Botanical Research Institute is an old friend; and the

help I have always had from its officials – Dr L. E. Codd, at the time Director; Dr R. A. Dyer, Dr Inez Verdoorn, Mrs A. Mauve, Mr David Hardy, and Mrs E. van Hoepen – unstinting. My warmest thanks go to them, and recently to Mrs van Hoepen for help in bringing botanical names up to date.

Especially, however, I remember Miss Mary Gunn, who was librarian at the Botanical Research Institute. Much of this book was based on her help and that of the librarians of the Transvaal Museum, Mrs Thelma Campbell and Mrs May Thomas. They always did more than was ever asked, and around this whole chapters were written.

The written words, in books, magazines, newspapers and letters, of many people helped to make this book. I cannot hope to note them all, but I list my principal sources of references. Some of them, such as the old journals and the folk-lore gathered by the Bleeks, are now great Africana. I remember with especially vivid pleasure the old *Cape Monthly Magazines* and the Reverend Robert Godfrey's *Bird Lore of the Eastern Cape Province*.

At the time this book first went to press Professor Vernon Forbes' *Pioneer Travellers in South Africa* had not yet been published, so that although I was able later to use his text in checking proofs, I was not able to use this splendid book for reference generally.

My thanks go to all who helped with the illustrations of our little recorded creatures and plants of the Karoo – Dick Findlay for his paintings; Professor C. J. Uys, Dr R. Bigalke, Mr Dick Wolff, Mr T. C. Robertson, Mr John Visser, Mr Chris Pisart, the Africana Museum and Africana Library in Johannesburg, the Transvaal Museum, the National Zoological Gardens, the then Department of Information, SATOUR, the National Parks Board, and not least my husband, and David, my son.

Finally, I remember Sir William Collins, Billy to so many of his authors, the chairman of Collins Publishers in London, who was the first to read the original manuscript, and who came to Cranemere with his boundless enthusiasm, and was talked of for years afterwards by the people of the farm, as 'The Great Man'.

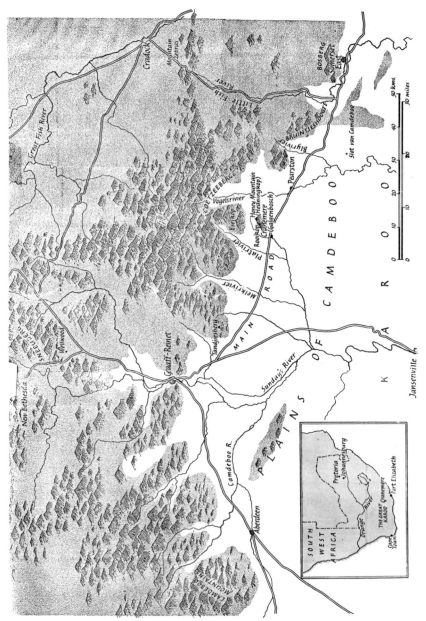

1 *Map of the Plains of Camdeboo*

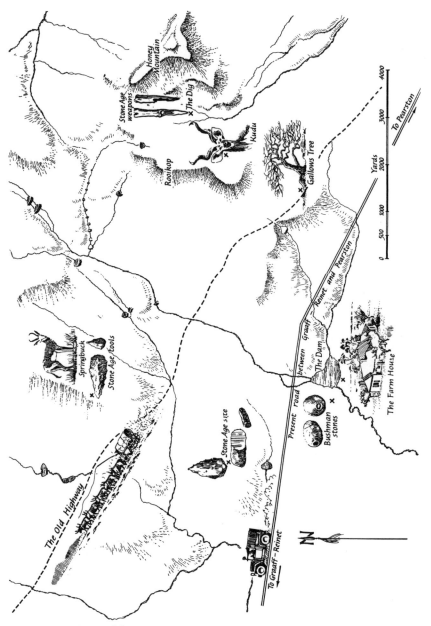

2 Detailed map of Cranemere

1. Karoo

Few people have the good fortune to be born in a desert. I was.

All my life I have been conscious of my luck. Not, indeed, that we of the Karoo often think of our land as desert. It is the travellers who have crossed our plateau for two hundred years, and our visitors of today, who have called it this – and still do.

They are right – or almost so! And like other deserts and semi-deserts of the world, ours is a country of life. We have only to walk or ride into the veld to know this and be caught up in its pattern: the squat, fat, angled plants; the hunting spiders that flicker between them; the ground squirrels upright beside their burrows; the vultures; the pale wild gladioli; the cobras; the scorpions; the mantis coloured like a flower; the black beetles rolling balls of dung; the koringkrieks lurching on immense and crooked legs. Here moves a steenbok, a duiker, a springbuck, a lark clapping its wings above us; here are the tracks of an ant-bear in the soil; red dust and a mottled egg upon it; arrowheads; the smell of rain, karoo bush, wild asparagus; mountains and hills floating in a mirage of water; a white hot sky; the sound of cicadas and wings and wind.

This home of my childhood lies towards the southern tip of Africa, on the eastern fringe of a vast plateau, the Great Karoo. It is in the heart of the plains with mountains rising steeply to the north, and like a far blue rim to the east and west. South, as far as we can see, there is only plain. It is a wide upland world, 2,500 feet above the sea and a hundred and fifty miles from it, almost midway between Cape Town and Johannesburg, just south of Olive Schreiner's famous Karoo farm, north and east of Pauline Smith's Little Karoo.

Our eastern corner of this Karoo was once known as the Plains of Camdeboo, an old name given to the country – the thirst-land – which rolled for a hundred miles or more from the eastern heights – the Bruintjeshoogte, famous in Cape history –

westward past Graaff-Reinet towards the Camdeboo Mountains, the Mountains of the Green Heights or Green Hollow. Nobody today knows for sure the exact meaning of this Hottentot word. Many early travellers described our plains under this name, and it remains vividly with me.

East lies the small town of Somerset East; west the small town of Graaff-Reinet; and in the eastern tip of the Plains is the tiny hamlet of Pearston. Ten miles from here is Cranemere, our family home, my father's and grandfather's, and today the home of my brother's family.

It is a country flooded by sun; lonely, sparse, wind-swept, treeless on the flats for many miles. In very good years thirteen inches of rain may fall in a year; in bad years three; and mostly it is somewhere between the two. After rain the Plains wave with grass and smell of honey and flowers; in drought they are desert. In between such times they are karoo – moorland, the early travellers called them – covered with low karoo bushes, little perennial daisy bushes with long, thin, wandering roots and tiny tough leaves that survive where grass cannot, and succulents of many kinds, breeding sheep with good bone and meat, and finest wool.

Away to the west the Plains merge with the Great Karoo proper stretching three hundred miles to the Swartberg, the Black Mountains. The early travellers who crossed this called it 'Carrow veld', the 'dreary waste', or simply 'the desert'. Some crossed it from curiosity, some from necessity, but they almost all reviled it.

'Karo', they recorded, was a Hottentot word meaning dry. It was. 'Denuded as porcupine quills,' said one bitterly of the little karoo bushes that covered the plain; 'sapless as a worn-out broom,' panted another, crawling in intolerable heat through a waste of sand and dry twigs. 'This monstrous landscape, this parched and arid plain,' stormed a third. 'Sirs, it would require a good pair of spectacles to see a blade of grass in this world,' proclaimed yet another.

For long this was the background to the young Cape Colony,

a barrier – treeless except along the river banks and near the mountains, waterless, grassless – between the bush, forest, and mountains of the coast and the grasslands of the north. And a most formidable barrier it proved.

Few written records have come down to us from the first settlers – they were more at home with a gun than a pen – but the early travellers wrote at length of the Karoo. If their journals are to be believed, few of them ever crossed it under happy conditions. They halted at Lioness Fountain, Hunger Fountain, Bare Place, Dry Foot Fountain, and a hundred more that bore such names. Weather – great frosts, great heat, great floods, great droughts – ruled their lives as it does ours today. If they were not baking they were freezing. Many wrote of the extreme cold and the sudden drops in temperature that left them by night shaking with misery. Some found the oil in their lamps became so thick they did not labour to trim them but chose to work by firelight instead. Others suffered tornadoes that overturned their wagons, threw down men and horses, and tore shrubs out of the ground.

The summer heat of this wide upland world can today scarcely be imagined by those even a hundred miles to the south. My first memories are of heat like the heat of blazing ovens; of shutters, and sunbeams making a hot bright path through a chink in a dark blind, of soil too hot to walk on barefoot and rocks too hot to touch. Heat, I suppose, is the most positive and formidable thing on the Karoo, and the beginning and sometimes the end of many a Karoo story.

The first explorers and naturalists who crossed the Karoo found the journey frightening, something to recount again and again. It seemed to them, looking across the smooth and arid plains, that the air trembled as though they were looking at a flame. They hid themselves in the shade of the wagons; they saw a tree miles ahead on an empty plain and dreamed of shade; they fastened their saddles and cloaks to the branches of the thorn trees they found along the rivers to cast a denser shade; they bound up their faces to protect them from the scorching winds.

Waterholes and fountains (springs) were the core of their lives. But waterholes did not always lie along the road; they were sometimes marked by pieces of white cloth tied on the branches of a nearby tree – and when there was a tree, as often as not a lion would be in occupation. They saw mirages, shimmering lakes enclosing floating mountains, and dreamed of water. They cast themselves down upon the edges of the muddy streams and drank like cattle. 'I came to a pool of mud,' cried one; 'the little water it contained was almost boiling . . . tears of delight came into my eyes.' Wild with thirst, he later shot a gemsbok in milk and milked her straight into his mouth. 'It was the sweetest beverage I ever tasted,' he swore.

Cattle like skeletons put their noses to the earth and licked such places as seemed even slightly damp. They died by the score. For more than two centuries the rough and lonely roads of the Karoo were made more desolate by the bleaching bones of cattle, horses, donkeys and mules that pulled the carts and wagons. I remember them, as do all my generation.

I watch our dogs running from one spot of shade to another in the veld and think of all the dogs of all the travellers and trekkers who crossed the Karoo. Every traveller had several and these suffered terribly unless their masters were humane enough to lift them into the over-crowded wagons. With the ground as hot as the side of a wood stove, they would rush along the track from bush to bush to find even the miserable shade cast by a bush too small to defend them from the scorching sun. They would wait with uneasy eyes until the wagons had passed them, and then, howling, would spring up and race ahead to another bush where they would lie for a few minutes, rushing on again in time to catch the wagons. Many a dog was crushed to death as it tried to keep in the shade of a moving wagon.

One traveller wrote that even his horses could not bear the blazing soil. He greased their hoofs and tied them in small bags made of skin.

When rain falls it comes, often enough, as a flood, and the land roars with the water, great solid banks of water tearing down empty river-beds and booming across the veld. Exhausted by a day's march, travellers welcomed with joy a river bank as a camping site, but sometimes they paid the price of ignorance and were swept away by a torrent born of a thunderstorm in the distant mountains. Even farmers sometimes could not resist building their homes near a river, and the story is still told of the baby in its wooden cradle that was floated away by a swollen river not thirty miles from Cranemere.

There were other troubles – Bushmen, horse-sickness, snakes, scorpions, spiders, a horde of insects of every kind. Gordon Cumming, the great red-haired Scotsman who slaughtered countless game in his journey across South Africa, was nearly killed by a puff-adder that slept the night beneath his pillow. He felt it moving under him but thought it was a mouse! My grandmother once shared her bed with a six-inch scorpion.

Flies were one of those minor horrors that could sweep almost everything else out of the mind. They were everywhere, hanging thickly from the ceilings of the farmhouses and covering every morsel of food. My father remembered as a boy visiting a Karoo neighbour and wondering at the big black balls hanging from the dark ceiling. They were flies.

There were fleas by the billion, and later travellers, stopping at the little iron-roofed inns, broiling in the Karoo heat, complained of bugs – 'B-Flats', they called them delicately.

'I shall sleep well tonight for I am tired,' a traveller remarked.

'That's fine,' said his host, rubbing his hands, 'for the B-Flats are sharp-set tonight.'

There were the locusts in vast swarms that darkened the air and demolished the crops of the settlers. There were then no man-made weapons against them, no way to evade this flying or hopping scourge. Their terrible order, their military precision, confounded the simple farmers who believed them super-insects, every troop with its commander-in-chief whom they obeyed, and for whose signal they waited to depart. They were indestructible.

There were the karoo caterpillars that, after rain, in their billions turned the karoo bushes into pulsating life, dark, wriggling, noisome. The locusts ate the grass and crops; the caterpillars ate the bushes. Between them they could make a desert in a year of rains.

This is the background of the Karoo that all South Africans know, and beyond which few progress. Yet into this forbidding land men and women came and settled: and from here many would never again go. My grandmother was among these.

Rain, however rare, makes life possible. Here on the Karoo we all know a great gentle rain (and it sometimes comes) after a great cruel drought: joy after rain colours the lives of the Karoo-born – and no doubt their souls – and it is certain that every man and woman stands an inch higher after the rains have come. Within days – hours, it seems – the dust-dry soil is engulfed in succulence, every bare twig covered with leaves, the plains enamelled with flowers, the air filled with scents. The mountains cascade water, the rivers and pools brim over, frogs bellow, birds fill the trees, and bees make honey all over the countryside. The great intricate web of Karoo life begins to function once again. Firm flesh covers the bones of starving animals; and men, women, and children cry, sing, and say their prayers.

2. Bushmen of the Sea

I do not know which was the first white family in our eastern Karoo or when it came, but the travellers of the late eighteenth and early nineteenth century found the settlers spread out on the gigantic landscape like a few shells on an empty beach.

Some were semi-nomadic, wandering across the veld with their wagons, flocks and herds, seeking good grazing and good water. Others had built themselves rude houses thatched with reeds and floored with mud and dung, where they lived a semi-permanent existence. Some found a congenial world in the east, in high mountainous country to the north of the village of Graaff-Reinet, in the Sneeuberg – the Snow Mountains; but they were forced by the cold to trek from here in the winter to the Karoo plains below. On the lower slopes some farmers existed all the year round, a tough, resilient people who had never seen the sea – and never seen a tree!

Some halted on our eastern Plains; and if they had loved the mountains of the western Cape they must have been happy here with the mountains in a grand amphitheatre to the north. Bruintjeshoogte, Swaershoek, Coetzeeberg, Tandjiesberg, even the Sneeuberg, they were (and still are) called, for one range runs into another and nobody, least of all the travellers or map-makers, was ever quite sure where one began and another ended.

Several rivers flowing from the mountains cut the Plains, the Blyrivier (glad river), the Vogelsrivier (bird river – the Voël of today), the Platrivier (flat river), and the Melkrivier (milk river), and many wry comments on these names have been passed down the years, for where, in drought at least, were the gladness, the birds, or the milk?

Some scientists today believe that two hundred years ago our Plains were pure grasslands and well watered, and that it is the white man and his sheep who have changed their face. Once they might have been this paradise, but clearly not two centuries ago when the first farmers trekked here, for by the 1780s the Plains between Bruintjeshoogte and Graaff-Reinet were already known as Karoo and were notorious for heat and dryness; in drought time no rivers ran, few pools of sweet water lay in the river-beds, while the water in the very fountains dried up. There was little shelter for men and horses and oxen, only a summer temperature at ground level of 150 degrees in the sun. Travellers pushed through the eastern Plains as fast as their animals could travel, stopping only at intervals to off-saddle their horses and let them roll on the ground for refreshment.

'Get off, sir, and let him roll,' was here a farmer's first greeting to a weary traveller. 'Put your car in the shearing-shed,' it is today; but in essence the greetings are the same.

The farmers who lived here were of necessity tough. To some travellers who met them they were turbulent adventurers, soldiers and sailors who had deserted or been discharged from the army and navy, eking out a living in a land without authority. 'The lawless freebooters of Bruintjeshoogte', they called them. I think of this today when I see the people of Pearston district in dark suits and moss crêpe demurely assembling for church on a Sunday.

To others they were the embodiment not of turbulence but of sloth. 'They have been known to receive travellers lying quite still and motionless excepting that they have very civilly pointed out the road by moving their foot to the right or left,' wrote a traveller about the farmers of Somerset East.

Frontiersmen without parallel, Theal, the South African historian, called them and their like, and their adaptability and bone-hard courage made them this. But they were more. If history – as opposed to prehistory – begins with the written word, they were the first makers of history in our eastern Karoo.

For many years here on the Plains they were wandering farmers only, grazing their animals after rain and moving on to find water in times of drought. The grazing was good; mixed karoo bushes on the flats and on the hills thick scrub, while after rain the Plains waved with grass. But even when the veld was rich in food farmers had to trek when the water supplies failed.

Here, between the Vogelsrivier and the Platrivier, intersected by the old trek road, lay a farm once named, appropriately enough, Droogerivier – Dry River, and later Galgenbosch or Gallows Tree – also, it is said, an appropriate name! This was the dismal place, the parched plain, the monstrous landscape of so many before. And this is the Cranemere of today.

Since I was a child I have believed that Cranemere – like all the Karoo – has within it a thousand stories; and even its beginning, as we know it, had a fine drama. It began rightly enough with water. Towards the southern boundary of the farm, some miles below the mountains, a number of natural pools formed in a wide hollow in which collected the run-off water from the mountains to the north, so that water lay here for longer than elsewhere in the neighbourhood. The pools had long been famous, for we believe the Bushmen used to hide in the koppies near them to shoot the game that came through a gap in the low hills to drink, and here for many years trekboers watered their stock.

Probably in the 1770s the land was issued as a loan place and became the temporary property of one farmer. Loan farms were apportioned in the simplest possible way and were held at a nominal rent. A man chose a piece of unoccupied land and set up a beacon. His land was that on every side of the beacon within half an hour's walk, and even if the transaction was managed officially, it was nevertheless a very supple affair.

'What was your beacon?' a farmer was asked at an enquiry.

'A bush,' he answered simply. 'It blew over.'

Perhaps Galgenbosch was issued in just such a manner, but all that we know of the first owners is that they were only able to use the farm after rain and that when the pools dried up they trekked. Never, apparently, did they think of doing otherwise until the farm became the property of Gerrit Lodewyk Coetzee. His name deserves to be famous on the Plains for he changed their history.

It is difficult to think of a time when the Karoo was without dams; in the early 1800s there was not a big man-made dam the length and breadth of the Plains. Coetzee's stepfather had been a trekboer temporarily owning Galgenbosch, and when the pools dried up he trekked. All things have a beginning and the dams of the eastern Plains were born in young Gerrit's mind. When Galgenbosch passed to him he turned his dream into reality. He built a dam where the natural pools lay.

With two oxen dragging an ox-hide on which the loose soil was piled, he made a low five-foot earthen wall in a gap between the two ridges of koppies and caught and held the water from the mountains. Rain fell, the dam filled (and the pools had now become a good stretch of water) and it held the water when the other pools over the countryside were dry. Coetzee, say the old records, was now able 'to live constantly on the spot with his flock'. Those nine words made history. Galgenbosch was the first permanently settled farm in the neighbourhood, and from every side the people of the Plains came to gape at the earthen wall that made this new life possible.

In 1843 Coetzee obtained the land permanently. We still sometimes look with pleasure at the title-deeds, old now and very worn, for they are part of our history and show it. The rich sonorous language tells of another age.

'By his Honour Colonel John Hare, Companion of the Most Honourable Military Order of the Bath, Knight of the Royal Guelphic Order of Honour, Lieutenant-Governor of the Eastern Division of the Colony of the Cape of Good Hope . . . in the name and on behalf of Her Majesty Victoria, by the Grace of God of the United Kingdom of Great Britain and Ireland, Queen, Defender of the Faith, I do hereby grant on perpetual quitrent unto Gerrit Lodewyk Coetzee a piece of land . . . Droge River, alias Galgenbosch . . . Given under my hand and public seal at Grahams Town this 4th day of November, 1843.'

In 1864 Coetzee sold the farm to John Bolleurs.

Bolleurs did well by the farm. He raised the dam wall and enlarged the dam so that it would not only water his stock but

3 Cranemere house as it is today

4 Shearing time on Cranemere. Alex Palmer and Konos sorting in the foreground.

5 *Rob sowing oats in the cracks of Cranemere dam in drought time.*

6 *Cranemere dam when full.*

feed them. The trekboers had always known that the small karoo bushes – those porcupine quills of the early observers – were unique. In good years animals, wild and domestic, throve on them, and even when they appeared no more than sticks, still they supported life. The early farmers had been content with this. Bolleurs was not. He grew lucerne and crops for fodder. If Coetzee had learnt how to keep his stock alive, Bolleurs learned how to keep them *fat*. He learned something more: that where there was water this astonishing desert burst into an exuberance of leaf, flower, and fruit; that out of this unleached soil an abundance could spring.

'He has secured so large a body of water as to enable him to cultivate hundreds of acres,' wrote the botanist John Croumbie Brown, 'and to supply, during the last drought, his neighbours for three miles below with water for their perishing flocks.'

The dam on Galgenbosch and the lands and gardens were quoted again and again in the mid-nineteenth century. Coetzee and Bolleurs, although they did not think of themselves as makers of history, yet helped to change a way of living. Like them, farmers in other parts of the Karoo were soon experimenting, and as they learned that water captured and made to work could make homes, so they settled down to rear families on one spot and to hand on their land to their children.

The Frontier Wars were coming to an end; merino sheep and Angora goats grazed the Plains alongside the fat-tailed sheep and Boer goats of the early colonists; farmers began to build dry walls of stones and occasionally fences to mark their boundaries, and permanent houses, and to plant gardens of vines, peach trees, oranges and lemons. The names of the farmers began to change. Once they had been only Dutch names, but now others were found right across the Plains and beyond, and among the old names such as Kruger, Botha, Nel, Coetzee, Trichardt and Lotter, there now appeared names like Hart, Stretch, Hobson, Featherstone, Parkes. The 'Bushmen of the Sea', as the Xhosa people called the first English (and the allusion was not complimentary), had arrived; unlike the Bushmen, they were there to stay.

George and Fanny Palmer, my grandparents, were among these, and they bought Galgenbosch in 1880. George was twenty-nine, Fanny twenty-six years old. They could have had no knowledge of Karoo conditions. George was the son of a farmer, Thomas Brown Palmer, who had emigrated from England many years before to settle in the Elands River Valley in the Uitenhage district of the Cape. He had longed for mountains and water and he had got them; and – what he did not bargain for – leopards as well.

Thomas came of a long line of sailors – his father was Captain John Palmer of the Royal Navy and his wife, Elizabeth Hawkins, was a descendant of Sir John Hawkins of the time of Queen Elizabeth. Their fathers had been midshipmen with the British fleet which took the Cape in 1795, and doubtless they had told their children of the new land they had seen. With fascination we – her great-grandchildren – remember that Elizabeth, reputed too delicate to survive the English winters, bore thirteen children on their remote farm, 'The Fountain'; and that when her six sons went out into the world they wore suits impeccably tailored by her.

George was born here in 1851. He was only a youth when diamonds were found but he made his first money transport-riding to the diamond fields, and later he was lucky there himself.

Frances Susannah, or Fanny as she was known throughout her life, was the daughter of a doctor, William Mawby, and his wife Anne, who had made a runaway marriage in England and been expelled from the bosom of Anne's – reputedly – noble family. They came first to Natal, then to the Orange Free State, and Fanny had one of those extraordinary childhoods that nineteenth-century South Africans seemed to take for granted, compounded equally of battle and lace doilies. Her early memories were of laagers and battle-cries; she grew up on horseback, and danger, fear and exhaustion were all familiar to her before she was in her teens; yet her father, writing to her at her convent school in the Cape and recounting her brothers' battles in the

Basuto wars, detailed without apparently any sense of the ludicrous those studies which would fit her for 'the life to which she would be called'. They included wax-flower-making, a good knowledge of the harmonium, dancing, French, German and Italian!

Probably Fanny was grateful for the dancing. At her first ball she met six stalwart young men. They were all Palmers, and she picked the one she wanted. She and George were married in 1875, her son Clifford was born two years later, and in 1880 she and George, with an adequate if modest sum of money, determined to find a permanent home and settle down. They had not the slightest idea where it would be. 'Anywhere in the world you want,' George had said to her, and they set off to see South Africa first.

In the Karoo the worst drought in living memory had just ended. In 1877 less than one inch of rain fell; the next year was hardly better, but in the autumn of 1879 the rains came and it rained for three months. Into this great, wide, newly washed world came George and Fanny Palmer with their cart and horses.

They were travelling between Somerset East and Graaff-Reinet but they had seen little to excite them; little except the feather beds at the inn at Bruintjeshoogte. These were famous in the eastern Karoo, for travellers stopping here and sleeping in the same great bed were lost in an ocean of feathers, their companions being invisible from the time they stepped into bed until they arose in the morning. And so, probably laughing for they were young and lively, they passed through Pearston and continued along the road that so many travellers before them had used. They passed close by the Gallows Tree that gave the farm its name, and perhaps it was here, or perhaps over Galbosnek, that Fanny said without warning and without hesitation, 'This is what I want.'

She lived until she was seventy-eight years old and she never changed her mind.

Perhaps it was the dam that decided her, that shock of delight that water can bring in a dry land. Perhaps she saw it in the mother-of-pearl light of early morning, or in the evening when the benison of wind and shadows fills the Plains. Perhaps it was the space and emptiness. Whatever it was, her decision was made, the farm was bought, and she and George established themselves at Galgenbosch.

This was a new and very strange world. 'The plants stand very thin in the Carrow-veld,' Thunberg, the botanist, had written a hundred years before; and they found this was true. Here was neither the bush and forest George knew, nor the grasslands of Fanny's home. It was an alien world of strange plants and animals, of dust and heat and sun, of floods and bitter extremes, and George, Fanny and Clifford loved it.

They owned twenty thousand acres of land but their home was a mud cottage. It had three rooms with outer walls nearly three feet thick, all made of mud and rubble (one of these, 34 inches wide, remains today as an inner wall), and a stout chimney which had probably been cleaned in the manner of the Karoo by sending a fowl down it. The kitchen was a small, smoky, mud-walled room standing well away from the cottage.

The floor was of mud and dung, and shone with ox blood, the famous floor polish of the old colonial farms. The roof was of reeds and the ceiling of reeds, straw and mud, bound with narrow leather thongs. Heavy wooden shutters kept out flies, snakes and air alike. The big wooden inner door was of yellowwood and its hinges were 37 inches long. The house was crude but immensely solid, and it had given shelter and hospitality to many people for a long time.

Unlike the farmhouses to the south and east, it does not seem ever to have been fortified. The first photographs show it as an unprotected thatched box standing on a plain empty of everything but a ridge of ironstone koppies.

Soon the house and the garden about it grew. The three rooms grew into thirteen, a high-ceilinged, rambling home, room leading into room, with a wide stoep running round three sides in the manner of Karoo houses, and big open fireplaces everywhere. There were no skilled builders. Many years later, when laying hot-water pipes in a new bathroom, the builder found that no two outside walls at the back of the house were on the same level.

In Fanny's time there were no bathrooms and no electric light. Even we, as children two generations later, bathed by candle-light in a hip-bath laboriously carried into our rooms and out again. There was no hot water except that heated on the wood stove. There was no refrigerator, no ice. Keeping food fresh and cool in summer was one of Fanny's major tasks.

The Specialist would have approved the sanitary arrangements. We had a splendid three-holer at the bottom of the garden, frequented not only by humans, but by wasps, immense hairy spiders, and bats which were a constant interest as they hung, charmingly decorative, upside down. Later, in the time of my brother Maurice, the building acquired a new status. For fifty years an old shell dating from Boer War days had propped open the dairy door. One day, after a newspaper report of the explosion of such a shell, it was carried down the garden and with due ceremony dropped down The Big Hole.

On a summer morning Fanny rose at four o'clock, and by candle-light she and her maids dusted, cleaned, polished and cooked. By nine the shutters were closed, the blinds drawn, and the coarse sheeting in front of every door to keep out the flies was dampened to cool the air. The stoeps were watered every morning and – until the fly season started – polished once a week with buttermilk.

One of my early recollections is the warm fresh smell of the damp cement in the early mornings and the clapping sounds of the zebra-skin mats being pulled about by the gaunt, beautiful old pagan woman in her full skirts and black turban who ran the dairy. Today it is still the right of the dairymaid to wash the stoeps and polish them with buttermilk. It has become one of the traditional jobs and she jealously guards her right to do it, but she no longer remembers why.

The house and its arrangements have changed somewhat

15

since Fanny's times, but the outbuildings are much the same – long whitewashed buildings with rows of rooms opening on to the farmyard, and heavy shutters. We had always taken these very much for granted until recently an architect exclaimed at their elegance; and they have, I suppose, the elegance of extreme simplicity.

Here were the incubator, and the Feather Room – in Fanny's time one of the most important rooms on the farm where the ostrich feathers were stored before they were packed and sent to Port Elizabeth. Today it still has the reed and mud ceiling of Fanny's day. Here was the dairy; the smithy where Rob Rafferty, manager for over forty years, shod the horses; the saddle-room, the store-room, the shearing-shed, the stables.

The site of the house had been carefully chosen. It had been built near the pools – the pools that Coetzee turned into a lake. Clearly neither beauty nor defence governed the site of the farmhouse: water did.

It was to govern the lives of George and Fanny and those of all who came after. From the first moment all their lives centred round the dam. One of the first things Fanny did was to change the name of the farm – no gallows trees for her – and she called the farm Cranemere after its two distinguishing features: the blue cranes by the thousand and the water that they flocked to in the dusk. The dam lay directly in front of the house only a hundred yards away, and at evening as they stood at their front door George and Fanny were almost deafened by the water birds, the honking of the wild geese, and above all the loud cries of the cranes.

George had not set foot over the threshold before he began plans to enlarge the dam. These plans were probably some of the first things that his son ever remembered, or his three grandchildren, my sister Iris, my brother Maurice and I, for plans to make the dam bigger, better, storm-proof, drought-proof, have echoed down the years. It is hard to say where one Palmer began and another ended, for one plan ran into another and what one plotted another accomplished. And the dam grew.

George knew it as a smallish earthen dam; my father left it with a weir of stone and cement 155 feet long, and a great steep wall of dolerite boulders and earth, with a capacity of 590 acre feet (just over 25 million cubic feet), all accomplished with a scotch cart and wagons. Maurice almost doubled its size.

For many years it was the biggest private dam in the Cape. It lay just south of the main road between Pearston and Graaff-Reinet and travellers used to stop first with their carts and horses and later with their cars, and look with surprise and some with disbelief at the stretch of water. We heard with pleasure of one traveller who often passed by who resolutely refused to believe it was real; there could not be such water in the Karoo – it was a mirage, he claimed, but a most unusual one for it was always there!

Everything depended on the dam. The animals and sometimes the people of the farm drank here. Its water grew the fodder crops and the food for the people. Here generations of children, black and white, have played. The water has never been clear but brown and very soft, and in it swam – still swim – the children of the farm and their dogs; fish and frogs and tortoises; on it are scores of water birds: beside it the plovers and other little birds; and when the water subsides and a low mat of vegetation grows in its place, insects by the million buzz along the edges. On a spring day it is a moving thing to stand among the butterflies feasting on these tiny flowers, to listen to the birds on the water and incessant sounds of life on the land – cows, lambs, children, bees, larks, tractors, pails, hoofbeats – with the desert plains on every hand.

So long as we can see the water, so long as a pool remains, no drought on Cranemere is insupportable; but when the dam dries and the surface flakes underfoot and cracks like a vast honeycomb, then even the illusion of life goes.

George saw his dam completely dry only once, but his son and grandson and great-grandson have seen it dry many times, for the water in almost any dam must come to an end if there is no rain in its catchment areas.

It is then that we turn to underground water. Not even this is independent of rainfall for it can disappear in drought, but it is far more reliable than surface water and thousands of people and millions of animals have survived on the Karoo because of the water below their feet.

The Karoo is a country of water-diviners. Not a great many men, it is true, claim to have the power of finding water, but it is an ability that here we all recognize and prize. One of the first big-time water-diviners a century ago, a man named Kohl, made a large sum of money in the eastern Karoo by divining for farmers mad for water, who were prepared to pay him anything he asked. Although he was not always successful, he appears to have had a gift. He found, for instance, most of the early water supply of the little Karoo town of Aberdeen. His instructions were followed in detail and nine feet below the surface, below four feet of soil and five of solid rock, a stream of water was found.

I do not know if he found the first underground water on Cranemere but it is possible. Certainly many of the underground streams on Cranemere have been found by diviners such as he, so that we owe a great debt to these unscientific and often simple men. Once my father, deciding to move with the times, obtained the services of a government geologist. It was an unnerving experience. He tramped the farm, returning cheerfully to say: 'You may as well give up, Mr Palmer. There is no water here at all.' Today Cranemere has some thirty functioning windmills, most of the underground streams having been found by diviners, some streams strong, some weak, and the water has been priceless.

Our childhood was punctuated by the arrival of these fascinating men. Our diviners differed in their choice of implement; some chose a forked twig of willow, some of thorn tree, some of quince. One worked with no more than a thick piece of bent wire, but the procedure was the same. They would hold one of the two prongs in either hand with the single end upwards and would march up and down over the area where it was hoped water would be found. Sometimes the twig would swing round, the end pointing earthwards, and the diviner would say in triumph, 'Here it is. Here's the water.'

All the diviners we had were honest men and believed without doubt that it was water that pulled the twig around in their hands. And who were we to disbelieve them when a borehole was sunk and as often as not the water would be there? If no water was found the diviners, of course, still claimed they were right: the water was there but the hole was not deep enough.

It was exciting to walk beside one of these men and watch him at work, and most dramatic when the twig held upwards so quietly and steadily suddenly snapped round and pointed towards the earth. The diviners declared that it turned quite independently of them and that however firmly they held the twig it would be forced round in their hands. I have no gift at all for water-divining, but once as a child I held one of the prongs and walked with the diviner holding the other prong; I myself felt the twig jump and turn within my clenched hand, and when I opened it my palm was red and scored.

Where the twig moved a pile of stones would be built and more often than not a borehole sunk. The clank-clank of the drilling machine sounding over the veld was the background to our early childhood. When water was found the whole family would celebrate, but a dud hole was like a death on the farm.

One of our most regular water-diviners lived a generation after George and Fanny. He was a friend of my father's and the power of water-divining had belonged to his ancestors – to the male line, for women seldom have the gift – as long as his family could remember. For him it was an uneasy gift. In some places he could neither sleep nor sit in comfort. There was one room in Cranemere house where he would never sleep for he declared a stream of water ran under the room and the vibrations upset him. Sometimes out in the car with my father he would suffer an attack of acute pins and needles when, he said, he was passing over water. Often diviners can only feel water that is running but one year this man suffered great discomfort sitting at the dining-room table. 'There's water underneath here,' he said. My father pulled up the floor and there was. Rain had oozed in under the boards and a pool had collected neatly under the diviner's chair.

A strong underground stream runs across Cranemere along an ironstone ridge from east to west and this has been a godsend in drought. One borehole along this stream was suggested by two water-divining brothers, Hans and Abraham Louw. They indicated a spot half-way up the hill next to the house, and my father started drilling. He drilled for 150 feet. He telephoned Abraham. 'It's no good. I'm stopping,' he said. 'No, Mr Palmer, you must not,' he cried. So my father drilled another fifteen feet. Once more he telephoned Abraham. 'You must not stop,' screamed Abraham. 'You must not. There *is* water there. I'm coming over now. Try, man, try!' Within half an hour, and before Abraham had arrived, my father struck water, strong sweet water that has given life through many droughts.

Later still, other holes were sunk further down this stream and turbines set up. It is one of the sights of the farm to walk down below the haystacks and watch the water gushing out, pure, clear and cold. Nobody can pass it by without touching it, and visitors on a summer's day have been known to plunge their faces and heads right into the stream.

With underground water Fanny made a garden and George planted trees. The garden was a tremendous task, for there was no deep soil near the house and it had all to be carted from some distance away and dumped at her door. The raised garden, laid out formally with rose-beds and orange trees and a big hedge of yellow jasmine as a boundary, was charming. It had a faintly Italian air, and Fanny delighted in it. Some of the big old-fashioned shrub roses she planted are still there, blooming well.

The unleached soil of the orchard and vegetable garden grew – and still grows – marvellous food: melons, huge white and purple figs, peaches, nectarines, apricots, plums, pears, quinces, strawberries, ruby and butter-coloured grapes, mulberries, loquats bigger than hens' eggs, pale as honey and as sweet; kohlrabi, scorzonera, salsify, brinjals (aubergines), sugar peas, green peppers. In the lands grow crops in rotation; wheat for bread, and pumpkins and mealies for white and black; the vegetable gardens of the servants; lucerne and oats for stock. Today the stud rams run here, the lambing ewes graze the oat lands, and the lucerne is a fodder bank for good times and bad.

Fanny used to boast she bought no food but tea, coffee, sugar and rice. To this my mother added walnuts, and Sita cheese. Even today very little food is bought. They were notable cooks, Fanny and my mother, and so is Sita, Maurice's wife. Fanny's pot-roasted venison and pou, her van der Hum made of brandy, syrup and naartjie peel, her pickled peaches, and many other dishes, are still remembered. Cranemere storeroom in her day was packed with bottled fruit and jams, just as it is today. The same sausages are made year by year of pork and mutton and venison, flavoured with coriander, lemon rind, garlic, black peppercorns and thyme, and their making remains one of the big events of the year.

The big Dutch oven, four feet high and made of bricks, still stands by the smithy, and here the farm bread was baked for eighty years. Tuesday and Friday were always baking days on the farm. The firing started at ten o'clock in the morning when branches of mimosa wood were lighted and left in the oven to burn into coals; the door was shut, and the oven slowly began to glow with heat. It was then opened, the coals raked out, the bread-pans put in with a bread-shovel, the door clamped down, and the bread left in a cooling oven to bake. The loaves were taken out after two or three hours and covered with a blanket, and they were spongy and soft-crusted and tasted of mimosa wood.

Abundance meant people and easy hospitality. Although there were long periods of loneliness and of complete isolation in bad weather, there were often people coming and going. Fanny and George entertained tremendously, for travel was slow and difficult and every traveller expected – and got – a bed and a meal. 'He believed in a free breakfast-table,' said George's obituary notice forty years later. He did: between them George and Fanny must have housed and fed half the eastern Karoo.

Whether there were visitors or not they changed ceremoniously for dinner every evening, and in silk and muslin and lace Fanny ate her dinner, her size two hand-made evening slippers resting on the dung floor. Tradition has it she clung to this custom whether floods or Boer forces were at her door, and whether her working day had been ten hours or eighteen. Recently an old lady visited Cranemere after an interval of sixty years. She was charmed to see it again and, laughing, told Sita, Fanny's granddaughter-in-law, the story of Fanny and the young manager who would not change for dinner. One day he received a parcel. A coloured maid bore it to him and there, under the eyes of the delighted houseparty, he opened it to pull out – a collar and tie.

Fanny and George were very gay in their younger days and danced a great deal in Fanny's drawing-room by the light of candles and lamps; and friends and neighbours came with their carts and horses, outspanned, danced till daybreak, and drove home with the sun. Every bed at such times was used and the boys dossed down on the floor. George and Fanny thought nothing of travelling many hours to a 'garden party', probably returning with several guests. Fanny used to tell how, as she was driving to Graaff-Reinet to a party and wearing a new Paris hat with ostrich plumes, the Melkrivier came down in flood as they were fording it. They escaped, but she watched her hat borne away, plumes bobbing, on the crest of the river.

Then, as today, visitors might equally have been tramps or prime ministers. Rhodes stopped here for several nights. George was then a member of the Cape House of Assembly and he and Rhodes were friends. They sat up round the fire until all hours talking, planning, and arguing. 'Rhodes was here,' wrote Fanny in her diary; 'another late night.'

She never knew of a morning how many people she would have to feed at night; nor, indeed, did my mother. There might be two or twelve. As a child, I remember twenty-nine people turning up unexpectedly to breakfast on their way to a great reunion of the Murray family at Graaff-Reinet, and my mother and Hannie, the housekeeper, coping easily. Some of them arrived late at night and I recall my astonishment next morning as I crept through the rooms at seeing several heads protruding from every bed.

Sometimes visitors stayed indefinitely. One winter morning a small bent man walked on to our stoep with a suitcase in one hand, an umbrella in the other. He was an itinerant house-painter walking from farm to farm looking for work, a fierce, bad-tempered, independent old man who, we learned as time went by, played chess, hated women, and followed the English county cricket scores with passion. He stayed with us for five years, and although he has been dead a long time his old room still bears his name.

Today, as in Fanny's day, the family may sit down alone to one meal and have fourteen the next: palaeontologists from America – or the local museum; wool buyers from France; half a dozen schoolboys and girls; a travelling salesman spreading out his wares on the tables and floors; a big-game hunter with a suitcase made of elephant ears; farmers and their wives who look at the Karoo through the dark soft eyes of their Huguenot ancestors.

It may be the local carpenter and we watch and listen to him with particular pleasure, with his solid good Scots face and his Afrikaans tongue. His name is Landman. His Scots great-grandfather was impressed into the British Navy, sailed to the Cape, and here, close enough to the coast to hear the breakers on the shore, he escaped. It was dense fog and he slipped over the ship's side unseen and swam towards land. Exhausted and half drowned, he crawled at length onto the sand. Then he got up on his knees, stretched out his arms to the fog-enshrouded land and cried in a great voice, 'Now am I a land man.' Landman is the name his family has borne ever since.

One day Sita, making quince jelly in the kitchen, looked up to see a woman in jeans and heavy boots standing in the doorway and sniffing the jelly. She and her husband were seeking their fortune cycling through South Africa, and now the wheel of their carrier had broken and they needed help. The carrier was a sturdy affair on wheels pulled behind her husband's bicycle, and on it was a large netted box in which sat, in great dignity, a fox-terrier and a ginger cat. They proved some of Cranemere's oddest and most touching guests through all the years.

Cecil Rhodes and they equally owed the hospitalities of their week-end to the waters of Cranemere; and if ghosts can see and feel, I hope the ghost of Gerrit Lodewyk Coetzee sees and is satisfied.

3. The Yellow and the Brown

When George and Fanny first knew the Plains the Hottentots were here, although the Bushmen who had once lived here too had vanished. The Bantu had arrived, here on our Plains mainly the Xhosa and Fingo people, and these races, the yellow and the brown, were Cranemere's labouring force and the background to its life.

The Hottentots were an ancient people. Their history, like that of the Bushmen, has been endlessly debated, although scientists today mostly believe they had a common origin in Southern Africa. That early common ancestor lived off the flesh of wild animals and the plants of the veld and bush, and from him evolved and separated those who kept flocks and herds. The Bushmen were the hunters and plant-gatherers and the Hottentots the herders. Were they perhaps bigger than the Bushmen because their food supply was more constant? Some anthropologists think it likely.

Strange and alien they must have been to the first Europeans who saw them, with their high cheekbones, flat noses, thick lips and peppercorn hair, their bodies smeared with fat, and their smell noticeable at 'a distance of twelve feet against the wind'; 'fierce', the observers called it. One of the company of Vasco da Gama, the Portuguese explorer, saw Hottentots at the Cape in 1497 and recorded, with apparent surprise, that their dogs barked the same as those in Portugal.

I remember the Hottentots of my childhood – no longer a pure race but still distinct – as yellow and grinning, shifty and light-fingered and fascinating, with stories to charm a duck off a pond. They still live all over the Karoo, the men working as herdsmen and gardeners, the women as domestic servants. In the mountains to the north there are some who never work at all, except as wandering sheep-shearers. The farmers call them the Hottentot gipsies, for they live on the roads with their carts and donkeys, never stopping in one place for more than a few days on end.

This was their homeland, but as far as we can tell it had never been that of the so-called Bantu. The earliest colonists never knew the Bantu – the blacks – as a settled people on our Plains but as hunters and marauding warriors. This dark-skinned, well-made, vigorous people was once popularly supposed to be part Negro, part Hamite, perhaps with a touch of Arab, who had pushed down Africa from the far north to south. Anthropologists tend now to believe them to have descended from the same far-off ancestral stock as Hottentots and Bushmen, and that these three races of Africa south of the Sahara owed their great differences in physique and culture to the fact that they had separated from one another so long before and had remained isolated and therefore had evolved along different lines.

Scientists know now that these black peoples were living in the Transvaal and Natal at least by AD 300. Some see the Nguni people – those inhabiting the great stretch of country between the eastern escarpment and the sea – as living in small communities, and grouping and separating at length into the Xhosa, Zulu, and other tribes known to us well in written history.

When Van Riebeeck landed in 1652 many hundreds of miles separated the mass of white and black – the Cape interior was still largely Hottentot and Bushman territory – although black hunting parties were probing the interior. (They were Xhosas, taking their name from a great chief, Xhosa, who lived possibly when Henry VIII was King of England.) In 1702 a Dutch party of hunters and explorers clashed with a Xhosa band near the Great Fish River six hundred miles east of Cape Town, and this seems to have been one of the very early meetings between the two races in South Africa.

The earliest Xhosa people to *settle* west of the Great Fish River lived almost on our doorstep. It is said that they made a home at Nojoli, the Somerset East of today, and their story has been told by the Reverend John Soga, himself descended from Xhosa warriors and councillors, in *The South-Eastern Bantu.*

It is a romantic tale. These first Xhosa clans were refugees fleeing to safety after a great battle near Umtata in the north, and with them, he believes, came the Ama-Gqunukebe. This tribe was born about AD 1700. Far to the north and west of our Plains of Camdeboo, near Umtata, lived a great Xhosa chief, Tshiwo, who had as councillor and executioner a man named Kwane – a strange man for executioner, for he spared his prisoners' lives, hiding them in the inaccessible country of the Gqunuqwas west of the St John's River. Here they lived, married Hottentot women, and reared families, until they grew into a clan in numbers.

A British officer, Cowper Rose, fighting in the Frontier Wars, told the story of this clan in 1829, 'doubtless taken down from the lips of some old Xhosa historian', as Soga said, and a wonderful story it is. He described how after many years – in a time of Tshiwo's need – Kwane gathered the hidden clan and brought them in strength to Tshiwo's kraal. Tshiwo's queen, looking towards the hills, saw the black forms and cried, 'What do I see, is it mimosa bushes? They grew not there yesterday;' and when she saw they were armed men she cried out again.

'Then Kwane came down with a hundred young men with their shields and assegais and their war plumes, and Kwane and his warriors kneeled before the chief and laid their arms at his feet, and then followed the aged men, and then aged women, the children and cattle, and Kwane said to Tshiwo, "These are the people you ordered me to destroy: behold, I have saved them." And Tshiwo took unto himself a portion of the people and of the cattle and gave the remainder to Kwane . . . and said unto him, "I adopt you as a son . . . and should a son of mine raise his assegai against you, raise yours against him for you are his equal."'

According to Soga, these Xhosa clans did not live for long at Somerset, but were defeated and ousted by a Xhosa army from Umtata which returned again to its northern home. But the first Xhosa, or part Xhosa, hunters across the Plains of Camdeboo

27

were possibly of Kwane's people, bringing to our Plains one of the great stories of South Africa.

Inevitably white and black met in numbers and the clash was appalling. Greed, rapacity, ruthlessness – writers ever since the First Frontier War have charged these things first to one side, then to the other. First one river was declared a boundary between white and black, then another and another, but quite fruitlessly: they were barriers by word alone. Blood and violence ruled the frontier for a hundred years, matched only – in modern times – by that of Red Indians and pioneers seven thousand miles away.

The Xhosas came streaming across the so-called boundaries, handsome, colourful and fierce, the seasoned warriors adorned with blue cranes' feathers; and even as far west as the Plains of Camdeboo they left death and smouldering ruins. The story is still told of a white boy, Louis Kotze, who in 1822 was murdered on Bruintjeshoogte by a Xhosa band. He had been taking a herd of cattle over the mountain and had stopped with a Hottentot boy to dig for the succulent roots of a kiepersol to quench his thirst when the band fell upon him and cut him to ribbons. His body was so mutilated that the pieces were later collected in a sack. His grave can still be seen.

The end of the Xhosa people as a warrior race brought peace to the Eastern Cape but it remains one of the tragedies of our history. The national suicide of the Ama-Xhosa, the history books call it. A Xhosa girl, sitting at the edge of a pool among the wild bananas, dreamed and watched the water. The waves of the Indian Ocean broke close to the pool and when the tide came in the water in the pool was troubled, and she saw visions in these movements. They foretold, she said, the victory of the Xhosas over the whites if they slaughtered their own cattle and emptied their grain bins. Chiefs and magicians spread the news: and the people believed, destroyed their food, and starved. A vision – or a strategy to fire the Xhosa spirit – miscarried, and half a nation perished in the months that followed. Hungry and desperate Xhosas poured into the Cape Colony to work for the whites, and in a generation they forgot the whistle of an assegai or the meaning of a headband with a blue crane's feather.

I expect the first Xhosa labourers on Cranemere were these refugees from hunger. In 1880, when George and Fanny arrived, the 'national suicide' was only twenty-four years past and white and black alike must have remembered it vividly, or the events which had made it possible. Yet here they lived easily together, these peoples who had fought each other so bitterly, and this I find an unexpected and interesting thing.

When Fanny set foot on Cranemere the feudal system sprang into life, this unfashionable system which – when it works – works so very well. George and Fanny, Clifford and Katinka, Maurice and Sita – they have cared for the land and people for a long time, and today some of the men and women who work for Maurice and Sita are the grandchildren and greatgrandchildren of those who worked for George and Fanny.

After months of newspapers and radios and politics at home and abroad, the goodwill of Cranemere brings great ease. There are few greater pleasures for me today than a return to Cranemere after a long absence and a reunion with the people, the welcome and questions, the Xhosa women trilling with laughter and gossip, the men, tremendously dignified – and I remember some of them as boys – arriving to pay a call of welcome with a gift of new potatoes from their gardens.

Every time I return I am struck by the good looks of our Xhosa people. As a race they are not black at all but brown, and the children, youth and maidens most comely. Sometimes they age extremely well, their brown lined faces acquiring much dignity and humour. As a child, I would sometimes go to their houses to talk to the old people, sitting in the sun at their doorways, and this was always an experience for I sensed a lively knowledge far beyond anything I knew. Between them they shared many hundred years of life, and old Jacob, the oldest of them all, was over a century when he died – over 110 years old, the doctor thought.

When I first introduced Jenks, my husband, to him, he said politely, 'So the Seur comes from Pretoria. And how does it go with Oom Paul these days?' The year was 1950 and Paul Kruger had been dead for forty-six years!

The old people were always surrounded by a swarm of young, little boys and girls and babies tumbling in the dust. To us they were often Joycey or Piet or Jan, but never among themselves for they called one another by the sonorous names of their own tongue: Nombulelo – I Give Thanks; Mbuyiselo – It Was Worth It; Khawulezile – It Went Well and Fast: Nonzima – It Went Badly; Nozipho – I Give It To You. There was once, Maurice recollects, a particularly lovely name that rolled off the tongue. It meant Born in the Veld. Sometimes they give us names, although we do not always know them. Sita is The Quick Worker; Maurice, Lord of All; Mary, their daughter, is Beautiful; Alex, their son, is The Good One.

Years ago there grew up in Cranemere house a small, solemn, clever little brown boy, Konos, who acted as butler until he became a man, when – according to Xhosa tradition – housework became *infra dig*. Even as tractor-driver in the lands and on the veld, he never lost his interest in the 'house' and family. On the day that David, my son, was born in Pretoria, a son was born on Cranemere to Maria, Konos's wife. They named him David after mine, and the farm today regards the children as two peas in one pod. 'As wild as two springbucks,' the people say indulgently.

One day in David's fifth year when we were visiting Cranemere a deputation met me in the kitchen. It was headed by Maggie, the matriarch, who had worked for my mother before Sita, and who considers our family matters as her own: and behind her clustered the maids.

'I wish to tell you something,' she pronounced, and I could see by her beaming face that it was something good. I waited. 'Master David is now of the farm,' she said 'and Hermanus [her husband and headman] has decided he must have a Xhosa name. He has named him. The name is Mphithizela.'

They had christened him Never Still, and it was the name my father had borne as a little boy eighty years before.

When Fanny ruled the farm there were many Xhosa people and even then they were detribalized. Many of them, it is true, had close relations in the Transkei and visited them sometimes, but none of them ever admitted a Transkei chief as theirs. Many of them were pagans. Today all the people of the farm are Christians and the little church, with its weekly meetings and festivities, is an important centre. Sometimes on a Thursday afternoon when I hear the voices of the women, for it is their afternoon, raised in extremely lively devotion, I think of the old pagan woman whom four generations of Palmers knew, who would not enter a church nor sleep on a bed, but who invited a witch-doctor to Cranemere, a dapper young man in a grey suit who rode a bicycle. I saw him one day dancing in his white paint and jackal-tails and monkey-skins and my heart missed a beat, and I knew why the old woman filled his bowl twice a day with her choicest food.

In Fanny's day Cranemere was a world of spirits. She herself knew them, for she (and my sister Iris) had their visitations, a ghostly traveller with cart and horses that would stop before the house. They heard the wheels and hoofs and the traveller's footsteps on the gravel and his knock upon the door. When they opened it there was never a soul.

But while we were not afraid to walk in the dark, our brown and yellow people were. They were terrified of the marsh lights, the will-o'-the-wisps, that were sometimes seen about the dam, for they believed them to be spirits. There was a certain road which was taboo at night, for close to it was a little stone hut where a man had been killed and which, they believed, his spirit haunted.

Close to Cranemere on the banks of the Melkrivier was another ruin where many people had seen strange things. A traveller between Graaff-Reinet and Pearston once spent a night in this half-empty ruin and was woken by the loud and merry sound of a Hottentot dance not six feet from where he lay

31

with his head upon his saddle. He struck a light with his tinder-box but immediately all was still. He settled himself again and the dancing recommenced, fast and lively, and the cottage vibrated with movement and laughter. He jumped up, saddled his horse, and rode forth into the night.

Time has not obliterated our ghosts. There are a great many graves upon the farm, every one unnamed, from the old bricked European graves to the more ancient ones, still piled with lichened stones, which may date from the time long ago when the Hottentots, and perhaps the Bushmen, used to place a stone on every grave they passed. Or perhaps they are the graves of the Bushmen's 'people of an earlier race'. Stories of ghosts still linger, and even now our people do not pass a grave happily at night. Probably there are many whites, too, who feel uneasy on a black night on this great plain surrounded by ancient bones and possibly ancient spirits.

I found it possible to believe, or half believe, these stories. Yet even in childhood I could never accept the tokoloshes. Many of the primitive Bantu people believe in these evil spirits. Ours was an unusual and villainous breed with horns and talons and shaggy hair and eyes in their big toes. They were said to live in the big koppie behind the African houses. They came forth at night to prowl about the houses and steal – if possible – the babies. Careful fathers, the Africans told us children, lighted fires before their doors at sunset so that there should be a pile of ashes through the night. Marauding tokoloshes would thus step in the ashes and be blinded.

Do they – devout Christians – have any regard for such things today? Or do they belong to the old magical past alone? I asked Maggie once. Her kind old face went blank. Then she laughed and said, 'Well, *I* have never seen one;' and that was as far as I got.

We did have a woman who practised magic, and not many years ago. She was a large, comely, smooth-faced woman who cast her spells successfully, it was said. She did great damage and caused many disturbances. There were some who feared her desperately, including a gaunt, miserable, neurotic creature who believed that the woman was killing her with magic.

I asked why she feared this and she told me a curious tale. She had sought the counsel of a wise woman in Graaff-Reinet who promised to show her the cause of her sickness. 'Throwing the bones' is the traditional means of divination among the interior tribes in South Africa, but this woman used 'a glass ball'. I had never heard of one of our people using a crystal ball before but it seems this one did. As the victim stared into it she saw a tiny, perfect picture – her enemy crossing the farmyard at Cranemere, and she said she could see even the stitches in her apron. 'I knew then I was right,' she said; and 'She always gets what she wants.'

The wretched creature's disease was later identified and treated; but I believe that if she had not taken the wise woman's antidote to bewitchment – I never learned what it was – she would have died of fear in spite of all that twentieth-century medicine could do.

Once our woman tried to bewitch me. She put a decoction in my coffee and when I emptied out my cup, grumbling that she must have left a cake of soap in the coffee-pot, she hid her face in her hands. It was little use, she told someone later, trying to influence a white. And she added she had never meant to harm me. It was a spell to make me give her a new silk petticoat.

Recently, after a long absence from Cranemere, she returned to visit. Sita told me about it afterwards. 'Do you know, she can make one think almost anything she wants,' she said. She added quietly, 'She is a remarkably clever woman, and I hope that she never comes back.'

Our Xhosa men still follow the custom of circumcision. It is a fascinating thing that this ancient practice can still persist in its old form amid our church, school, radio, antibiotics, and all the other trappings of their modern lives: but still, before any youth on Cranemere is judged a man, he must 'go into the veld' as did his ancestors.

When their time has come the youths – two usually go together – leave the inhabited part of the farm and go by themselves to some lonely spot. There they make a temporary hut, here is their school, and here the circumcision is done by a specially appointed person who sometimes travels miles to perform the operation.

He himself is an important part of the ceremony, for on the kind of man he is much of the future of the youth, it is believed, depends. Soga writes how one of the great Xhosa chiefs, Kreli, a beloved and respected man, was held to have a mild temper because he had had the right surgeon, whereas his father and his own son had fiery tempers because their surgeons had been less worthy: they 'developed a horn', so the Xhosas said.

While in the veld the young men paint themselves from head to foot with white clay, and this always comes from the same place and is collected by the same person year by year. They may be seen by no woman or girl during the period, may drink no water and eat no meat or salt. Every day the little boys on the farm take them watery food: coffee, tea, vegetables, fruit. Every day one of the young married men cares for their wounds, and these invariably heal without infection. They use in their treatment – never a modern drug – the dry outside scales of the gifbol, the poison bulb, which grows all over South Africa and is probably one of our oldest healers.

Often, when we were children, certain parts of the farm were forbidden to my sister and me because here the young men were 'in the veld'. Sometimes we came upon them unexpectedly and it was impossible to avoid them as they stood like bright white statues among the small grey bushes, but then my father taught us to turn our faces away and pretend we had not seen them.

After several weeks they return as new people with new clothes and blankets, for they may wear nothing they have ever worn before. Now they are men and may marry; and I do not think it is only fancy that they bear themselves with a new pride. As a child, I used to think that their backs were straighter.

It has often seemed to me that the Xhosa children resemble their parents far more than do ours. Often, returning to Cranemere, I can tell from a glance at a small brown boy or girl who their fathers and mothers are, and sometimes their grandparents. I look with particular delight at one small girl for here is Olifant, her great-grandfather, living again.

Olifant lived on Cranemere for over half a century; and today when we talk of our Xhosa people to strangers we usually think first of him. We children never knew him as a young man. To us he had always been bent and wiry, his face criss-crossed with wrinkles, his eyes sparking; a great old clown, tumbling and dancing for the children, laughing from his toes, and in his cups filling the world with noise. We loved him and he loved us, a rollicking, uncomplicated, unpolitical relationship unquestioned then by any.

Europeans have often remarked on the affinity that the Hottentots and Bantu of South Africa have with animals. Early travellers marvelled at it. Burchell wondered at his Hottentots, who knew every individual sheep in a great flock, allotting to each ewe its rightful lamb; and within a matter of hours knowing intimately every ox in a new team.

Cattle were the most loved and coveted treasures of the Xhosas and many observers described how the men would run along talking to their oxen like children, telling them their complaints and hovering over them with covetous fondness. The cattle, like dogs, responded. Theal, the historian, tells how they would come to a call or a whistle; lie down at an order, run in a circle, or dance in rows.

Olifant showed, in all completeness, what the relationship of a man and an animal may be, and he stood for all those Xhosa men for whom their animals had been joy and pride. He differed from them in one way only: his love was not cattle but mules.

Mules and horses were an important part of Cranemere before the days of motor-cars and tractors and George would have only the best of them. His cart-horses were Punch and Hamlet, Devil's Skin and Satan, splendidly fast and strong, and with these he used to fly into Pearston, the stones and dust spurting on every side. His mules matched them in excellence. He finally acquired a team of twelve great handsome animals bred in Montevideo and these were famous in the district. When any cart or wagon in the neighbourhood seemed irretrievably stuck, someone would always say, 'Send for Palmer's mules,' and they always did the trick.

Olifant lavished on these mules, and on every succeeding mule that lived on Cranemere, the most passionate and tender love. He tended them and their harness with devotion. He would talk to them, coax them, scold them, flatter them, joke with them, telling them his difficulties and his joys, and as they turned their heads and moved their ears it was clear they listened and understood.

The Anglo-Boer War was a time of great tribulation for Olifant, for four of his mules were commandeered by the British Army and one was stolen by a Boer neighbour, who rode away on it to join Malan's commando. There remain today some of the letters concerning this mule, endless correspondence between the Palmers and the British forces who finally acquired the animal, my grandfather (doubtless driven to desperation by Olifant's swimming eyes) finally offering to charter a truck to transport the mule to the nearest station to the farm!

Olifant had his day. The war ended and, as Cranemere's representative, he went forth to claim his darlings from the great military compound in the north-eastern Karoo where had been herded the thousands of mules commandeered by the military throughout the war. He had not seen his mules for two years.

Shaking with excitement, he presented his credentials. 'I have come for my mules, Baas,' he said.

The officer looked at the thousands of milling animals and laughed. 'You can have any four mules,' he said, 'but you'll never see your own again, you know.'

'I want *my* mules,' said Olifant, and he climbed onto the high fence around the compound to look down on the sea of backs below him.

'There's my mule,' he screamed, 'and there, and there, and there,' and he called them by name – 'Dapper, Kaptein, September, Zwartman,' and out of the mass streamed his mules towards him, the gates were flung open for them, and Olifant and they embraced and it was difficult to tell whose were the tears and whose the neighs.

Years later when I was a schoolchild coming back from boarding-school in Port Elizabeth, Olifant would sometimes be sent to meet me in Pearston and I would travel back the last ten miles with him by mule wagon. I remember lying on my back in the bottom of the wagon, eating cold green mealies and tossing the cobs into the veld, looking at the pale Karoo sky above with the little kestrels swooping, and listening to Olifant gossiping with his mules. If queens know greater pleasures they are lucky indeed.

Olifant must have been a very old man when he died. He was buried on a windy afternoon with a wild yellow sunset and I remember that my father wept.

Olifant was a great story-teller, like many of the people of the Plains. Today we still recall some of the stories we heard from him and the other black and brown and yellow people we knew as children; tales of magic, of a dog with a tail of fire that was known to hunt by night along the farm road; of bones that talked; of animals with speech; of *die ou volk*, the old Cape lions; and as we talk of them I think how the stories of our Plains have that same classic touch we find in all the great folk-tales of the world.

Sometimes their tales were no longer African at all, but tales transported six thousand miles, so delightful to our people that they had absorbed them and made them their own. We listened raptly, for a Baron Münchhausen adventure on the lips of a Xhosa herd on an African evening was enchantment.

'This,' Olifant would say, 'happened to my brother;' and he would tell us some story like the adventure with the baboons.

'One day,' he would say, 'my brother was herding goats. But it was hot and he went to sleep under a witgat tree. When he woke up the goats were gone. So he jumped up and got on his horse in a hurry, and galloped across the veld after them. He rode and he rode, and after a while he came to a valley with a krantz [precipice] on either side, and when he was in the middle of the valley he found he was in a fix. High up on the rocks the baboons were jumping about and shouting, and when they saw him below them they started to roll down stones on top of him.

'Well, my brother was very lucky to get out of that valley alive, but he did. And on the other side he came to a dam. My poor horse must be thirsty after the baboons, he thought, and he took him to the edge and let him drink. And he drank and he drank. He drank until the level of the water in the dam began to fall. And presently there was no water left at all. He had drunk the dam dry.

'"Magtig!" thought my brother sitting on the horse's back; "Now this is a strange thing." Then he turned his head and looked behind him and saw the reason for it all. The stones the baboons had thrown had cut his horse in half and the water had passed clean through him and was running down the slope in a stream.'

Here Olifant would pause triumphantly for our applause.

A Hottentot near Graaff-Reinet once told the classic among tales and it was of how he had met the Devil. He was shooting on the flats, and after an exhausting day, for the springbuck were wild and there was little cover higher than a karoo bush, he sat down and lit his marrow-bone pipe. The tobacco and dagga were strong and good and he sat pleasurably until dusk drew in and he heard the dikkop and the night-owl crying, and saw an object moving slowly towards him.

He thought it was a jackal and fingered his gun, but when it drew closer he saw it was a black goat – 'and yet not exactly that either, for I saw,' said he, 'it had a man's head.'

He knew then it could be none but the Devil. Shuddering with horror, he yet determined to brave it out for there was no chance of escape.

The Devil approached. 'Good day, nephew,' he said, holding out his hoof.

'Good day, uncle,' he gasped out.

'What is nephew doing here?' the Devil asked.

'I'm watching for those buck,' he jerked out as best he could.

'So!' said the Devil. 'But what is that that you have in your mouth?'

'Only my pipe that I am smoking, uncle.'

'Then just give me a whiff too, will you, old brother,' coaxed the Devil.

The trembling man took the pipe out of his mouth but found that in his agitation he had let it go out. Immediately a brilliant plan leaped to mind. His gun was loaded and with it he would end the Evil One for ever.

'Stop a bit, uncle,' he said, 'this is my tinder-box,' and he pointed to his gun. 'I'll just strike a light for uncle with it.'

He put the muzzle of the gun into the bowl of the pipe, telling the Devil that when he pressed the trigger he was to draw in his breath, and so light the pipe. At the last moment he pointed the barrel straight at the Devil's head and fired.

'Bang, bang,' roared the gun.

'I heard his skull crack as the slugs crushed it, as I thought, to a jelly,' he recounted later, 'but to my surprise, when the smoke had cleared away he quietly took the pipe out of his mouth and with his two hoofs squeezed his head into shape again, exclaiming while he rubbed his mouth with his hoof, "Good gracious! Allamastig! What strong tobacco!"'

4. The Forgotten Highway

A great highway once traversed Cranemere. Today it is forgotten, as are the people who travelled it. Yet together they illumined history.

This old road stretched north of the present road between Pearston and Graaff-Reinet, across the Plains and through the heart of Cranemere. *Die ou wapad* – the old wagon-road, the people of our countryside call it without remembering the significance of the name, for once this was a trek road, the most northern road across the Cape Colony from east to west, and the highway used by all early travellers between Cape and frontier by the northern route.

It is now almost completely overgrown by karoo bush, and although it can be picked out on an aerial map, in the veld itself it can be traced only with difficulty and in parts it has vanished. Not a plaque, not a stone, recalls its great past, and now none of the people of the Plains remember its time of greatness or in how many old journals or tales of exploration it figured.

Nor do they remember the people who travelled the road and helped to make the story of the Plains, people who often never lived here and of whom we know little, but who are with us still in unexpected things: in the name of a plant, an animal, a bird, a mountain, in a piece of knowledge that is a legacy from them to us.

They lived perhaps two hundred years ago. Many of them knew Cranemere; some crossed and recrossed it. I remember still the frenzy of excitement with which I first discovered them, not from history books but from the old journals which still remain our very great adventure stories.

The first great eastern trek route from the settled, well-established Cape roughly followed the coast for several hundred miles, much of it through well-wooded country with elephant and buffalo, gorgeous birds and strange plants; but sooner or later when these adventurers – in the fine old spirit of the word – reached the end of this route, little known as it might be, they longed for the sights and perhaps the perils of the unknown. Between the Sundays River and what are now the cities of Port Elizabeth and Grahamstown many turned north towards the Karoo, cracking their whips at the fords of rivers to frighten away the lions and marvelling at the rich animal and bird life.

The old trek route passed Kommadagga and wound its way to the Little Fish River to a spot near where the village of Somerset East stands today. This was an enchanting post, green and leafy, lush grassland at the foot of the loveliest mountain in Africa, the Boschberg – the Mountain of Trees – flowing with waterfalls and garlanded with wild flowers. It was a botanist's paradise as William Burchell, one of the world's great naturalists, was to find. From here the trek route back to the Cape lay north-west, over the mountain of Bruintjeshoogte; and suddenly, almost over the brow of the mountain and a bare fifteen miles from the Little Fish River, the grass and the water were gone. This was Karoo. This, to them, was desert. The travellers tightened their belts and cheered themselves as best they could, for between here and the village of Graaff-Reinet sixty miles away they were lucky to find good water. The Blyrivier, the Vogelsrivier, the Melkrivier – all were likely to be dry in drought.

It was a desert plain, the travellers wrote, yet alive with game – springbuck, eland, kudu, wildebeest, steenbok, quagga; and where there was game there were lions. This stretch of country was accounted one of the most dangerous in the whole colony, and it was a toss-up whether travellers along this road would go by day, enduring the great heat, or by night, risking the lions. It was with the utmost delight they finally heard the loud croakings of frogs and knew that the Sundays River and the village of Graaff-Reinet were at hand.

When the first travellers ventured here at the end of the eighteenth century the eastern Plains lay in the district of Stellenbosch. Soon the district became Graaff-Reinet, then Uitenhage, and Somerset East, all great names in early Cape history. Today it is Pearston, taking its name from the little village that stands on the banks of the Vogelsrivier near the ford where the travellers once crossed.

Somerset East was then not dreamed of; Graaff-Reinet was a little village with half a dozen houses built of mud where it was difficult to remain in a lighted room by night for the bats that came out of the thatched roofs by the thousand and blew out the lighted candles by the wind they caused. Twenty years later it was the most picturesque town in the Cape, an oasis on the river, with flat-roofed, white-washed houses and wide streets planted with orange and lemon trees, vines, oleanders, pomegranates, and great quince hedges bent down with fruit.

It hummed with life. Here was a church, school, court of law, a smith, a wagon-maker, shops, and traders in ostrich feathers, hides, soap and butter. Later Graaff-Reinet was to lie on a main road to the north, but at the turn of the eighteenth century the north was almost unknown territory.

Ten miles west of the Vogelsrivier near the old wagon-road is a large red hill covered with small succulent trees, the Spekboomkop of the old maps, and the Rooikop – the Red Head – of today. Close to this grew a witgat tree not fifteen feet tall but with a thick, seamed, milk-white trunk and a dense grey-green crown of tough little leaves. This was the Gallows Tree which gave the farm its early name, and it was a landmark along the road.

Here came the first frontiersmen. Louis Trichardt, the voortrekker, and his family passed here; the Prinsloo family, the Kruger family, relations of Paul Kruger; Coenraad Buys, the flamboyant rebel. Two of the very great botanists and naturalists in South African history, Thunberg and Sparrman, planned to cross the Plains of Camdeboo by this road, but changed their routes on account of drought and horsesickness. Swellengrebel, accompanied by two friends and a wandering artist, was one of the very earliest of whom we have any record to make this trip.

Great botanists such as Zeyher, Ecklon, Drège and Marloth

7 *The two Davids measuring the gigantic thorns of the Karoo thorn tree.*

8 *Maggie, the cook, and Emily about to put dough in Cranemere's old Dutch oven.*

9 *William Burchell*

10 *The interior of Burchell's famous wagon, from a copy of his drawing in the Gubbins Library, University of the Witwatersrand.*

probably knew the farm; almost certainly MacOwan and Bolus did. Robert Broom, one of the world's greatest palaeontologists, hunted fossils, lizards, spiders, insects, and plants on the Plains and in the mountains beyond.

Governors, officials, explorers, the friends of kings and the humblest shepherds – they all passed over Galgenbosch and some camped on it or just beyond its boundaries.

Carl Thunberg stopped short of Galgenbosch. He is sometimes called the 'father of Cape botany' and science owes him a great debt. He was one of the great pioneer botanists and collectors and left a fine journal. It is a pity that he never completed his trip across the northern route as he had planned, for his descriptions would have been illuminating.

Andrew Sparrman was a Swedish medical doctor with a talent for natural history. He got as far as Bruintjeshoogte, overlooking the Plains of Camdeboo, before turning back. He was a man of considerable courage and observation and his journal reads like a racketing good adventure story. It was one of the earliest best-sellers on Africa and was translated from the Swedish into English, French and German, and ran through several editions. It is pleasant to know that this is so, for he worked hard to get to Africa, and his equipment for his trip was spartan compared to that of other travellers.

He partly financed his expedition by translating a Swedish doctor's treatise on the diseases of children while cruising in the South Seas in stormy weather, clinging with his legs round the foot of the table and holding fast with one hand, thus steadying himself to write with the other. Was ever money to see the sights of Africa raised in a more unlikely way?

He took with him into unknown country not a well-seasoned colonist, but a youth, Immelman, suffering from lung disease, who was eager for new sights. They each had a horse, and a baggage-wagon between them, which provided no proper place to sleep so that they travelled hard, sleeping on the ground with saddles for their pillows and their greatcoats over them. When it rained they sometimes slept under the wagon, but this was extremely hazardous, for the oxen were tied to the wagon and they had to creep in and out among their legs, hoping that the legs they squeezed between belonged to the gentlest of them. Sometimes they lay inside the wagon, Sparrman on a wooden chest (with a round top!) and his companion between the chest and the body of the wagon on several bundles of paper.

They did try some of the colonists' houses. It was a choice, Sparrman wrote dourly, between high winds and rain, and 'an host of fleas'.

The baggage that the explorers and collectors took with them as necessary for their lives and studies in this new land makes fascinating reading. There were certain things they all took: clothes, food – although the kind varied considerably from one to the other; arms of various kinds and ammunition; tools, medicines; tobacco for the Hottentots and other things the Hottentots loved such as beads, tinder-boxes, knives. Some took liquor, but Sparrman's only supply was an oaken cask of brandy to preserve snakes, and even this was a great embarrassment to him for he had to guard it carefully from his Hottentots. Great was his relief when he caught his first serpent and put it alive into the cask in the presence of his company. If they drank that brandy, Immelman told them, they would burst with snake poison. 'They gave us plainly to perceive that they envied the venomous creature the pleasure of being drowned in so delicious an element,' said Sparrman.

Sparrman took with him, also, reams of paper for drying plants, pins for insects, and a supply of special needles with which, together with fair words, he hoped to bribe the farmers' daughters to help him collect insects in the veld. They must have found him an odd young man for on at least one occasion he pinned his 'little beasts' to the brim of his hat, and was pleased at the reaction! And so he travelled the country, collecting and noting everything, people, animals, birds, insects, stories; 'suppling' his throat with ostrich eggs, planning to hunt the unicorn, calling himself the child of a great man, Jan Company – for what Hottentot in the interior had ever heard of the

Dutch East India Company? For all his imagination and high spirits, he remains a trustworthy observer.

One of the very first travellers to pass over the wagon-road on the Plains of Camdeboo was a Hollander, Hendrik Swellengrebel, the son of a former governor of the Cape. Although born in Cape Town, he lived in Holland, collecting as a hobby exotic plants, many from the Cape. He made three famous journeys through the Cape and one took him in 1776 across the Karoo; with him went two friends, one a Pieter Cloete who wrote an account of his trip, an artist, and a number of servants. Swellengrebel never once referred to the artist – Johannes Schumacher – by name. An artist was not, apparently, worthy of this courtesy. Today Schumacher's works are Africana!

This was a small, mobile, lightly equipped party, and it entered the Karoo not from the east, but from the west. 'Quiet, clear, pleasant weather,' wrote Pieter Cloete crossing the Plains of Camdeboo (there were few who ever seemed to write thus).

They hunted springbuck, buffalo, quagga and wild pigs here, and saw the fresh manure and spoor of a rhinoceros. Schumacher shows something of this countryside in his intimate little paintings of the flat-topped mountains of the Karoo, some rising into peaks, the wooded slopes of the Boschberg, the plains, and of the wild animals they hunted.

Colonel Robert Gordon, who passed over the Plains of Camdeboo twice between 1777 and 1779, was not only the greatest traveller and explorer of the Cape in his day but a very accomplished man, one of those who would have shone in any bright and gallant circle of Europe. Tall, handsome, elegant, abounding in energy and learning, a soldier, an engineer, an artist, every visitor and scientist to the Cape clamoured for his friendship and his help; and equally was it said that in the interior every Hottentot trusted him. He had learnt their language and probably knew them better than any other man in Africa.

He was born in Holland in 1743, the son of a soldier of Scots extraction and a Dutch mother. As commander of the military forces at the Cape, he was an ardent supporter of the Prince of Orange, and when the Cape was taken by the British in 1795 he committed suicide.

The fate of his journals makes an enthralling story. After his death they disappeared, and for a hundred and fifty years all efforts to trace them were a failure. I used to imagine idly to myself that one day we would find them in the loft above the guinea-fowl room on Cranemere, in some old box, keeping company with the owls. The truth was as improbable.

In the 1960s the director of the South African Archives, Dr A. Kieser, lunching with the director of the Staffordshire County Archives in England, asked him – 'to keep the conversation going' – if he had any Dutch documents. He had, he said, but he could not understand them. They inspected them after lunch. They were Gordon's travel diaries and a treatise on the Hottentots, perhaps some of the most valuable Africana finds ever made.

In addition to his journal Gordon left nearly four hundred paintings of plants, trees, birds and animals, as well as a number of natives, reptiles, fish, landscapes, and the first charts and views ever made of the Orange River. The British Government was urged to buy these but refused, and they were bought privately. In 1913 when they again came up for sale South Africa was not interested, and they are now in the Rijks Museum in Amsterdam.

At the present time nothing of Gordon's remains in South Africa, and yet strangely enough one of his possessions has, in a roundabout way, been returned to us. He was one of the first importers of merino sheep. On his death these were taken to Australia and formed the basis of the great Australian sheep industry, and from the Australian flocks they sired came rams sent in their turn to South Africa.

Gordon had as his good friend and companion on some of his travels the Governor of the Cape, Baron Joachim van Plettenberg, who was the first head of the Government to appear on the eastern border. Theirs was a large official party and a leisurely journey, described by the Governor himself in his journal. They passed through the Plains of Camdeboo on an October day in 1778, and it was no desert for they saw it after rain.

Although the little karoo bushes were there, it was above all a world of grass and van Plettenberg wrote of the beautiful far-stretched meadows and the plains rich in grasses on which the cattle doted.

Shortly after Gordon's last visit to the Karoo there appeared on the scene one of the most ludicrous, engaging, and colourful young men ever to ride the 'desart' or recount his adventures. He was François le Vaillant, a French ornithologist of world fame, who arrived at the Cape in 1781 when he was twenty-eight years old. Everything about him was extraordinary, including his introduction to South Africa – his goods were blown up by the British while still aboard his ship, leaving him 'nothing but the clothes he wore, ten ducats, and his fowling-piece'.

Colonel Gordon, as always, was a friend to all naturalists and travellers, and he helped Le Vaillant in Cape Town, so that when he finally set off he was well prepared in every way. Not for him the spartan necessities of Sparrman – he had two large covered wagons, tents, tools, five large boxes, a whole cabinet for his butterflies, 'curiosities' for the Hottentots and natives, 500 lbs. of gunpowder and a huge supply of lead and tin bullets, sixteen guns, several pairs of double-barrelled pistols, a large scimitar and a poniard. He carried for himself a large mattress, everything needed for a mobile kitchen, and linen of every kind (he changed his clothes at least three times a day).

His three most unusual possessions were a dressing-box, a baboon, and a cock, and all three were quite vital to his travels. The first carried his finery, which he used freely to impress the Hottentots; the baboon was his companion and the 'taster' in the veld of all the new foods; and the cock was his clock in the mornings. It roosted on his wagon or his tent, never leaving the vicinity of the camp, growing so much an inmate that the pack of dogs would spring to its aid if it were in trouble.

Le Vaillant recounts many adventures, some of them probably true, for no man could travel in this country without seeing and doing strange things, but Le Vaillant added an extra touch of exuberance. Along the coastal route he met elephants and buffalo and battled with them bravely (using their fat later for candles and for his night lamp); he met strange Hottentots ('my engaging behaviour had secured me the friendship and confidence of these honest savages'); he fired off his guns all one night to keep the lions at bay. Near the Sundays River he turned northwards to the Karoo, travelled along the Vogelsrivier in great heat, and across Bruintjeshoogte to the Great Fish River.

What a treat he must have been for the Hottentots. He had grown an immense beard to prove to any hostile native that he was not one of the 'detested' farmers ('I was received as an extraordinary being, and as a man of a new species'); he loaded his hair with powder, he combed his black beard so that it hung down in the most graceful manner possible; he dressed himself in a dark brown hunting-frock with steel buttons which reflected the light of the sun. Under this he wore a white vest and in place of boots a pair of nankeen drawers (which appeared to him equally noble); he wore, too, shoes with large brilliant silver buckles, knee buckles as a clasp on his hat, a magnificent plume of ostrich feathers, and he carried two pairs of pistols and a gun.

Le Vaillant probably travelled as far as Tarkastad, where he turned back again and prepared himself to go westwards past the Snow Mountains, the haunt of Bushmen, as he wrote, which made his brave attendants tremble, but not, he suggested, himself! He spent New Year's Day, 1783, on the Little Fish River, crossed Bruintjeshoogte three days later, and began an eventful crossing of the Plains of Camdeboo.

On his right towered what he took to be the Sneeuberg but which on modern maps are named the Swaershoek and the Coetzeeberg, the true Sneeuberg being many miles to the northwest. His mistake has confused many authorities on his travels, including the late Captain C. H. B. Grant of the British Museum of Natural History in London, but Le Vaillant was not to blame. These were not the true Snow Mountains but locally they were often called by this famous name. Moreover, as he advanced towards them in 'excessive heat', he saw there were still traces of snow upon them, and this probably clinched the matter for him.

Le Vaillant did not rush across the Plains of Camdeboo as did so many others. He set up a fortified camp on the Platrivier, perhaps a mile beyond Galgenbosch, and enjoyed many adventures here. He mentioned no farmers or Europeans at all and the country he described was wild and deserted.

His first adventure with lions was probably on Galgenbosch – on Cranemere – itself, just east of the river, when a lion and lioness attacked his oxen at night; 'an useful hint to me,' he wrote, 'never to travel during the night in countries with which I was so little acquainted and which, as I afterwards learned, are the most dangerous to be passed in all Africa.' He heard the lions roaring at night, and saw at dawn and dusk the leopards on the banks of the river; he shot eland here, saw traces of rhino, and hunted Bushmen in the mountains.

He did not admire the country, the parched sands and the rocks of the mountains piled on each other in hideous forms. He complained equally of the rain – the dreadful storm and the torrents which swept down from the mountains, the cascades and cataracts that fell with a horrid noise and covered the plains with vapour and foam – and the insupportable heat which he survived only by his own ingenuity, by soaking his beard and his hat, and by lapping water like a dog which he swore gave him wonderful ease!

A grim trek back across the Karoo brought him at last to the beginnings of civilization. People flocked to see him and hear his tales, to beg for a glimpse of his wagon-loads of gold dust and jewels and 'that magnificent precious stone, superior to the diamond and as large as an egg, found in the head of an enormous serpent' with which he was supposed somewhere in the Eastern Cape to have fought a most desperate and bloody battle. He laughed at the reputation he had earned but obviously felt it was his due. Almost the last we hear of this flamboyant young man in the first volume of his travels is of his falling down upon his knees before the doubtless pretty young miss who had offered to cut his beard and 'devoting his head as a sacrifice'.

It is not easy from his journal to believe that Le Vaillant was a scientist, but he was. His wagons when he returned were not full of gold dust and precious stones but of birds, and they filled everything, even his tea, coffee, and sugar chests. Even if many of his statements were incorrect, his contribution to South African ornithology was great and his *Histoire Naturelle des Oiseaux d'Afrique* is a rare, beautiful and precious book.

The next traveller of note over the Plains seems to have been John Barrow. He must have been an unusual man for, coming from a humble home in Lancashire, he died a baronet with Point Barrow, Cape Barrow and Barrow Straits in the North Polar Seas named after him. He came to the Cape as private secretary to Earl Macartney, who became governor of the Cape Colony in 1797, and was sent by him to the interior to make a first-hand report on conditions. His visit was to appear as one of curiosity, science, and of botanical research rather than an official survey, but it remains a valuable comment on the country at the time. That it is not even more important is because Barrow, although extremely able, appears also to have been a bigoted young man, intolerant and arrogant, and much he wrote of the people he met was biased.

Henry Lichtenstein followed. He was a doctor of medicine and philosophy and professor of natural history in the University of Berlin, and he came out to the Cape as tutor to the thirteen-year-old son of the Governor, General J. W. Janssens, for the Cape was once more under Dutch rule. He seems to have been a nice young man but not a humble one. 'With a cheerful heart and placid confidence in my future fate, I quitted my native country, my parents, my brethren, my friends, and blessed, even at that moment, the determined resolution with which I was enabled to engage in the career prompted by my genius,' he wrote.

In 1803 he set out on a journey into the interior of the Cape with a vast official party headed by de Mist, the Commissary-General, and including his nineteen-year-old daughter, the Lady Augusta – Julie – who, although warned in lurid terms of the dangers ahead, insisted on joining the party. It sounds a very unwieldy affair with its numerous officials, its surgeon, book-keeper, soldiers, Hottentots and slaves, and – its most unlikely members to explore the wilds of Africa – two gentlemen-of-the-chamber and two ladies-in-waiting, and a French horn player whose job it was to collect the cavalcade and keep it together.

The thought of this ponderous procession disciplined by the horn player and ambling through our desert with its ladies and sheep and butterfly-nets enchants me. Perhaps it is the most unusual gathering our Plains have ever seen.

The baggage filled six wagons and held every luxury and necessity. Lichtenstein, who went as naturalist to the expedition, took all the scientific equipment he needed, including a microscope, butterfly-nets, a huge amount of paper for drying plants, a cask of brandy for preserving reptiles, and a complete library. He read Goethe, Lessing, Schiller, Tasso, and Sterne's *Sentimental Journey,* and surely Africa has seldom been explored with odder literature as guidance.

Leaving the southern route, the party struck northward and Lichtenstein describes much of the country to both sides of Bruintjeshoogte. He found the Plains of Camdeboo arid, hot and bare, and the landscape monstrous. They travelled through a wood full of lions and were told that on their account the road should never be travelled by night.

Lichtenstein's journal is today considered good and accurate but it is in parts rather stodgy. It is, however, enlivened by a charmingly Germanic description of the Lady Augusta, who was patient and intelligent, with a richly stored mind and a singular union of feminine softness and tenderness of heart with a manly resolution and firmness of mind. And she was punctual! Lichtenstein paid her the greatest compliment he apparently knew. 'It is not less incredible than true,' he wrote, 'that through the whole journey, which was extended to nearly six months, never was at any time the least delay occasioned either by her or her female attendants, never was any regulation whatever broken.' Lichtenstein was obviously charmed. He had a strong-featured, sensitive face with a dimple in his chin and large expressive eyes; it is difficult to believe that punctuality was the only plane on which they travelled the desert together.

The Reverend John Campbell, who crossed the Plains nine years after Lichtenstein, was a missionary sent by the London Missionary Society to inspect their settlements. Travelling via Grahamstown, he struck north and then west, crossing Bruintjeshoogte and recording how steep and dangerous the road was and so came to the plains beyond the Vogelsrivier, a red country, he said, covered with heath mixed with grass – and this is very much how a traveller of today might find it. He made the same mistake as Le Vaillant, calling the mountains on his right the Snow Mountains, and like him he found the heat oppressive.

His party halted at the Galgenbosch itself – the Hang-bush as he called it – near a small pool of water the colour of soap-suds, and found here small temporary huts of branches of leaves made by some natives who had attempted to settle in country to the north and were now fleeing from the Bushmen towards their own country in the east. In the cool of the afternoon they travelled on towards Graaff-Reinet, admiring the wonderful forms of the mountains to the north of them, and they risked the danger of lions by night in order to reach the next water. It was Lions' Fountain!

Campbell passed through Graaff-Reinet and continued to Klaarwater and Litakun (near the present Kuruman) in the north, famous names in missionary history. It had rained, and the farmers talking to him of his journey said that the marks of his wagon-wheels would be visible for four years to come. He travelled therefore by the most level and direct way he could, for he felt he was 'commencing a path which perhaps may be travelled for hundreds of years to come'.

In Graaff-Reinet Campbell met William Burchell. He did not know it but he was meeting one of the most unusual men of his time, whose reputation has only become greater with the years. He was a botanist, a naturalist and ecologist of the first order, a superb collector, an artist, and a writer of grace, humour and accuracy. His journal, which appeared in two volumes in 1822 and 1824, is said to be the most valuable and accurate work on South Africa published up to the first quarter of the nineteenth century, and one of the classics of English travel. Even today it makes wonderful reading.

What started Burchell on his way to becoming the greatest of all South Africa's naturalists is a mystery. He was born on the outskirts of London in 1781 and his father was nothing more dashing than a market-gardener. What was there in a background of carrots and peas to make a youth yearn for exotic plants and animals 6 000 miles away? He worked at Kew and perhaps it was only a natural interest in botany that finally guided him to South Africa, perhaps it was the dismal end of his love affair, or his meeting on St Helena with Lichtenstein back from his journeys in the Cape. Whatever it was, Burchell landed in Cape Town in 1810, and in 1811 set out on his travels to the interior.

A long journey in the Africa of his day, without any companion or maps or knowledge of the country or of native languages, was a hazardous undertaking and Burchell seems a most unlikely person to have undertaken it. He was a small, gentle man; he had, he confessed in his journal, never slept a night in the open, had no love of hunting, and hated to shoot even the animals and birds he needed for his specimens. 'It is not easy to suppress that natural reluctance we feel at taking away the life of anything so innocent and pleasing as the bird that entertains us by its happy warbling,' he wrote.

His hobbies were painting and music. He carried his flute with him on his travels and in Graaff-Reinet he found with delight an organ. His Hottentot servant blew the bellows for him while he played. He drank his half-glass of wine when he could; flew the English flag upon his wagon of a Sunday, and carried with him and read deeply his copious library, which contained books on everything from natural philosophy and mineralogy to mathematics. His closest companions were his dogs, of which he had an immense pack.

Besides his travelling, scientific and painting equipment, he had with him a straw hat ornamented with twelve strings of beads as a gift for a chief, and a bag of peach-stones which he distributed in the interior. If he had travelled thus in America he would almost certainly have created a legend of himself as a Willie Peachstones, but in this country no popular tale of him remains.

In his own words, he wished to explore 'the less frequented or unknown parts of Africa, for the purpose of becoming acquainted with its inhabitants, and of increasing my own knowledge by the addition of whatever facts I might have the opportunity of observing'. This odd young man (and he had so many unusual and outstanding qualities that he was odd) succeeded tremendously. In his great trek which lasted four years he covered 4 500 miles and collected more than 63 000 objects 'in every branch of natural history'. Moreover, he systematically listed his 40 000 plants, noting the place and date of their discovery, and this in itself was unique for his day. He did not shine as a botanist only for he discovered and described the white rhinoceros, and described and drew many other animals. So – collecting, painting, drying snakeskins in his plant press, making maps and taking sights with his sextant, interested in everything from the beetles on his path to the people he met – he travelled, noting everything with scrupulous accuracy.

He went first north through the Great Karoo to the interior, and here he visited Klaarwater, the Griquatown of today, and Litakun or Litakoo, and the territory around, making a journey to Graaff-Reinet and back again to the interior, then finally back through Graaff-Reinet, where Campbell met him, across Galgenbosch and the eastern Plains of Camdeboo to Bruintjeshoogte and the Boschberg, down the Kommadagga road, and so back on a leisurely journey along the coast.

He passed over the Plains of Camdeboo in May 1813, collecting as he went, and on to the Boschberg, where he made a rich haul. It is a tragedy that the third volume of Burchell's travels was either never written (although he had planned it) or was lost, so that we shall never know this eastern Karoo as Burchell saw it. The plant specimens that he collected here, however, are safe at the Royal Botanic Garden at Kew.

Lord Charles Somerset, aristocratic governor of the Cape, and his two daughters journeyed over the Plains of Camdeboo in a leisurely official tour in 1817. With them went one of the most extraordinary persons in South African history, Dr James Barry, about whom the most far-fetched and romantic stories are told. The bare facts are fantastic enough. Dr James Barry obtained the degree of M.D. of Edinburgh University and then entered the army, arriving at the Cape in 1815 as surgeon. After a long and distinguished service here, a Colonial Medical Inspector and favourite of Lord Charles, Barry returned to England on pension, and there died in 1815. Although there had been rumours, only then was it found for sure that Barry was a woman. She had succeeded in impersonating a man for almost a lifetime of seventy years, a lifetime which included every horror of primitive surgery and possibly a good deal of danger. It is said she fought a duel at the Cape.

Thomas Pringle, the dreamy, courageous poet and journalist, also passed this way with his wife and sister on a frightful ox-wagon journey to Cape Town through the Karoo. He had little to say of the Plains of Camdeboo; indeed his account of this trip is noteworthy mainly for the fact that this poet, capable of fancy and eloquence, referred to his wife throughout as 'my female companion' or 'Mrs P'.

After him came five travellers of note, as diverse as men and women may be.

In the early 1830s Robert Moffat and his wife Mary, travelling the hard desert road between Litakun and Grahamstown, passed over Galgenbosch. They were two of the most remarkable people in the history of Southern Africa, and it is a pity that they should be remembered today largely because of their association with David Livingstone. They had as much courage as their renowned son-in-law, and their stories, even if they made no headlines, are crammed with astonishing incident and achievement.

Robert's story in South Africa started in 1817, when as a still growing youth he landed in Cape Town in the service of the London Missionary Society and trekked north to Namaqualand by ox-wagon.

He wrote later of the loneliness and discomforts in the twelve months which followed when he travelled about Namaqualand preaching, with his Bible and hymn-book in a blanket on the back of his saddle, always searching for water, eating when he could, and when he could find no food binding his stomach with a thong to prevent the gnawing of hunger, thrusting his head into old ant-hills excavated by ant-bears to have something solid between his fevered brain and the sun. I do not think South Africa has seen a more heroic figure than this stalwart young Scot, herding his cattle through the desert and singing as he marched, 'Here I raise my Ebenezer, hither by Thy help I'm come'; preaching, teaching, disputing the water-holes with the lions, and when his loneliness grew too heavy for him, lying on the rocks with his violin and playing his mother's favourite hymn.

His salary at this time, he records, was £25 a year.

Moffat deserved a good wife and he got one. Two years after he landed in South Africa Mary Smith of Dunkinfield followed him out and the two were married in Cape Town. It proved not only a happy marriage but a remarkable partnership.

The portraits of Robert and Mary taken at the age of twenty-four show two handsome, intelligent young people, Robert somewhat of a dandy with a curl waving across his forehead, Mary a pretty, plump girl with a firm chin, dark curls, and a white frilled cap. Together these two, praising the Lord loudly and continuously for the privilege accorded them, travelled into the little known country beyond the Orange River to raise a mission station at Kuruman that was not only a great outpost of Christianity but for years the heart of many expeditions to the interior of Southern Africa. Here, too, they brought wagons, ploughs, spades, harrows, grain, fruit – and a printing press.

Moffat travelled widely – itinerating, he called it – and Mary either went with him or stayed to run the station, bear innumerable children, and adopt the waifs and strays about her – two Bushman children and a babe abandoned on a hillside whom she reared in her own household.

When Robert and Mary travelled to Grahamstown in 1830 they were taking their eldest children to school near Grahamstown, Robert was planning to have printed parts of the New Testament he had translated for his people, and Mary was starting a new chapter in her adventurous life – the journeying to and fro over many years to see her children, journeys often made quite alone except for her native servants, through an unmapped, turbulent, war-torn land. Sometimes she waited a month or more for the Orange River to subside, crossing it finally on a raft of willow logs, and often she listened by night to the lions. There were continual rumours of native wars and invasions. These were the things that sent so many travellers and colonists of her time hysterical with excitement and fear. Mary simply remarks, 'It was no pleasing task to take such a journey alone' – which seems to me one of the understatements of South African history.

Robert preached for the last time at Kuruman in 1870 and the countryside turned out in force to touch his hands, and Mary's. He and Mary returned to Britain after more than fifty years' service in Africa, Mary to die almost at once. Moffat lived until he was eighty-eight, and when he died he could have claimed that not only had Moselekatse, the great Matebele chief, listened to his words, but so had a queen and an emperor.

The Moffats left no record that I can find of their journeys over the Plains of Camdeboo, but a link nevertheless remains. Andrew Murray, the famous pastor of Graaff-Reinet, and his wife, gave great hospitality to the Moffat family and in the old

Murray home – now a museum – Mary's favourite chair is still preserved. It is known as Mary Moffat's chair.

I would rather have seen it than Livingstone's tomb in Westminister Abbey.

There was yet another Mary Moffat, the eldest daughter on whose behalf her mother undertook that first journey through the eastern Karoo. She was then a child of ten, destined fifteen years later to become the wife of the greatest explorer of his day, David Livingstone. Livingstone described her as 'a little, thick, black-haired girl, sturdy and all I want'.

It was just as well that she was sturdy with little of the romantic, for she followed Livingstone through Africa, died of fever, 'a willing sacrifice', at the age of forty-one, and was buried under a great baobab on the banks of the Zambezi River. I went on a sentimental journey once to see her grave. It is a remote and alien spot, but perhaps as fitting a grave as any for an African-born.

It was Moffat in the first place who had brought Livingstone to Africa. Nine years after he made his first trek across the Plains of Camdeboo he visited England, talking widely at missionary meetings, and here David Livingstone, then a medical student, heard him and was fascinated. Thereafter he too yearned after Africa, and in 1841 he landed in Cape Town as a missionary of the London Missionary Society.

His first journey inland took him from Uitenhage over the western fringe of the Plains of Camdeboo some thirty miles west of Galgenbosch to Graaff-Reinet and Kuruman, but alas! it seems he was a travel snob. The journeys and sights he records with such enthusiasm later were all of unknown Africa: the Karoo was inhabited by whites – if sparsely – and so presumably not worthy of attention; and this I find hard to forgive.

On this first trip he was an unknown medical missionary, a serious young man with a background of poverty and grinding work. World fame – the days of 'the unconquerable Scot' – still lay ahead and were surely undreamed of as he trekked with his oxen across the Karoo.

Captain William Cornwallis Harris, who crossed the Karoo shortly after the Moffats' first trip, was a dashing young soldier with a passion for shooting and for wild-life. He arrived at the Cape in 1836 on two years' leave from the Indian army in company with a friend and an Indian servant. From Port Elizabeth and Grahamstown he struck north, crossing Bruintjeshoogte and the Plains of Camdeboo on his journey to the interior. He was one of the earliest Europeans to cross the Transvaal, and to understand something of his feat it must be realized that he explored this almost unknown country before the voortrekkers had crossed the Vaal. He actually met the first trekkers in the Orange Free State on their way north when he was on his return journey to the Cape.

He had wonderful adventures, including a meeting with the Matabele Chief Moselekatse, but he himself would probably have said his greatest achievement was the shooting of the sable antelope. His was the first description of this fine antelope, and for a long time it was known as the Harris buck. All the travellers used their beds as places of greatest safety for their treasures; it is noteworthy that the sable skin and head travelled back to civilization in Harris's bed!

Harris's collection of wild animal trophies made a great stir in London at the time, but today we remember him mainly for his journal and his exquisite paintings. From his writing and his portrait he appears a robust and lively young man and anything as delicate and ethereal as these paintings of wild animals in an accurate and yet strangely dreamlike setting is surprising. 'I never moved without drawing materials in my hunting cap,' he said. 'Nearly all my sketches were made under a bush in the open air and completed on my knees in the wagon amid rain and wind.'

The people of the Karoo may remember Harris for his description of Somerset East, where the rats ate up half his goods, and the 'lady' from whom he begged a wagon, who ate her peas with a knife and offered him none.

It is lucky indeed that the Somerset rats did not eat the bribe he carried in his baggage for the chief Moselekatse. It was a greatcoat of duffel, a coarse shaggy cloth, surmounted by six capes and provided with beige bone buttons, a ponderous brazen clasp in the shape of a crest, and lined and trimmed throughout with scarlet shalloon 'in a manner calculated to captivate the taste of the most despotic and capricious of savages'. It did. This fabulous coat and the gift of a rich Persian carpet, a red woollen nightcap and a pyjama cord, were probably the reason why Harris and his party were looked on with favour and allowed to return alive. They are some of the oddest items of baggage ever to have been transported across the Karoo, but not as improbable as Nesserwanjee, the dignified and loyal Indian servant – Harris's 'Parsee' and the Hottentots' 'cow-worshipper', who ate no beef and wore a turban and a pair of red silk braces.

Fifteen years later yet another unusual traveller crossed the Plains of Camdeboo. He was Nathaniel James Merriman, Archdeacon and later Bishop of Grahamstown, Oxford graduate, close friend of Gladstone, and father of John Xavier, later prime minister of the Cape Colony. He was a man of distinction in more ways than one, but probably his greatest feat was the crossing of the Karoo *on foot*.

Merriman had the task of supervising the Anglican Church in the whole of the eastern part of the Cape Colony, and he chose to visit the far-flung parts of his territory in this way partly from his love of simplicity, partly because he often could not afford to travel in any other way, so that the Dutch farmers saw an astonishing and dismaying sight – a man who claimed to be a minister of the church, sometimes with a bag slung over his shoulder, sometimes attended by a servant, sometimes with a pack-horse, marching across the veld like a tramp.

They reacted at the start with suspicion and animosity. 'They cannot believe that a predikant would walk,' wrote Merriman with wry amusement. 'They never knew or heard of such a thing, and take him for an impostor – a discharged soldier – a convict. It is vain to tell them that our Lord and Master and His holy apostles walked. It may have been so. But they know that predikants don't walk.' The almost never-failing hospitality of these men failed in his case, and he records sleeping in a vegetable store-room after roasting and eating some of the potatoes he found on the floor.

In 1849 he trudged across the Plains of Camdeboo, where the rivers were dry and the huge plains parched, with a packet of biltong sandwiches and some naartjies, wondering at the mirages of water and forests on the way; meeting a farmer who spurned him because he had no horse; spending a night at Galgenbosch and rejoicing at the hospitality of a farmer who could speak English. He does not mention his name but it was Gerrit Lodewyk Coetzee, and Merriman slept in the mud-walled cottage below the dam.

Looking back, he is a tremendous figure striding over the Karoo, sometimes forty miles in a day; wading a river with his trousers and drawers round his neck and his cassock round his waist, with his Bible and prayer-book under one arm and a knobkerrie to which his shoes and socks had been fastened in the other. It is good to think that as time went on, as he walked his thousands of miles (and he reached Cape Town to the south and Bloemfontein to the north) he became known, respected, and no doubt greatly enjoyed, as the walking parson.

One day we followed the old road for miles in the veld, losing it for a stretch, finding it again and losing it once more. The two Davids ranged widely, searching for things of interest, and suddenly David Pretoria called, 'Look at this; it's tiny and heavy as lead.'

It *was* lead, a leaden musket-ball slightly flattened at one end. I remembered the huge supply of lead bullets of which Le Vaillant had boasted. This could have been one of his. Perhaps this was one of the bullets he had fired at the lions that attacked his wagons here on Cranemere.

We passed the bullet from hand to hand, considering this extravaganza: and history stirred about us.

5. The Bushmen of the Veld

These first early travellers who crossed Cranemere wrote of the Bushmen. As far as we know these – and perhaps the Hottentots – were the first modern men, *Homo sapiens*, to have lived upon our Plains. They were the point where history and prehistory fused, modern yet Stone Age Man – Late Stone Age – a fascinating and bewildering combination.

They left their marks all over Cranemere. Long ago a Bushman hide-out used to stand on the top of the low ridge of koppies overlooking the gap through which the game passed to drink at the pools below – the pools that later became Cranemere dam. It was made of five great smooth slabs of brown stone, three walls and a barred stone roof, so small that it was only when we were young that we could crouch in it with ease. It could hardly be distinguished from its rocky background. An old witgat tree stood close to it and this we would use as a beacon, yet not until we were on top of the shelter did we ever see it. Here generations of Bushman hunters had hidden to the lee of the south-easter, the great prevailing wind of summer, and from here had made their kill. This stone box, solid and shining, was a link of which we never tired, a link across the centuries with the first of sapient man.

Sometimes we found other traces that the Bushmen had lived here before us. In the mountains close to Cranemere were paintings in rocky shelters, and in a cliff overhanging the Vogelsrivier to the south-east were little caves or hide-outs scooped out of the face of the rock, which today the Xhosa people call 'the Bushman houses'. The Bushmen or their ancestors had worked the heavy round bored stones, weights for their digging sticks, that had been found near the rock shelter. The rounded stones with sides worn satin-smooth, and the long narrow stones with smooth abraded ends that we found near the Rooikop and on the veld and koppies, were fashioned by them for grinding paint and bulbs and seeds. Once we found two lying together, one round, one long, a Stone Age pestle and mortar. And all over the farm we found tiny flakes, little chips of sandstone and shale, shaped and pointed, sometimes not even an inch long, which had been Bushman tools or those of their forefathers. Once we found six tiny tanged arrowheads lying together.

Where had they come from, this tiny race of mysterious men? Their slanting, almond, Chinese eyes suggested an origin far from Southern Africa and the early colonists talked of them wonderingly and fearfully as 'Chinese Hottentots'. Some said they were gipsies from Egypt; others that they were the missing link, as Gibbon put it, 'the connecting link between rational and irrational creation'.

Some early scientists believed that they originated in the far north-east and were driven south by stronger races, until here in the southern end of Africa they found safety and a glorious home. Modern research does not bear this out, and it is now widely held that their origin is here in Southern Africa.

When the Dutch arrived in South Africa the Bushmen were for the most part in the interior and the Hottentots in the coastal areas. Matched in build, weapons and perhaps in numbers, they had continued to exist in the same land. Now the two claws of a great pincer, the whites from the south and west and the blacks from the north and east, were slowly closing on the Bushman and his days in his native land were numbered.

It has become the fashion to regard the vanished Bushman as a sort of primeval innocent, and in a modern world that singularly lacks the free, the gay, and simple, it is not difficult to understand his attraction. He may have been these things, but he also proved himself the most ferocious neighbour.

The Bushmen did not roam the country widely but, it is claimed, they remained within their 'own' territory, killing their own game, hunting for bulbs and roots, and drinking at their own places, and they defended these things with their lives. It is believed the Cape Bushmen lived in small family parties within these territories, which traditionally belonged to them alone.

Sometimes their areas were very large and they moved from one part to another, which was easy enough for their huts were only branches and leaves or skins, their clothes were skins, and their only domestic animals were dogs. Once they probably owned Cranemere pools and the animals that drank here by absolute right of inheritance.

The settlers needed water and food too, and they took them, drinking and watering their flocks and herds, and killing the game, and they knew no boundaries at all. The Bushman responded with a courage and ferocity that made his name a byword, and the fight was on. It was to continue in the Cape until the Bushmen as a fighting force were destroyed.

This was savage war. It is easy to understand why the Bushmen were terrifying opponents, for their weapons – their famous poisoned arrows – must have appeared almost magical to white and black alike. Once truly hit by a Bushman arrow, a man never recovered unless the limb where he had been hit were immediately hacked off. Sitting round a camp fire at night, riding near a thicket, a bush, a gully, a rock, no man journeying across the Karoo, no farmer tending his animals, was ever safe. At the end of the eighteenth century Barrow wrote of the extraordinary conditions under which the farmers of the Snow Mountains just north of Cranemere lived.

'If he has occasion to go to the distance of 500 yards from his house, he is under the necessity of carrying a musket. He can neither plough, nor sow, nor reap without being under arms. If he would gather a few greens in the garden he must take his gun in hand.'

The colonists claimed that the Bushmen killed indiscriminately and plundered cattle and sheep by the thousand. Those they could not drive away they often killed or maimed most brutally. A farmer, returning from a day's work to find his house burnt down, his wife and children dead, a favourite horse dying in agony with its entrails ripped out, or his cattle with great gaping wounds, would be in no mood for mercy.

Lichtenstein in 1803 saw the Bushman fires close to him on

the slopes of the mountains when he camped near the present site of Pearston. The Bushmen had been on a marauding raid and had carried away a number of cattle from the farmers, perhaps from Cranemere itself. Even in 1813 a family party of Xhosas, who had penetrated to the Snow Mountains, turned back in terror to their own country to escape the Bushmen, and camped a night at a pool of water near the Gallows Tree. Today the farm north-east of Cranemere still bears the name of Bosjesmansfontein – Bushman's Fountain. Once the old spring near Cranemere mountain must have been a Bushman fountain too. We know nothing of that last Bushman who here defended his spring and pools against the first trekkers, but we like to think that some of the stone tools we have found belonged to him.

The colonists soon learned to regard the Bushmen as vermin, the most dangerous animals of all. In the 1790s a Graaff-Reinet farmer, when asked if he had found the Bushmen troublesome on the road, replied 'with as much composure and indifference as if he had been speaking of partridges' that he had only shot four. Barrow claimed that one colonist had boasted to him that he himself had killed nearly three hundred.

It was not only the Dutch colonists who regarded the Bushmen as game. Le Vaillant, the French ornithologist, for example, hunted Bushmen in the Coetzeeberg on the very edge of Cranemere. He had pitched his camp in excruciating heat in an open spot so that the Bushmen should not surprise him, and his Hottentots kept constant watch, for, he said, 'A Hottentot dreads a Boschman much more than a lion.' From here he hunted them, and although he admired the way they flew over the rocks with the nimbleness of monkeys, it did not stop him from shooting at them.

An English farmer recorded that as a child he had seen his father and two Boers go out to shoot a Bushman. It is a gallant and pitiful story that must have been repeated many times in the Karoo. The Bushman had dug a hole for himself and in this, part of the veld, as always, he lay shooting his arrows at the three men. They advanced slowly towards him, protected by an enormous shield of double ox-hide. The farmer in the middle held this, and the two on either side their rifles, which they fired as they walked, and as they moved they knew that one touch of an arrow in an unguarded foot or hand, and they were dead men. An arrow did indeed pierce one man's hat, but he was uninjured. The Bushman was finally killed, and when they examined his little body they found he had cut through the skin of his finger-tips with the constant pulling of his bow-string.

Farmers hunted the Bushmen in small groups, or in commandos. Barrow says that one such party near Graaff-Reinet 'prepared themselves for the enterprise by singing three or four hymns by William Sluiter and drinking each a glass of brandy'. They probably needed both.

Many of the Bushmen taken prisoner died or finally escaped, for they often found captivity unbearable, even when they were employed as servants by humane and kindly men. This was not invariably so, for there are always human relationships which endure in unlikely circumstances. One little Bushman boy, whose parents had been killed, was brought up in Graaff-Reinet in a home 'towards the sunset', and here he learned to garden in company with his master's sons. His master was kind and he followed him wherever he went. Another Bushman child saved his master in the veld from an attacking lion by jumping at the animal and waving a skin in its face (and it should be recorded that in his turn the farmer saved the same child from death or mauling by a lion).

A little Bushman boy reached Scotland in the middle of the nineteenth century. His name was Ruyter and the hunter Gordon Cumming found him in the Karoo near Colesberg and took him back to Britain. I have never learnt what became of him although I have often wondered.

Not all early writers distinguished clearly between Bushmen and Hottentots. This is not surprising, for they were somewhat alike in appearance and today many anthropologists consider them akin. The Bushmen, however, were smaller than the Hottentots. By our standards they were tiny – the Bushman arm, it is recorded, was the shortest in the world. G. E. Cory, the historian, described their colour as a dirty yellow. Sir Laurens van der Post, their most ardent modern champion, describes it as a lovely Provençal apricot. Cory says the men were on an average four feet six, and the women four. Their countenances were crafty and repulsive, with large prominent cheekbones and receding chins, beardless, the hair on their heads like isolated peppercorns, their stomachs protruding, their hinder parts thick, their limbs thin and wiry. Sir Laurens says they were robust and well-formed, their eyes clear and shining like those of an antelope, their faces heart-shaped, their ears Pan-like and altogether beautiful in build and movement!

So there it is – we can make our own choice.

Theal, the great South African historian, added a touch that many have corroborated: 'Demeanour that of perfect independence,' he wrote.

The early knowledge of the Cape Bushmen we have today we owe largely to four remarkable people with great hearts and imaginations – a German with a bent for languages, Wilhelm Bleek; his daughter, Dorothea; his sister-in-law, Lucy Lloyd; and a writer, anthropologist, and geologist, George Stow. They rescued, before it had entirely disappeared, a wonderful harvest of Bushman language, fact, legend and art, and this is the basis of much of our knowledge of Cape Bushmen today.

Bleek arrived in South Africa as a young man in 1852. Soon after his arrival Sir George Grey, Governor of the Cape and a man with an immense curiosity about all the rich and novel things around him, asked him to catalogue his library, and for the first time Bleek became interested in Bushmen. He began to study and record the Bushman language. At this time the only Bushmen near Cape Town were the convicts working on the breakwater, many of them serving a sentence for no more than poaching offences. Bleek used to go down and talk to them; finally he was allowed to employ some of them as servants; and here in his home he studied them and learned from them. He died when he was only forty-eight but Lucy and Dorothea continued with his work.

The three of them collected a very large amount of Bushman lore, particularly between 1870 and 1880, and this was fortunate, because when Dorothea met the children of these Bushmen thirty years later they remembered none of it; it had been entirely forgotten.

Dorothea also completed the Bushman dictionary that her father had started.

In the 1860s Bleek and George Stow met. Stow's first introduction to the Bushman had, however, come in a roundabout way through a Port Elizabeth friend, Dr Richard Rubidge, whose hobby was climbing Karoo mountains hunting for fossils, and he interested Stow, too, in his work. While Stow was searching for fossils he first discovered Bushman relics. Today Bushman art is recognized as one of the most curious and beautiful inheritances of Africa, but then it was virtually unknown. Stow was struck by the elegance and beauty of the paintings, hidden away in shelters and on rocks in remote mountains of the Cape. He determined to copy the paintings for himself, and with paper and crayons he set out to explore the mountains.

Between the years 1867 and 1882 he copied many paintings as accurately as he could. Sometimes he found the actual specimens of the Bushman paint still existing in the caves. Although he worked in his tent and under the roughest conditions, he was very accurate, as Dorothea Bleek was to find years later when she climbed up to the shelters and compared Stow's copies of the paintings with the originals.

Bleek at the very start of his work on Bushmen had been interested in the fact that the missionaries had not been able to influence them at all. Many writers have recorded this extreme independence of spirit. The Bleeks were to record other things and to claim that all those captive Bushmen who worked for them had not only independence but honesty, loyalty, and a fine courtesy. Never did they steal so much as a pocket-knife or a peach off a tree while in their home. They noted again and again that this monogamous people made good husbands and wives; and loving parents.

It is a picture of curious intensity, the Bleeks, their convict Bushmen and their families, living together bound not only by legal ties but by sympathy and affection, working, laughing, telling stories, the children playing, all of them, even to the small children, sharing in the Sunday music (the Dead March from *Saul* was the Bushman favourite, Dorothea remembered).

But they did not really belong to any home, however gentle; they belonged to the wind, the veld and the mountains, and it is here we think of them for they were part of these things as no one else in Africa has ever been. They hunted for food and they made their kill often enough in the very likeness of the wild animals, disguised in ostrich plumes, or a buck's skin, or a buck's horns. Burchell saw one with a large cap made of springbuck skin, stretching far back behind his head and resembling a springbuck's back. It was worn when stalking game and Burchell called it a 'becreeping cap', anglicizing an Afrikaans word and creating a name picturesque enough to stand in its own right.

The Bleeks recorded one of the most interesting things of all about the Bushmen: their awareness of the wild animals about them, not a twentieth-century awareness and perhaps not even purely human. They felt animal 'messages', they told the Bleeks, messages that were within their bodies, a tapping within that heralded the approach of game and which was never false. A man would feel a tapping at his ribs and know the springbuck were coming, for what he was feeling in his ribs was the black hair on the sides of the springbuck. 'I feel the springbuck sensation,' he would say.

I remember still my feeling of incredulous fascination at first reading in Bleek's *Bushman Folklore* of this strange awareness.'We have a sensation in our feet, as we feel the rustling of the feet of the springbuck with which the springbuck come, making the bushes rustle. We feel in this manner, we have a sensation in our heads when we are about to chop the springbuck horns. We have a sensation in our face on account of the blackness of the stripe on the face of the springbuck: we feel a sensation in our eyes, on account of the black marks on the eyes of the spring-buck.'

In his own body the Bushman could feel the buck scratching itself with its horns; and a sensation in the calves of his legs and behind his back where the blood of the slaughtered buck would drip as he carried it. He was *Homo sapiens*, modern man, but he was also part of the animal world. It is said that like a wild animal he could, even as a child, find his way to any place where he had been before.

The Bushmen, of course, were tremendous hunters. They had, said the colonists, eyes like telescopes, and with these, their poisoned arrows and terrible relentless trot, they made their kills. They killed the springbuck with bow and arrows but they ran down the bigger game, killing the exhausted beasts with spears, and they could, it was claimed, keep up their trot for four days on end.

Their bows were small – there was no need for them to be powerful – and here on the Karoo they made them of the karee or gwarrie trees that still grow widely. The arrows were usually of the common wild reed with bone or sometimes flint arrow-heads, and later sometimes of iron. On the tips of these the poison was spread.

They were very fine toxicologists and their poisons first-class. The colonists knew this and modern science bears it out. Cape Bushmen are supposed to have used animal and vegetable poisons together, extracting the poison sacs from snakes, drying the poison and pounding it, and mixing it with the juice of poisonous bulbs. On Cranemere we still often see the yellow cobras our Bushmen once used with such efficiency, and the poison bulb, with its innocent blue-green fan of leaves, that they pounded for its deadly juice. This poison was never instantaneous in its effects, but it always worked. A Bushman with his patient, horrifying trot would follow a wounded animal in the sure knowledge that in the end it would drop.

Meat was the most important food. So like the animals in some ways, the Bushmen had the taboos and the courtesies of men, and the cutting up of the meat, its division, and eating, were attended by great ceremonial. Women were not allowed to eat the meat of any part of the lynx or the meat of shoulder-blades; children might not eat the tip of a springbuck's tail. Jackal's heart was forbidden them lest they should become timid like a jackal, but a leopard's heart was believed to give them courage. The meat of the great bustard and ostrich eggs were delicacies and often reserved for old men; and the children of the man who made a kill were entitled to the marrow of the bones of the slaughtered buck. None of them, men or women, ate the baboon because 'it was so like a man', or the hyena because it ate human corpses.

They ate Bushman rice, the larvae of ants; locusts, gum from the thorn trees, and their greatest delicacy was wild honey. Possibly Honey Mountain owes its name to them. The women dug for roots with digging sticks, hard pointed sticks weighted with a perforated stone, and carried their water in ostrich egg-shells. Here on the Karoo they probably made their digging sticks of the tough wood of the wild olive trees from which our farmers still sometimes make their fence posts. They ate enormously when there was food, and when there was none they simply went without, their enormous buttocks – so folk-lore has it – acting as camels' humps in this dry land.

Burchell, who was always honest even about the people he liked and respected (and he liked the Bushmen), recorded 'a little affair' that upset his stomach. A Bushman woman, he said, who carried a child on her back seemed to be eagerly in search of something which she saw between the folds of her kaross (a rug made of skin or fur), and the twists of her leather bracelets and necklace. 'I noticed that her hand was frequently lifted to her mouth or held out to her babe. I discovered, not without some strong sensations,' he wrote, 'that the object of her active and earnest pursuit were certain little crawling things, which, though in England viewed with disgust, were here sought for with complacence, and presented by an affec-tionate mother to her tender infant, who held out its little innocent hand to receive them as bonbons.'

Clothing, it seems, was far less important to the Bushmen than food. They dressed in skins and Dorothea Bleek suggests that it was only in later days that they wore even these. But their ornaments were painstakingly made. The women wore arm or leg bracelets of leather or bark or twisted hair, such as the tail hairs of a wildebeest, and ostrich-egg beads which they wore as headbands, as necklaces, or even in long strings round their waists. When I look at these in a museum today I am struck by their delicacy and beauty. How very feminine the Bushman women must have looked in their finery.

They could have seen little beautiful in the white man's appearance, with one exception. Burchell described their passionate admiration of his umbrella!

For the rest they painted, sang, danced and acted, and told each other stories. A story was 'like the wind, it comes from a far-off quarter, and we feel it', they told the Bleeks. It is their gaiety, their art, and these fabulous stories of men and animals, the wind, the sun, the moon and the stars, that so enchant today. It is sometimes hard to believe they belong not only to the dawn of modern man, but to the days of Queen Victoria.

Everyone who has read of Bushman lore knows its unlikely central figure – the praying mantis, a creature with extraordinary powers. It was Mantis who made an eland out of a shoe and fed it on honey, who changed springbuck into human beings, who performed innumerable magic, crazy acts that the Bleeks recorded.

But he was not a god. Cape Bushmen, it is said, never prayed to him, but they did pray to the sun, the moon, and the stars, and they told a host of stories about them all; how the Milky Way was made by 'a girl of the ancient race' who wished for a little light and threw wood ashes into the sky, which became the Milky Way; how she made the stars by throwing scented roots into the air.

Stars were supposed to govern the finding of food, and the Bushmen prayed to certain stars for certain foods. Canopus, Dorothea Bleek records in *Bushman Folklore*, was the star of the ant's larvae.

'O Star coming there
Let me dig out ants' food
With this stick,'
they prayed.

The jewelled constellation of Orion, so warm and splendid in the southern summer sky, was for them made up of tortoises hung upon a stick, the sword of males, the belt of females, possibly because when Orion becomes visible in spring the tortoises are active in the veld. Jupiter was 'Dawn's Heart'.

They prayed to the moon – and I think of them here on the Cranemere plains with their right hands upraised to the night sky declaiming in their clicking tongue:

'Ho, Moon lying there
Let me kill a springbuck
Tomorrow.'

They made many stories about the moon for it was a magical thing, dying and yet returning again. Of course they worshipped it, for there can be few things more likely to be worshipped than an African moon shining on a great plain.

And what of themselves after death? Did they see themselves in the waxing and waning moon, I have wondered? Stow records that Cape Bushmen believed in a form of life after death. Some believed in a place on the banks of the Orange River to which they all would go. Those who had lived a good life would travel easily and feast on locusts and honey, but those who had not would go on their heads and live only upon flies – and to Karoo dwellers this has great point. The cutting off of the joint of the little finger of one hand was said to ensure a good journey.

Normally when a Bushman died he was buried in a sleeping position with his knees drawn up towards his breast, and his possessions were placed around him. Some time ago an old man working for our neighbour, Edgar Hobson, was collecting stones near the Cranemere boundary when he came upon a small skeleton. It lay beneath a rough heap of stones that he had not recognized as a grave at all, the knees drawn up to the chin, and beads above the head. The well-preserved skull showed it to

have been a young Bushman girl, but what fascinated the palaeontologist Professor Raymond Dart was that here, in her mountain grave a hundred and fifty miles from the sea, the beads had
been made of sea-shells.

Naturally the most important thing in the life of the Bushman
was rain. Dorothea Bleek found that most Bushman tales of
rebirth were connected with water. Rain itself was to him a
tremendous and supernatural being to be treated with great
respect. Lucy Lloyd in her preface to *Bushman Folklore* told how
she once brought home a splendid red fungus, later asking a
Bushman servant to throw it away lest it decay. A tremendous
storm followed and this, the Bushman felt, was caused by her
lack of respect. '*Throw* it away,' she had said instead of 'put it
gently down'. It was 'a rain's thing', and the rain was showing
its resentment of incivility. Frogs, tortoises, fish and snakes were
also rain's things, to be feared and respected.

The Bushmen, we are told, danced at all times when they
were happy but most of all after rain, so that our arid plains and
hills must, after rain, have known dances of especial fervour,
with men dancing the night away, stamping while the women
clapped and sang, or imitating the wild animals, leaping and
prancing and copying their movements, disguised with the
horns or heads of the animals themselves. On their ankles would
have been the dancing rattles, made of springbuck ears filled
with seed or broken ostrich egg-shell; they would have sounded
these, and played upon their bows, and beaten their drums
made of the thigh-skin of the springbuck that roamed the flats,
Hottentot instruments which they had made their own.

These are things of long ago learnt only from books. It is the
direct link that usually makes the greatest impact on us now, the
enduring clues to the Bushman past; where these links survive
they are of exceptional interest. Not long ago archaeologists,
studying the Late Stone Age fresh-water shell middens fairly
close to us in the upper reaches of the Fish River, found that
these followed the same pattern as the coastal middens, while a
few ornaments made of sea-shells were also found. So these

11 Robert and Mary Moffat at the time of their marriage in 1819.

12 How the early travellers crossed the Karoo, from a drawing by Burchell.

13 William Cornwallis Harris

14 A Cornwallis Harris painting of gemsbok.

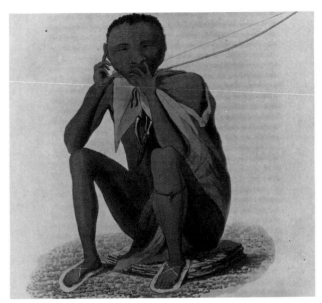

15 Burchell's painting, from his Travels in Africa, *of a Bushman playing on the* gorah.

16 Bushmen were tiny men and David, aged nine, can barely sit upright in a 'Bushman house' in the mountains.

17 *A portion of the strange painting – perhaps of a Bushman ritual dance – in the mountains above Cranemere. The second figure from the left is disguised as an ostrich.*

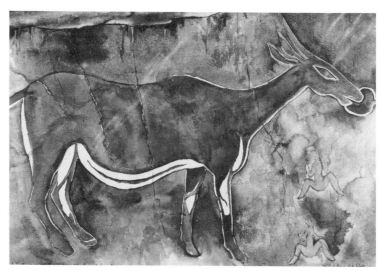

18 *Unique among Bushman paintings is this of a bushbuck browsing, from the mountains above Cranemere. Experts say that the white outlining, the eye and the leaf show an individual technique which sets it apart from the usual Bushman art.*

Bushmen had been travellers! What, then, of the claim of the early writers that the Bushmen never moved beyond their own territory? They could not surely have 'owned' almost two hundred miles of land. Had they perhaps owned *routes* to and from the coast? And what a fascinating thing if it were so.

Three young scientists recently investigating a bundle of bedding litter from the floor of Scott's Cave – a Late Stone Age site in the Gamtoos Valley south of Cranemere – happened on a fresh set of clues. They were Janette and Hilary Deacon, archaeologists, and Michael Wells, botanist, and not only did they study the beads, pottery and implements in their yard of debris – normal procedure – but they studied scientifically the plant remains, and with rising excitement knew that they had hit on something new.

Even at the start they realized that this first detailed botanical study of Stone Age debris in South Africa could perhaps throw a new light on the Late Stone Age; on foods, clothing, bedding, on living habits generally; perhaps even on seasonal movements and migrations, and they thought that the contribution might finally be considerable.

We had taken a bag of worked stones to the Albany Museum in Grahamstown – our local museum and one of considerable standing – when we saw the box of litter and learned its nature. The three scientists were awaiting the results of the carbon dating of the material, but in the meantime were playing detectives with enthusiasm.

'Look,' said Michael Wells, and he picked a handful of husks out of the debris. 'Tritonias! And they are not lying sideways as if dropped at random. They are squashed upon their bottoms, showing that force was used upon them. Surely they were crushed for food.'

I picked out a fragment of boerboon pod, still easily identifiable. 'There are many of those,' he said, 'but not a seed. Pods but not seeds – the seeds were obviously used, and probably as food.'

There were remains of elephant's foot, valued in modern

medicine, leaves and wood of wild olive, and grasses of various kinds. There were small hard lengths of stick, the ends clearly cut and each one showing an indent. 'After I'd picked up several I thought: I've seen this before,' said Wells. 'I had. They were all the same. They had all been tied in the same way and probably formed the edge of a mat. They were bits of cyperus, the common sedge, so now we can guess what they made their mats of. And we know what they used for their string and rope. It was the same sedge.'

Around Cranemere itself lay other clues to Bushman life which we had never suspected, and they were for us the greatest interest of all. They were Bushman paintings and they were quite unknown.

Since Stow first copied the Bushman paintings in the Eastern Cape, paintings have been recorded many times from many parts of the country, although very few from the Karoo. It is true that the second earliest copy of a Bushman painting ever made was of one in our countryside – in the Sneeuberg – made possibly by the famous Colonel Gordon himself. But on the whole our area is considered poor in rock art, and in our district only four sites were known in 1952 when C. van Riet Lowe published *The Distribution of Prehistoric Rock Engravings and Paintings in South Africa*.

In a dramatic flush our artist friend, Dick Findlay, opened up a new area of Bushman art – and in an unusual form – in the mountains about us.

It all had its beginnings in a morning's expedition. A few miles north of Cranemere on a neighbouring farm stands a typical Karoo mountain, Eselkop or Donkey's Head, rough, steep and stony, and here, we had been told as children, was a rock shelter with Bushman paintings, unknown to anyone but the farmer who owned the land, the men and women who worked for him, and a few neighbours. We had longed to see it but never had.

One winter morning we climbed up to it. The shelter was

half-way up the mountain facing south over the Plains. We toiled up the mountainside, slipping on the loose stones and the shiny wandering roots of the spekboom, until presently Koeltas, our guide, led us round the side of a krantz by a pathway as narrow as a bit of string. It was a typical Bushman shelter formed ages past by the weathering of the sandstone, so that there was now an overhang twenty feet wide and a hundred feet long forming the roof and protecting the wall beneath it. Once a spring had bubbled in a corner of the shelter and a damp spot still marked the place. What a vantage point and what a stronghold! From here the Bushmen had watched the game and later the colonists and their flocks and herds below; and with a sudden lift of excitement I thought: it was into this mountain Le Vaillant chased the Bushmen nearly two hundred years ago – what are the odds, into this very cave?

Then we turned to the paintings. At one time the whole face of the rock wall had been adorned with these, not paintings of animals but of human figures. We knew that most of them had disappeared. For many years the shelter had been used as a goat kraal and here a long time ago a party of baboon hunters had by accident set alight to the goat manure which lay feet thick upon the floor. It smouldered for weeks and in the intense heat whole slabs of surface rock cracked off and were destroyed. When the fire burned itself out the paintings had gone.

We looked at the wall sadly: it seemed there was nothing left at all. But as we moved along, lightly touching the cream and brown surface of the rock, and our eyes grew accustomed to the subtle colours, we saw in a few parts outlines, first a suspicion and then clearly, and there was revealed a group of human figures apparently engaged in some ceremonial.

The Bushman artists painted – beside their wonderful animals – people with long narrow bodies, oddly stylized, hunting, dancing, marching, fighting, but rarely any plants or birds. This was a typical painting. Every man portrayed an animal. There were those with bucks' horns, with a jackal head, a cat face, and one disguised in ostrich form. One had a bow and quiver and a hand drawn with great detail, and one was declaiming, or conducting some ancient ceremony. All the figures were red-brown on a creamy-brown background and of great elegance and finish. 'Chic,' Dick Findlay was to call them later, 'old and very chic.'

How old were they? We argued among ourselves. A. R. Willcox in his book, *The Rock Art of South Africa,* believes an age of five centuries for the oldest *surviving* Bushman art is certain; an age of twenty centuries possible. Walter Battiss, the artist whose copies of rock paintings are famous, believes them older.

Why did they paint? For magical reasons? Today it is sometimes believed that the hallucinatory experiences of the Bushman medicine men are depicted in many paintings and this is a fascinating explanation of some of the strange features that have puzzled people.

We talked of the paintings for weeks afterwards, and of how all over South Africa paintings such as these must be vanishing. Back in Pretoria I asked Dick if he would copy them for us so that some permanent record would remain. 'It's my hobby, I'd love to,' he replied. We had known him for long but had never guessed this!

So he went to Cranemere, climbed the mountain and copied the paintings. When he had finished them he said, 'There must be more.' If there were we did not know of them. Sita and Maurice thought a while and then began to telephone the farmers in the mountains. Sometimes one, sometimes another, had heard of a painting near by, and when Dick later met the men they were often able to give him yet another clue. He followed every hint, sometimes finding paintings close about us. Then he would say, 'Yes, but there must be *more.*' There were. He raced about the countryside – this country believed barren of rock art – finding more and still more paintings, and he questioned and climbed (often with Mary and Patrick Carfax, Sita's nephew, as guides) and sweated and painted. As the months passed he made the six-hundred-mile trip to Cranemere again and again and every time he found new sites.

One night we spread his paintings over the floor and on our hands and knees we pored over them, figures of men and animals of all kinds, ant-bear, elephant, lion, bushbuck, springbuck, gemsbuck. With us was Walter Battiss. He looked with attention at the copy of a lioness Dick had done in our mountains. The painting is unknown, for even the farmer who guided Dick had found it only by accident when hunting for dassies as a boy. It represents a big orange-gold lioness padding across the veld and in movement and colour it is very lovely. It is a shaded polychrome and it interested Battiss immensely, for polychromes are rare in the Karoo where the animals are usually simple in outline and of one colour; and moreover it had been expertly painted by a master hand.

Then he began to tell us his theory that among the Bushmen, as with us today, great creative artists were rare, that they travelled perhaps hundreds of miles, and that their paintings, widely distant, could be pinpointed today because of their individual styles and peculiarities. Talking of this, he turned over Dick's paintings until he came upon a copy of a bushbuck copied in the mountains above us, and he stopped abruptly and said with sharp pleasure, 'But this is new, this is individual. I have never seen this artist before. Dick, this is a *new* artist.'

The painting was fairly large, 19 by 12 inches, and the buck, of a deep red, was outlined heavily in white, which in itself was unusual. The brilliant almond eye, the ears, the sweeping curved tail, were also outlined; and it was browsing on a leaf marked in white – a bold, beautiful painting by a man who had used tricks no Bushman artist had before.

Sita has a copy, traced and painted by Dick on a piece of butcher's wrapping paper, the only paper Pearston could provide! It hangs in her museum that houses everything of unusual interest on Cranemere; and every time she looks at it she thinks of this artist and of Battiss's words, 'It's the best thing to come out of the Karoo.'

6. The Beginning

As children on Cranemere we all believed the Bushmen the beginning of history on our Plains, followed in their turn by the settlers and Bantu. History and prehistory merged and none of us, I think, ever looked further. Although we knew of the palaeontological treasures of the Karoo it was very vaguely, like some old myth, far away and divorced from life. One spring morning we took a header into the prehistory of 200 million years before. We have not since emerged.

Like the story of the Bushman paintings, it started with an expedition. Just north of Cranemere in the Graaff-Reinet district not twenty miles across the mountains as the crow flies is the farm Wellwood, owned by Dr Sidney Rubidge, an old friend of the Palmer family. For years Dr Rubidge, to the merriment of a large part of the neighbourhood, had been collecting fossils – mostly fossil reptiles – from the Karoo around. 'They think I'm a bit touched,' he said; but he went on collecting. Talking at random of the curiosities of the Karoo, we thought one day of Dr Rubidge's fossils and determined to see them.

How easily and unknowingly one can take a step that can embroider a new interest into a life – or lives. There should have been a pricking in our thumbs the morning we went to see the fossils, but we had no warning at all. Mrs Rubidge gave us a sumptuous Karoo tea and then we walked to the museum close by. Two hours later we reeled into our car. We were drunk – drunk with fossils. We could think only of the story they told. As we had stretched out our hand to touch a tiny reptile no bigger than a squirrel we had looked at our fingers enclosing the little skull and marvelled that these, our fingers, had come from that; that we were the heirs of that little lizard of 180 million years ago. For the story Dr Rubidge's fossils showed us was the story of the beginning of man himself.

The story began here on our Karoo. Looking across our

parched and ancient plains, it is easy to believe they have been here since time began and that the first life – a desert life – crawled here in aridity, sand and heat. Travelling through the quivering air of the Plains of Camdeboo, it is almost impossible to believe that there was ever a time when the climate of this land was different, when the Karoo was mainly swamps and lakes. Yet the Karoo was once a vast lake fed by a huge river, possibly larger than the Nile, which meandered across the country from the north, spreading a great sea of mud over the land. Here lived and died the millions of reptiles big and small which lived in this remote muddy world, here they left their bones, and here in course of time the climate changed and the mud became shale, holding within it these bones, themselves become like rock in hardness. These are Dr Rubidge's fossils of today.

Fanny Palmer as an old woman told us something of the early story of the Plains, yet I never heard her talk of these creatures of the ancient swamps. She died before their full significance was known and so missed a story that would have thrilled her.

It is a tremendous and an alien story unfolded here about us, and Fanny – although she did not know the story – knew the man who was to tell it.

His name was Robert Broom and he was to become one of the very great palaeontologists of the world. When Fanny knew him he was a doctor in Pearston doing a routine medical job attending to coughs and colds and broken bones, and nobody, not even Fanny who admired his drive and passionate interest in the world about him, foresaw the scientist who was to begin by asserting that these ancient reptiles of the Karoo were the ancestors of man and to end many years later by unearthing their descendants, the 'Southern Apes', *Australopithecus*, links between ape and man. The bones that Broom saw as he drove about the dusty roads, followed the shale stream-beds across the plains, and climbed the hillsides, were those of these first creatures that ceased to be wholly reptile and displayed the first unaccountable traits that belonged to the warm-blooded creatures of the world.

When Broom came to Pearston in 1900 palaeontology, or the Science of Ancient Life, was still a young science. Darwin's *Origin of Species* that rocked the scientific world was only forty-one years old. Before that time it had been generally accepted that man had been created in the world in the shape of man. It was true that through the centuries there had been men, such as Darwin's own grandfather, who had glimpsed the modern theory behind evolution, but they were only glimpses.

From early times men had noted the odd plant and animal shapes in rocks. Some believed them to be a form of rocky life; or to have spontaneously generated in the rocks, or even to have grown from germs dropped from the stars. Men such as Herodotus or Leonardo da Vinci who guessed their true source were not deemed by many to be either wise or good. Palaeontology as an accepted respectable science was not born until the late eighteenth century, and it was not until the mid-nineteenth century that the suspicion arose that man could have had an ape for an ancestor, let alone a reptile. Nineteenth-century scientists such as Owen, Cope, and Seeley had suggested a new line of thought, but it was only a suggestion.

Even well into the twentieth century scientists argued about the origin of mammals, some believing mammals had arisen directly from amphibians. Today, the fact that science generally acknowledges that mammals arose from reptiles is largely due to Broom's work on the Karoo specimens started in Pearston in 1900 and helped in great measure by Dr Rubidge and his fossil collection.

In South Africa little was known of the young science of palaeontology. The first of the mammal-like reptiles, or Therapsids as these famous fossil reptiles of the Karoo are known, had been discovered in 1838, and at the time there was hardly a soul in South Africa who cared a straw. Andrew Geddes Bain, South Africa's first geologist and greatest roadmaker, was building a military road north of the village of Fort Beaufort. During blasting operations he noticed in the rock what he took to be teeth and fragments of bone and these he extracted carefully and sent to the Geological Society of London, who referred them to Sir Richard Owen, noted British palaeontologist.

'The result was so novel,' said Owen afterwards, 'that Mr Bain was asked to persevere,' and he was given financial help by the Geological Society and the British Museum.

Bain, and later his son Thomas and a few other enthusiasts, continued to collect fossils in the years that followed. Owen was interested in what he termed 'these huge herbivorous dragons', but even he failed to realize that their bones were a momentous discovery. It was in 1838 that Bain found what he called the Blinkwater Monster, the first fossil specimen of the 'Cheek-Lizard', *Pareiasaurus*, now the best known of the giant fossil reptiles of the Karoo, a huge, heavy, slow-moving creature. Owen had described some of Bain's finds in 1846 but this remarkable one – was it perhaps too remarkable – he left undescribed for thirty-eight years, earning for himself the wrath of later scientists.

Incidentally, although a cast of the skull remains, the original skull, which weighed nearly 100 pounds, has mysteriously disappeared from the British Museum.

Broom was later to describe this ancient dragon as something between a crocodile and a hippopotamus with a broad, rather flat head and wide bony cheeks with knobs. It had small cutting teeth and great curved claws, and it was undoubtedly a digging creature, living not on flesh but on plants. Broom called it one of Nature's most successful experiments, for it lived in great numbers – a very similar creature was even found as far away as north Russia – and survived for over 30 million years! And its bones were literally strewn over parts of the Karoo.

Owen had realized that these new fossil reptiles had certain mammalian characteristics. In 1870 an American palaeontologist, Edward Cope, obtaining a good skull, observed with fascination these same details. Interest began to mount. In the 1880s Professor H. G. Seeley, a famous British scientist, examined the collection that the Bains, father and son, had sent to England. 'I learned the wonderful natures of the animals,' he said; and in 1889, brimming over with anticipation, he was off to South Africa to visit the Karoo for himself, to collect fossils, and complete his knowledge of the skeleton of the great 'Cheek-Lizard'. Up till then it had been known by scientists from its skull, an incomplete vertebral column, and a few bones. He longed to find a complete skeleton, and he did.

He was lucky to have Thomas Bain as guide and assistant, and they travelled through the Great Karoo north of Prince Albert Road, noting many fossils as they went. The farmers knew of his coming and had gathered a collection of bones to show him. He was somewhat dismayed, for he had had experience of this type of collecting in which the easily transportable skull and bones were severed from the rest of the skeleton, and the whole thus lost for ever. He had found fifty skulls in the British Museum with no indication of the bodies to which they had belonged, and he was afraid this would be his luck in South Africa. He need not have worried. Later, one collector alone in this area was to send three dozen skeletons to the Cape Town Museum. But Seeley could not foresee this and great was his thrill to find a skeleton 'just as it had been complete in the flesh, left upon the surface of the country, lying embedded in the rock and only needing to be taken out and carried away'.

He looked at his 'lizard' bones with deep excitement. Would they reveal any closer connection with mammals or not? He soon found out. As the matrix was cleared away (a terrific job for the rock was iron-hard) and the bones were laid bare, he pounced on them eagerly. 'I found to my amazement that although the proportions of the bones and the forelimbs were extremely heavy, heavier perhaps than in any other known mammals, yet the forms of the bones were entirely mammalian,' he wrote. 'The time went on, and the sun rose higher: we cleared away the hind limb, and I then had the pleasure of laying bare what was hitherto unknown — the bones of the ankle joints.' He found to his delight a perfectly new type of ankle formation, with the feet terminating in great curved claws.

Now all that remained was to transport this clawed dragon to civilization. This 'carrying away', as other early fossil hunters were to find, was a chancy affair, with little skilled help and many difficulties, but at last the fragments were gathered up, and they filled several large cases. A procession of mule wagons bore away what Seeley trusted would some day be one of the most prized ornaments of the British Museum.

Later on this same trip, no longer geographically in the Karoo but geologically in these same Karoo beds, Seeley saw some of the most remarkable creatures of all. At Aliwal North he saw fossil bones which might have been those of either a reptile or a mammal; he could not tell which for sure. Dr Kannemeyer, a famous fossil collector of his day, had found a number of such specimens. 'When we took the skulls of these wonderful animals,' wrote Seeley, 'we found that, reptiles though they may be, they had lost all the distinctive characteristics in the skull of the reptilian with one or two exceptions that we could not examine, and had acquired in other cases the character of the skull of the mammalia.'

It was a notable expedition for him and for science generally.

Thomas Bain, who helped Seeley on this trip, had gained a great deal of his knowledge through his famous father, Andrew. The two of them, together with Dr William Guybon Atherstone, were the three great pioneers among the fossil hunters of the Karoo, forerunners of Dr Rubidge. Atherstone was a great figure in his day. He identified the first diamond discovered in South Africa and was the first doctor on the African continent to perform an operation using ether as an anaesthetic. He seems to have tackled everything with the most uninhibited zest.

The Karoo was for him a world of marvels. 'Were not the plains around us strewn with the buried bones of giants of a former world, extinct creatures known but by the scattered remnants of their stony skeletons lying here and there whitening in the sun?' he wrote from the Great Karoo in the 1870s. 'Reptiles of wondrous form and monstrous size – far-famed dicynodons, some with ivory tusks like walruses, without teeth, some with both tusks and teeth, and some (the largest) without either . . . gigantic creatures . . . Printed thanks I received for a wagon-load sent to the British Museum . . . Amongst them was one vertebra measuring nearly six inches across.' And then a typical wisecrack: 'This is a country in which no blotting-paper is required for the ink dries faster than you can write.'

Even on official business, bouncing over the Karoo in his cart, he could not bear to pass a likely stone but, leaping out, would turn over the rocks until night fell, when he would pack up his fossil treasures by the light of his bivouac fire.

Fossil-hunting was not always a serious business for him. Collecting at the foot of the Swartberg one day, he and Thomas Bain were accosted by a young farmer with a load of hay. Atherstone was on his knees with his hands full of fossils when a shadow loomed over him and a voice drawled, 'What goes on? Are you hunting for gold?'

Atherstone handed him a bit of the rock with a beautiful orthis and some small, perfect trilobites, red on the grey rock.

'A fossil bush-louse,' he said.

'Good heavens! And this is Bosluis Kloof,' the man exclaimed.

'Of course,' Atherstone replied. 'That is why they gave it the name. Look! Here are hundreds, thousands in the rock.'

'I see them with my eyes,' remarked the farmer, 'but how did they get in the rock?'

Here Bain joined them. 'Don't you know all about the Flood and the animals that were in the Ark?' he asked. 'Here, what do you think this is?' showing him a small fossil in a rock, looking exactly like a rusty screw.

'That must certainly be a screw of the Ark,' said the farmer with astonishment, 'but *magtig*, how rusty!'

'Think of the *time* elapsed since then,' said Atherstone.

'*Ja, dit is waar*,' said the man. 'It is wonderful. Really, if I had not seen it with my own eyes I would *never* have believed it!' And he strode off with his bundle of hay.

Atherstone used to recount the story of the screw of the Ark with joy.

There were other early collectors, such as Joseph Orpen who, while surveying at Harrismith, found the first fossil dinosaur known outside Europe, and Dr D. R. Kannemeyer of Burghersdorp who discovered the mammal-like creatures that had so impressed Seeley; Alfred – 'Gogga' – Brown, the gentle hermit who looked like Darwin and kept tortoises; Albert Higgins, Arthur Putterill, John Whaits, and W. van der Byl. Several of these collected in the Karoo itself. The Reverend John Whaits was a railway clergyman with a good eye for fossils and wherever he travelled he collected treasures. Many of his best finds came from Beaufort West and Graaff-Reinet. Van der Byl lived on the farm Abraham's Kraal in the Prince Albert district close to Jan Willemsfontein and Versfontein, where in 1871 Atherstone had made great discoveries. He made Abraham's Kraal a famous name in palaeontology.

In spite of the work of such men, little was known of the South African fossils. Scientists of world reputation such as Owen, Cope and Seeley had stimulated a certain interest in the mammal-like reptiles of the Karoo, but it was not until the arrival of Broom that they were thrust upon the world.

Modern science may find holes in Broom's knowledge but his work on the Karoo reptiles remains unsurpassed in scope, detail, vigour, and vision.

Broom was born in 1866 in Paisley, Scotland, where his father designed material and shawl patterns. Even as a small child he collected with passion everything within reach, and this was to continue throughout his life. At Glasgow University he studied with brilliance chemistry, botany (winning a prize as the best first-year student) and medicine, taking his degree as doctor of medicine in 1889. He also found time to be an ardent supporter and assistant secretary of the Natural History Society.

He was interested in everything and in many scientific problems, including the origin of mammals. Soon he was off to Australia to study marsupials and to collect extinct species, bones and lizards, but the stories of the mammal-like reptiles of the Karoo fascinated him, and he finally found them irresistible. In 1897 he arrived in Cape Town, and it is interesting to find that almost at once he was collecting again, first golden moles in

Little Namaqualand where he practised as a doctor, then lizard embryos.

In 1900, only two years after he had first seen Karoo fossils for himself, Broom arrived in Pearston – erupted, the people were later to say – with his scientific and collecting paraphernalia, his butterfly-net, his books, and the most ardent, overriding, thrustful collecting mania the Karoo, or perhaps for that matter the world, has ever seen. He chose Pearston deliberately because it lay on the edge of the richest fossil-bearing country in the world. He planned to explore it, and at the same time to determine for himself if possible the origin of mammals, and with these two modest ambitions in mind he settled down here as medical doctor for three years.

He was thirty-four years old. His immaculate professional clothes were the only decorous thing about him and he rocked the district. He did what he wanted, when he wanted, and how he wanted, helped along by what colleagues were later to call a sixth sense and the absolute assurance that God was on his side. He began to collect everything. It is almost impossible to turn up natural history reports of this time without finding Broom's name: bees, flies, wasps, spiders, lizards, plants of all kinds, fossils – he collected them omnivorously. 'When one has gone fossil-hunting and has drawn a blank, as often happens,' he was to say afterwards, 'it cheers one to discover a new or rare lizard or mammal or to find a new plant.'

Later he was to collect equally successfully books, pictures, stamps, letters of famous people and stories.

There are endless tales of Broom at this time and his errands of mercy which ended up as collector's sprees. He attended Fanny Palmer, and successfully brought at least one Palmer relative into the world, but there are nevertheless farmers and their wives in the district who still claim they should have been delivered by Broom but were not. Unable to resist the temptation of a new locality, he was sometimes 'over the randjie' hunting for a fossil at the vital moment. It is said he once forgot a broken leg when he saw a new butterfly at the side of the road!

During these years he received a letter that interested him greatly. It was from two brothers, C. J. M. and James Kitching, who had heard that he was looking for bones in rocks and wrote to say that they knew of some in a river-bed near New Bethesda, a tiny village near Graaff-Reinet and not many miles from Pearston. The letter had momentous consequences. Broom visited the village. What had been in C. J. M. Kitching a random interest in fossils became a fixed and burning enthusiasm, and many of the mammal-like reptiles he collected in the following years were finally to grace one of the great museums of the world, the American Museum of Natural History. Broom the scientist, and Kitching the road-builder – their paths were often to cross again and with what a burgeoning of palaeontological knowledge of the Karoo!

Now Broom began to explore the Karoo for himself.

Geologists have divided the shale and sandstone deposits of the Karoo into various beds or series and these are again subdivided into zones. Each layer or bed has within it the fossil remains of the creatures of that age, and like a page of a book each layer tells part of a continuous story of these creatures and their descendants.

The first of these beds was deposited some 250 million years or more ago, the last about 150 million years ago, and they reach roughly from Permian to Triassic times. The fossils from this immense period indicate the origin of tortoises, lizards and birds, and above all of mammals, and although the early beds are not so rich in fossil remains, the upper beds, known as the Beaufort and Stormberg series, are fabulously rich. It was the beds of the Beaufort series that Broom explored with ardour as he drove over the wide level plains from which rose the typical mountains and hills of the Karoo, crowned with dolerite.

He found the slopes of these mountains and the beds of rivers and streams were a wonderful hunting-ground for fossils. Not that fossils were found everywhere. While he found some beautifully preserved in the shales around Pearston (at least one of these is now in the American Museum of Natural History) and

Bruintjeshoogte, the richest areas were to the north and west, roughly as far west as Prince Albert.

He was later to estimate that in the whole Karoo formation there were preserved the fossil remains of at least 800 000 000 000 animals, of which at any time at least a million specimens were lying on the surface to be picked up. And of this one million probably 100 000 were weathered into dust every two or three years and a fresh 100 000 exposed.

Broom thus found in the Karoo a collecting ground without parallel. Years later when Professor Camp from California was hunting fossils in the Karoo, Broom directed him to a farm where he collected 100 skulls in one day! In 1889 Professor Seeley, travelling east of Prince Albert, had seen fossil bones lying in the very roadway. In this area, it was said, the farmers used the large fossil skulls and bones beneath their tables as foot-stools.

Our own Plains are not considered particularly rich in fossils compared with other areas in the Karoo. Yet recently James Kitching – son of C. J. M. Kitching – who as a child had collected fossils with Broom and is now a noted palaeontologist in his own right – found eight fine fossil reptiles on Cranemere in an afternoon, some lying on the surface of the ground, and a few miles away two large fossil reptiles which had been used to prop up a fence. Close to Pearston his brother, who had had car trouble and was walking idly about waiting for a mechanic to help him, picked up two fine fossils at his feet.

No wonder Broom had chosen the Karoo.

He did not stay in Pearston for long but in 1903 went to the Victoria College at Stellenbosch as Professor of Geology and Zoology. Here, in seven years, he published ninety-six scientific papers, and every holiday and every available moment was spent in the Karoo. Soon, although all official help was denied him, he began to make a unique private collection of fossils. South Africa officially was not interested in fossils, so that finally he sent his collection to the United States. Several overseas trips alternated with periods of work both in England and South Africa, and honours began to fall upon him. In 1928, for instance, the Royal Society of London awarded him one of the two Royal Medals for his work on fossil reptiles and on the origin of mammals. For a short while he returned to medical practice and in this time wrote nineteen papers and three full-length scientific books.

Finances had always been a problem, and in 1934 when a post was offered him at the Transvaal Museum he took it, and became a full-time scientist. But soon the origin of man was to supplant in importance that of mammals in his mind, and his tremendous enthusiasm was directed into a new channel.

A new crop of legends grew about him here – of his courage, for he was a doughty fighter as many scientists learned; of his absent-mindedness; of his uncanny sixth sense. Colleagues remembered how when a fossil was still almost hidden in matrix he would often know what it would turn out to be – to the fury of the orthodox.

To some he was naturally anathema; to others he was the great old man of science. His friends remember him not only with respect but with delight. Kitching, his face lighting with laughter, remembers Broom hunting fossils in the blue gravel – the diamond gravel – of the Vaal and returning boiling with anger.

'What, no luck?' someone asked.

'Bloody diamonds,' Broom stormed, 'and nothing else.'

He was now an old man. During the last years of his life at the Transvaal Museum time became an obsession with him. 'What do you want? Go away. There's no time to talk,' he would snap at visitors. Few men can ever have filled a life so full.

During the years when he was exploring the Karoo fossils he revealed a world of almost legendary creatures that once lived on the Karoo, from the size of a mouse to that of a dragon. There were the great carnivorous creatures that preyed upon the 'Cheek-Lizard'. Broom obtained the skull of one from the Reverend J. D. Vorster, a minister of the Dutch Reformed Church, from Fraserburg Road Station. It was probably twenty feet long with a skull three feet long and enormous front and eye teeth. 'It was large and powerful enough,' said Broom, 'to have played with the nine-foot-long Pareiasaurs as a fox-terrier does with a rat.' He named it *Eudinosuchus vorsteri* in honour of the minister.

Not all the reptiles were as forbidding. The early Dicynodon, that is, 'double dog-toothed' fauna of the order of *Anomodonts*, were small and sluggish. Although their skeletons are very like those of mammals, their appearance sounds very unmammal-like indeed: heavy, short-legged and scaly, with horny beaks like a tortoise and sometimes with two gently curving tusks. Over a hundred forms of Dicynodonts are known, and they too must have been a most successful brand of reptile for they lasted for some 20 million years. Their horny beaks appear, unexpectedly, to have been a most successful adaptation.

Later Dicynodonts were larger but never huge. One common form was short-legged, short-tailed, large-headed and tusked, and on these lived many species of carnivorous reptiles such as the Gorgonopsians or 'Terrible Eyes', long-legged, sharp-toothed, active creatures. Broom considered it was probably due to them that it was so extremely rare to find a Dicynodon skull together with its bones, for aeons ago when they made a kill these flesh-eating dragons dragged away the bones to some safe retreat as do carnivores today, leaving only the skulls. Skulls have been picked up by the hundred, but the very few small skeletons found were probably those of animals that had been drowned and preserved in the mud.

Gorgonopsians are not only common in the Karoo, for very similar species have been found in Russia. Broom estimated the Russian forms were twice as large as a lion, the Karoo ones somewhat the build of a hyena, although some were much larger. They must all have been quite frightful in appearance.

One of the most interesting forms of Anomodont was *Lystro-saurus*. It was a large aquatic animal, described by Broom as a reptilian seal, but its large eyes and nostrils were placed near the top of the head so that it could look over the water and breathe with very little of the head exposed. It was very abundant in parts. This, together with many of the other reptiles, is in Dr

Rubidge's museum; and that first morning we paused, as we have done every time we have visited the museum since, and looked at it with awe for it is one of the most spectacular examples of adaptation to environment that can be imagined.

The different faunas did not all exist together through the millions of years; while some lived side by side, others died out and were followed by new forms, and Broom saw the evidence of this clearly in the zones of the Karoo beds.

The great 'Cheek-Lizards', the Pareiasaurs, which had excited Seeley, were found, for example, in the lowest and oldest zone of the Beaufort series; but in the next zone, the Endothiodon, there are very few, a great many other creatures having superseded them; instead, there are many Gorgonopsians, many 'Double Dog-Tooths', a very few Therocephalians or 'Wild Beast Heads', and a type of Anomodont called *Endothiodon* which gave the zone its name. In the zone to follow, Cistecephalus, there are great numbers of 'Double Dog-Tooths', 'Terrible Eyes', and 'Wild Beast Heads'. In the next zone comes *Lystrosaurus* with its eyes on the top of its head, and a number of small Cynodonts or 'Dog-Tooths' with mammal-like jaws and teeth. The following zone is Cynognathus, yielding the genus *Kannemeyeria*, to which belong large mammal-like reptiles. I once handled a tooth of a Kannemeyeria. It was nearly two inches long with a huge base and a rough point. But that point had been made by man, Stone Age Man, who had used as a tool the nearest and best material at hand!

Above Kannemeyeria in the Molteno beds there are plant remains and a few mammal-like reptiles. Now in the Stormberg beds come, among others, the Dinosaurs, primitive lizards, and crocodiles, and the creatures that were almost mammals, the Ictidosaurians, which needed only the slightest change in the jaw structure to be true mammals. Some scientists have counted them reptile, some mammal; it has been largely a matter of pay your money and take your choice.

By 1933 Broom had no doubt not only that the later types of animals were more mammal-like than the early ones, but that he could point to *all* the principal stages in their evolution. Although in Permian and Triassic times there had been many mammal-like groups of reptiles, they all, he thought, ultimately perished – with the exception of one. This was a line of 'small generalized Therocephalians' which eventually gave rise to the Ictidosaurians.

In Upper Triassic times he believed some small Ictidosaurian developed hair, the bones of the jaw becoming slightly changed, and the heart four-chambered. This was the first mammal.

All these great changes had originated, he felt, not in the herbivorous creatures – for although they survived for a long time they were of use mainly as food and never evolved into higher types – but in the small early carnivores and omnivores. It was probably these little creatures that gave Broom his greatest thrill among the Karoo reptiles, for he saw in them the line which led to Ictidosaurians and to warm-blooded animals, the direct ancestors of man, whereas many of the larger and better-known carnivores he described as 'remote cousins' only, the creatures that had mammal-like characteristics but which finally perished.

Broom thought these small carnivores among the most important reptiles that had ever been discovered. They are, however, rare and are known today from comparatively few specimens. In South African museums there are only a couple of dozen good skulls and one tiny skeleton.

When the Mesozoic Era, the era of the reptiles, ended the reptiles were swept off the face of the earth, leaving only a few survivors. It was a gigantic and world-wide cataclysm, a mystery that has never been satisfactorily solved, although many reasons have been suggested such as a major change in climate. But it *did* happen: the great and the fierce vanished, leaving only their bones, and those creatures that remained to cling tenaciously to life were small and probably quick and furtive. They were the humble, and at the same time the great, survivors and from them came the first true mammals, themselves possibly no larger than a mouse. From them in time erupted the hundreds of species of mammals that filled the world, and from one of these, as modern scientists believe, the line from which arose Man himself.

One of the most remarkable fossils that Broom ever handled was a one-and-a-half-inch-long skull and it threw him into transports of delight. It belonged to Dr Rubidge and is today the gem of his collection. Broom named the little animal, no larger than a field mouse, *Millerina rubidgei*, afterwards changed to *Milleretta rubidgei*, pronouncing it to be the first well-preserved skull ever discovered of the group of reptiles that 'may have had as one of its members the ancestor of all mammal-like reptiles'. He said 'may' but he had no hesitation later in describing Rubidge's *Milleretta* as 'the seed of the mammal race'.

The story goes that Broom, absent-minded always, carried this precious skull around in his pocket for several weeks; and as he pulled his handkerchief or papers out of his pocket, the skull would often enough pop out too.

Dr Rubidge's collection of fossils – they are nearly all local – were manna to Broom. Several times a year for many years he arrived at Wellwood vibrating with anticipation and Dr Rubidge usually had something to show him. Sometimes the finds were momentous. Dr Rubidge himself collected, sometimes helped by Peggy, his daughter, and others, notably C. J. Kitching who was superintending a road-making gang near by and whom Broom pronounced to be the greatest fossil-hunter in the world, and his young son James who was later to be dubbed 'the greatest fossil-*finder*'.

James Kitching today remembers Broom on those electrifying visits sitting on their kitchen table in a go-to-hell collar and a silk tie, digging away at a piece of matrix with his mother's scissors, drinking coffee out of his saucer, and talking endlessly of fossils. He was a tutor without parallel, and there are palaeontologists today who claim that Broom passed on something of his sixth sense in the field to the boy who helped him. James himself believes that the astonishing ability to see an almost invisible fossil in the veld is an inheritance from his father, for it is shared by all his brothers. In fact, James's is probably a Broom-Kitching legacy and unique.

'Did you yourself start when you were a boy?' we asked Dr Rubidge.

'No,' he replied, 'oh no, I was a middle-aged man.' Then he told us how eighty years before, a great-uncle of his, Dr Richard Nathaniel Rubidge (he who had first introduced Stow to fossil-collecting), had roamed over Wellwood in a frock-coat, a starched shirt, and a top hat, looking for fossils. He remembers today that the story had delighted him but it had not inspired him to collect on his own. It was his daughter Peggy as a ten-year-old child who started him on his collecting. As a young man riding over the veld he had noted stones within which were embedded bones. Sometimes he picked them up and carried them home, but they meant nothing to him and his interest was perfunctory. It was in the 1930s that he first looked with atten-tion at his 'bony stones'. 'What is a fossil?' Peggy asked one day. He had just happened on a newspaper reference to the antiquity of fossils and her question roused him.

'Let's go and see,' he said.

They found several fossils that day and it was Peggy and a young friend, Frank Collins, who made the discovery that was to shake him into a lifelong interest. It was a large rock with parallel 'bones' at its tip, each about two inches long, and he thought they were part of a fossil paw. They brought the rock home and Dr Rubidge spent every odd moment for a month knocking away the matrix around the fossil with a carpenter's hammer and a farm chisel. 'It makes me shudder now to think how I did it,' he says. Slowly there were revealed features like a horse's snout, while the claws of the 'paw' were shown to be teeth.

This was his introduction to Broom. Broom swooped upon his find to pronounce it a new species of a large carnivorous reptile which had lived possibly 200 million years ago. He named it *Dinogorgon rubidgei*. 'Now you are immortalized,' he said to Dr

Rubidge. 'The name will endure as long as does human culture.'

Here was a new interest connected, however remotely, with present-day life, even, Dr Rubidge felt, with his very farm animals. 'No designer of any gadget, no inventor, nor any explorer into a new field of science could have experienced a more profound sensation. I became obsessed,' said Dr Rubidge. 'I had one fossil.' And then he looked at us and smiled. 'Now I wanted two.'

He was off; and the hobby he loved soon began to develop into something more. Ten years later Broom was to say, 'His collection is in my opinion scientifically more important than the whole world's collection of South African reptiles put together . . . Some day the work of Rubidge and Kitching will be regarded as forming one of the most glorious pages in South African history and science.'

Until his son Richard took over the farm Dr Rubidge could only collect fossils in his spare time. 'I was afraid if I wasn't always there Wellwood would melt away,' he says ruefully today. But in spite of this his collection grew. By 1934 he had discovered over 30 new genera and over 70 new species of Permian reptiles.

Today he has some 800 skulls, including 104 type-specimens. Thirty-three have been named in his honour, and several after Peggy. The most valuable fossil scientifically still remains *Milleretta rubidgei*, but *Leavachia duvenhagei* is a close second – again an early link between reptile and mammal. The skeleton of this little creature, some 18 inches long including the tail, remains the only one of its kind yet found, and is judged to be 200 million years old. Its skull is almost complete and its small delicate hand was described by Broom as the most perfect ever found in a fossil.

The 'Wicked Rubidge' (*Rubidgea atrox*) is another famous fossil and the first of a new family to be described. Broom thought the skull the most perfectly preserved of any South African fossil reptile in any museum. This large skull, some 20 inches in length, was that of a large reptile found near New Bethesda and it was carnivorous as the tremendous teeth and fangs indicate.

The name of a little Hottentot boy, Hans Wessels, who made coffee for the fossil-hunters, is honoured here – 'A skilled little Tottie with a number three shoe,' as Dr Rubidge remembers him with a smile. Dr Rubidge with three young boys stopped one day to look for fossils at a gravel outcrop near Murraysburg where a road-gang was working. No boy could be with Dr Rubidge without becoming fossil-conscious and they piled out of the car shouting, '*Dié is myne – Dié is myne – Dié is myne*' – 'This is mine.' Everyone found something. Hans's find had had its snout taken off by the tractor, but he bundled the pieces into a grain-bag. 'Put the skull together,' said Dr Rubidge jokingly, 'and perhaps your name will be famous.'

Little Hans to everyone's surprise sat down at home and worked and fitted for two weeks until the skull was complete. Broom found it was a new species, and at Dr Rubidge's request he named it after Hans.

One of the great 'Cheek-Lizards' is here, *Pareiasaurus rubidgei*. It is remarkable for its cusped teeth, every one of which is still covered with brown, lustrous, perfectly preserved enamel. When I first saw it I found it hard to believe they had never been polished.

Here, too, is *Platycyclops crassus*, a huge animal with a skull 28 inches long and 20 broad, with a great 'third eye' in the middle of its forehead. This fossil (and its name) fascinated us, as did Broom's explanation of that 'eye' – not a true eye, he guessed, but possibly another sense: and modern science tends to show that once again Broom was probably right.

We paused in front of a huge creature with its great teeth exposed in a fearful grin. 'I used to call him Old Smiler to myself,' Dr Rubidge told us. 'I used often to come in and sit down and say "Goodnight, Old Smiler", so I was greatly amused when Dr Broom gave him his scientific name, *Smilesaurus ferox*.'

Once we stood petrified at a face that gazed at us, not from empty sockets but from ancient, evil, dragon's eyes. Dr Rubidge was delighted. 'I had the eyes specially moulded,' he said, 'and when I slip them into the sockets the creature lives. Some scientists have been really angry: they say, "You make a mockery of science", but in the whole museum it is always the face with the eyes that people look at first.'

Dr Rubidge talks constantly of Broom. 'He was the greatest mind I have ever known,' he says. Here the two of them spent many hours together (and here Dr Rubidge still keeps Broom's desk and basket-chair just as they were once used). In Broom's absence Dr Rubidge would collect all the new specimens, perhaps thirty or more at a time. He loves to remember how Broom would arrive, rush to the museum, and without reference to a single note or book would reel off their names.

'Don't you ever need a reference book? Don't you ever make a mistake without them?' he once asked, and Broom made the typical Broom reply, 'I sometimes make mistakes but not as many as other people.'

Dr Rubidge told us once, 'I would ask visiting scientists about some Karoo fossil here and they would say, "Oh, that's Broom's field; ask him!" But all the world was Broom's backyard. He would come in here and spot something sent me from America, Europe or North Africa, and he would recognize it and name it instantly. Sometimes I thought there was nothing he did not know.'

He remembers Broom's identification and assembling of *Leavachia duvenhagei*, the fossil skeleton with the exquisite hand, as one of his most incredible achievements. Duvenhage, a water-borer, was drilling for water near Wellwood and had been asked to watch for fossils. One day he brought a chunk of rock containing a fossil skull and this Dr Rubidge put in the museum. Days later he brought him a fossil with a few ribs and vertebrae showing, the rest of the skeleton being hidden in the matrix. This he housed in a different place. When Broom arrived he looked at the skull and said immediately, 'I've seen what fits this.' And he had. The day before he had seen Duvenhage's other find and instantly and positively, although both skeleton and skull were enclosed in matrix and he had seen them at different places and at different times, he knew they belonged together. Duvenhage admitted when questioned that the two *had* been found together but he had never thought to say so. The elation of Broom and Rubidge was even greater than usual when the fossil was cleaned up from the bottom side to expose the hand.

Both Broom and Dr Rubidge pondered the significance of the fossils they handled daily. Broom could never resist a wisecrack.

'Here,' said he one day to a pretty girl he was showing round the exhibits, and he held out on the palm of his hand the tiny rat-like skull of *Milleretta*, 'here is your great-grandfather!'

But this was not his only approach. He was basically a deeply religious man. He believed – and the clearer the story of evolution became to him the more firmly he believed it – that it did not happen by chance, that 'some intelligent controlling power' had specially guided one line to result in man: and by this he meant more than physical man. The evolution of man's body, he thought, was complete. *This* was not the end and aim of the great venture over the millions of centuries, but the evolution of man's *personality*. There were many, wrote Broom, who would not agree with him: and almost one can read between his words, 'A fig for them.'

Seen as Broom saw it, *Milleretta* is not an inglorious ancestor but a splendid one, a one-and-a-half-inch-long testimony to the glory and omnipotence of God. It pleases Dr Rubidge to think so. Evolution is a theory still frowned on by many in South Africa and some at least of his visitors adhere to the letter of the Bible.

'Are they shocked at what they see and hear here?' I asked Dr Rubidge once.

'I explain to them,' he said, and I could imagine his gentle enthusiasm, 'that in my opinion the Bible and science tell the same story but in different ways: one tells it in poetry and one in fact. Most people go away satisfied.'

Broom died in 1951. He was the most regular visitor and ardent collaborator and Dr Rubidge mourns him. 'My lonely pursuit', he now calls his fossil-hunting.

Broom laid the stone for the Rubidge museum in 1943. It stands near the homestead, dwarfed by the great orange trees for which Wellwood is famous, and it is visited by perhaps one person in every hundred from the country round. It is the sad story of the prophet in his own country. There are those, of course, who know the experience, half real, half not of this world at all, of looking upon the great dragons and at the same time the tiny creatures that were the seed of mammals, of knowing them and touching them and listening to Dr Rubidge gently and lovingly telling their stories. But they are mostly scientists from Johannesburg, Cape Town and Pretoria, from all over Europe, from Oxford and Cambridge, London and New York and Washington.

None of these, it is certain, ever forgets this tiny, rich, remote museum, and the one show-case that Broom once described as scientifically the most valuable in the world. All covet the contents, but Dr Rubidge has decided his fossils are to remain in perpetuity in the Karoo country from which they come.

7. Stilettos and Almond Stones

'This long, splendid, and laborious past.'

Abbé Breuil

Once we had seen the Rubidge fossils we longed to find some on Cranemere.

I do not believe there is such a thing as a mild interest in fossil-hunting. It is all or nothing. Either a man passes a fossil by with complete indifference, or he is enwrapped in its cold glamour. Dr Rubidge had shown us a new world and we were enslaved. Wherever we walked in the veld we looked: we hunted along the dry shale beds of the streams and on the mountainsides; but we found very little. Dr Rubidge's fossils had been cleaned: ours were still encased in matrix and looked as often as not exactly like the rocks about them. We must have walked a dozen times over a lump of rock without noticing the irregularity on its surface. It was James Kitching who was later to walk the way we had, see the mark of the tusks upon the surface, and find it the skull of a baby 'Wing-head' that had lived 200 million years ago.

The remains of these mammal-like reptiles lay, we knew, on every side of us, and their remote and bizarre story filled our minds. We did not give a thought to its sequel – the story of the emergence of man from ape, and modern man from prehistoric man, for the Karoo had figured very little in this later chapter. We had, of course, picked up stone Bushman artefacts – but the Bushman was modern man, even if the first of modern man in Southern Africa. We did not once, I think, try to fill that gap between our mammal-like reptiles and the Bushman. We were content with our own fantastic chapter of the evolution story. Who could ask for better?

But in other parts of Southern Africa gaps in that story were being filled.

An Australian anatomist found what is believed to be the Missing Link and it came from a spot three hundred and fifty miles from Cranemere. His name, as the whole world should know, was Professor Raymond Dart, and his find came from Taung (then Taungs) in the northern Cape.

That find has been described and redescribed, but its drama remains as strong and fresh as in the year 1924 when Dart pieced together, from a box of bone-bearing rocks unearthed in a lime-quarry at Taung, the face of a child that was to set the scientific world by the ears. 'My Taungs Baby', he called it, and Taungs Baby was the name it was to bear for kings and scientists, the man-in-the-street and the music-hall audience for many years after.

It was a face not quite human, yet not the face of an ape. Those rounded eye-sockets, those neat canine teeth, that forehead, were those of a human child; and Dart guessed from the shape of the skull that it had walked upright, or nearly upright. But its brain was the size of that of a chimpanzee.

Dart guessed, with what passionate excitement we may imagine, that here was a creature between ape and man. He called it the Southern Ape, *Australopithecus*, and coined one of the most significant words of twentieth-century science.

In 1924 few guessed that significance; few gave the child a second's serious thought. The child was a chimp; Dart was a joke.

Not to Broom. With that same passion that had unearthed the link between reptile and mammal, Broom recognized the link between ape and man. Dart, in his book *Adventures with the Missing Link*, records that soon after his discovery was announced Broom burst into his laboratory and dropped upon his knees before the Taungs skull – 'in adoration of our ancestor', he put it.

When Broom determined the world should accept a fact, it usually did, sooner or later. But he needed very concrete evidence and he set himself to get it. At the age of seventy he went hunting in a cave not far from Johannesburg – the Sterkfontein caves – and found the bones of an adult creature clearly related to the Taung baby, and it was to prove only the first of many finds that he and later Dr John Robinson, his assistant, were to make of different types of ape-men.

What Dart had formulated, Broom proved. Here on the Transvaal highveld had lived perhaps two and a half million years ago a creature between ape and man, in popular terms the 'Missing Link'. He called his find *Plesianthropus transvaalensis*, but it was later found to be the same species as the Taung child and therefore *Australopithecus*. It is now *Australopithecus africanus*, but those who remember the rousing days will never forget the name *Plesianthropus*, because of the famous specimen that Broom and Robinson found at Sterkfontein in the 1940s and which was hailed around the world – sometimes rapturously, sometimes with laughter – as 'Mrs Ples'.

Since those days the remains of many australopithecines have been found in various sites, and here we remember the other early names associated with them in South Africa, names like Tobias, Brain, Kitching, Hughes, and others (in the 1980s some are still in the forefront of the story of man).

Further afield, there were the discoveries of, among others, Mary Leakey's phenomenally robust *A. boeisei* in East Africa – its popular name, 'Dear Boy', flew around the world as had that of Mrs Ples.

There were the momentous discoveries in Ethiopia by the anthropologist D. C. Johanson and others, of fossil remains, above all of the skeleton known as 'Lucy', that some scientists think is *A. africanus* and others a new species, *A. afarensis*, the Southern Ape of Afar. Drama and publicity attended its discovery. On a blazing day in 1974, Johanson and a colleague, walking across a little gully in the desert of Afar north-east of Addis Ababa, picked up some fossil bones lying on the surface of the soil, which were to provide 'the oldest, most complete, best-preserved skeleton of any erect-walking human ancestor ever found'. They knew as they picked them up that the bones were hominid, and they howled and hugged one another, and jumped up and down, half mad with excitement, only stopping when they suddenly thought they might jump on a fossil and destroy it.

Lucy was over three million years old, perhaps half a million years older than the ape-man of Sterkfontein.

These scientists and others have all helped to establish the validity of the ape-man, and yet his nature is still not clearly known. How could it be otherwise in our greatest guessing-game of history? Was he the ancestor of man? Many scientists today believe *A. africanus* was, although other robust forms of contemporary ape-men, bigger than he (of different species) found in South and East Africa, were not; they had, it is thought, separated some two and a half million years ago into a line which in the end ran dead.

Could ape-man have fashioned a bone tool from the animal he had killed, or could he at least have used one? Experts differ about this. What they do accept is that there was a man-like creature who lived from two and a half million years ago to about one and a half million years ago, *who could make stone tools*. He was in line of descent from Australopithecus (and for over one million years he lived in South and East Africa at the same time as the ape-man). He had, however, a bigger brain, and scientists suggested this, and his tool-making ability, in the name they gave him, *Homo* (admitting him into the genus of man) and *habilis*. He was the 'handy man', the first of men.

What *he* gave rise to was a bigger man with a bigger brain who could not only fashion stone tools but who could make and use fire and possibly could talk. Scientists called him *Homo erectus*, 'upright man', and he lived in many parts of Africa, and also in Asia.

The first specimen known was discovered not in Africa at all but in Java in the early 1890s by a young Dutch doctor, Eugene Dubois, who had set out to find the Missing Link. He thought he had, and called his find *Pithecanthropus erectus*, the 'erect ape-man'. But ape-man he was not – he was man, if not the earliest yet still man towards the beginning of his story. Later his fossil remains were found in Africa, first in North and then in East Africa, where they were largely associated with the work of the famous Leakey family. They have also been found in South Africa at Swartkrans, a site very close to Sterkfontein.

The great fascination of upright man for us is that most fossil experts see him as the immediate ancestor of modern man, *Homo sapiens*.

The first, primitive, far-off *Homo sapiens*, with brains bigger than that of *Homo erectus*, and their increasing skills, lived widely in Europe, in Asia and in Africa. Today they are seen as belonging to four great subspecies or groups. Neanderthal Man – *Homo sapiens neanderthalensis* – we have known from childhood, for he serves as the model for almost every Stone Age illustration we know, with his large eyebrow ridge and great jaws. The first specimen to be described scientifically was found in a limestone cave in the Neander Valley in Western Germany more than a century ago. The uproar it caused lasted down the years, for if some scientists recognized it as ancient man, others claimed it as an individual affected with idiocy and rickets, 'a cossack who came from Russia in 1814' or as a man resembling a sub-normal modern Irishman!

From Java came *Homo sapiens soloensis*, and from Southern Africa two more subspecies.

In 1921 a fossil skull was found at Broken Hill in what was then Northern Rhodesia, which delighted scientists for it was one of the most complete fossil skulls ever discovered. It represented a very primitive man indeed, clearly a relative of Neanderthal Man. He was certainly rather gorilla-like; and in another way very human. He had suffered from toothache. He was known as Broken Hill, Kabwe or Rhodesian Man, *Homo sapiens rhodesiensis*.

Other fossil remains of this subspecies were found later in South Africa at various sites – at the Cave of Hearths in the northern Transvaal, and in the Cape on the wind-blown dunes near Saldanha Bay close to the village of Hopefield. This was the Hopefield skull.

19 *Dr Robert Broom working on a Karoo fossil – one of the few photos ever taken of the great scientist at work.*

Dr Broom with the fossil skeleton of a carnivorous monster perhaps 200 million years old.

20 *Dr Rubidge with the gigantic skull of an extinct Karoo reptile, Platycyclops.*

21 *An intact fossil skeleton of a small Karoo reptile, Dicynodon, over 150 million years old.*

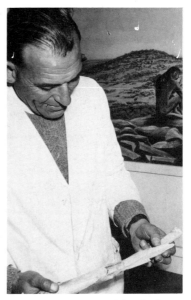

22 *Dr Rubidge displays the skull of the minute reptile* Milleretta rubidgei – *the earliest link between reptile and mammal.*

23 *James Kitching examining the Cranemere bone stiletto.*

24 *The beginning of the Mountain Dig where Sita saw the first Stone Age bone which had lain there for thousands of years.*

25 The skull of the **Milleretta rubidgei.**

Primitive man's pestle and mortar for grinding seeds and pigments, found on Cranemere.

'The most perfect hand in palaeontology' – *the hand of the little* **Leavachia duvenhagei.'**

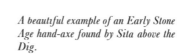

A beautiful example of an Early Stone Age hand-axe found by Sita above the Dig.

Three hundred miles north of Cranemere in the middle of the great grassy plains is Bloemfontein, capital of the Orange Free State. Near here, at Florisbad, a skull was found in the 1930s that was thought to belong to South Africa's early Middle Stone Age, which began perhaps forty thousand years ago. It intrigued South African palaeontologists because, although it showed its kinship to Rhodesian man, it had certain differences. These led some scientists to place it in the fourth group or subspecies, to which belong many of the later human fossil remains found in South Africa.

One of the most notable was made just before the First World War by two farmers digging a trench near Potchefstroom on the Transvaal highveld. It was a human fossil skull, the first ever to be found in South Africa and became known as the Boskop skull. It had certain notable features – its brain capacity, for one, was larger than that of many men and women of today. Other fossil remains belonging to this fourth subspecies came from sites that proved to be both romance and history – Border Cave at Ingwavuma in KwaZulu with its colourful and stirring story, and others in the Transvaal, and in the Cape as at Fish Hoek, Klasies River Mouth and Matjies River.

All these fossil remains have one thing in common that separates them from those of other groups of *Homo sapiens* – in form they are modern.

It is possible that they represent the oldest – the first – of modern men for some of the fossil remains, although modern in form, are ancient in time – some may be 100 000 years or more of age which is far older than fossils of modern-looking man in other parts of the world, and if the dating is correct it could mean – and the thought is revolutionary for many – that he arose, not in Europe or in Asia as we have been taught, but here in our veld and bush, in the caves of our mountains and our sea shore.

So it is that scientists, with increasing enthusiasm, are exploring the possibility that modern man arose in Southern Africa. It is the extraordinary climax to a very long story, the millions of years that went to man's making, and the fraction of time that is the chapter of modern man – 'the last tick of the clock', in Dr Rubidge's words.

This, briefly, is the story of the bones. But there is also the story of the stones. All over South Africa, in greater quantities than anywhere else in the world, lie the stones worked as tools by early man. In their size and shape and fashioning they tell the story of man's need and how he met it, of his prehistoric wit and drive and vision. They are found as well in many other parts of the world, made at different times in different patterns so that an expert, seeing a stone of a certain shape, can say with authority that it belongs to such-and-such a Stone Age period. Sometimes Stone Age men in Africa made tools identical with those of prehistoric man of the same period in Europe or Asia. Thousands of miles divided them in flesh, but not in mind. This is surely one of the most fascinating of all angles on early man.

What man first guessed that within a crude stone lay a shape he could use, his for the making? Perhaps he was born here on our South African veld where huge quantities of fine-grained stones litter the plains and koppies. Certainly his descendants used stone with great skill for hunting, killing, preparing their food, digging, pounding, scraping, scooping, cutting. They selected their stones and from these knocked chips – flakes to archaeologists – off the parent stone or core. A good Stone Age workman learned to strike a core in such a way that he produced a flake of a certain shape, and this he sometimes further trimmed to give it a good cutting edge.

In South Africa we commonly talk of the Early, Middle, and Late Stone Ages to describe the various periods of the great Stone Age in Southern Africa when man, true man, was evolving. Dr Revil Mason, the archaeologist, compares – very roughly, he insists – the European Lower and Middle Palaeolithic with our Early Stone Age; the European Upper Palaeolithic with our Middle Stone Age; and the Mesolithic with our Late Stone Age (and happy we can be with our simple terms).

Our Early Stone Age man made heavy, often handsome, tools such as hand-axes and cleavers; and chips for cutting and scraping. Their Middle Stone Age descendants favoured lighter tools, and by the Late Stone Age these had been reduced still further in size, for some of the flakes of this period are tiny. Some archaeologists believe that outside influences helped to shape our Stone cultures, but others maintain this is untrue; that as man developed here, so did the products of his hands and mind; and that his culture from Early Stone Age to the Bushman is indigenous.

It is just over a century since a farmer in the eastern Cape, Thomas Holden Bowker, made the first collection in South Africa of stones that had been shaped by Stone Age men. Desmond Clark, telling the story in *The Prehistory of Southern Africa*, recounts that Bowker as a boy had mounted these small flakes as heads of his own arrows!

Bowker made his collection in 1858. A year later in Europe a French antiquary, Boucher de Perthes, won a twenty-year-old battle by proving to the scientific world that the worked flints discovered at two sites in France were ancient, dating from a period 'before the Flood'. One of the sites, St Acheul, was to be intimately linked with South Africa, for this French site gave its name to an Early Stone Age culture which existed here in South Africa – here on Cranemere – just as it did six thousand miles away in France.

De Perthes would have recognized Bowker's finds as important. Even at the Cape Bowker's collection aroused interest and in 1866 Sir Langham Dale, Superintendent-General of Education, discovered worked stones near his home in the Cape Flats which he sent to experts in England. Certainly by the 1880s worked stones were generally recognized and held an interest for many in the Cape Colony. Fanny and George Palmer treasured several big worked Late Stone Age stones that they had picked up on Cranemere.

Tremendous sites of Stone Age tools are known today in South Africa – although seldom in the Karoo – and naturally most of the tools and weapons from these are of stone. The less durable materials – bone, leather, wood – are seldom found, and scientists long for them. Only under very special circumstances have bones survived, such as in a limestone cave or in a few places where they were not only quickly covered with silt but where the soil was rich in lime and the climate dry yet not too dry, and the bones were preserved by the minerals drawn upwards towards the surface of the soil.

This was a background we knew, but at a distance.

On a cold blustery winter day we found on Cranemere a Stone Age deposit which was to prove the first of its kind in the Karoo and to provide one of the finest Middle Stone Age bone weapons ever found in South Africa. In one day we found ourselves not on the outskirts of the story of man in Africa, but at the very heart of it, and to all of us, from the children upwards, it was a rousing event.

What we found did not make an orderly story with a clear beginning and end, for it progressed in a series of erratic leaps and bounds and we do not yet know the end.

One afternoon we drove up to Honey Mountain to hunt for fossils. It is the most remote and most lovely part of the farm, where a shallow valley between the mountain and the Rooikop leads to the plains below. We all climbed out of the lorry to spread over the veld in various directions, bent on our own discoveries.

I followed a narrow stream-bed gently upwards over brilliantly clean blue shale in crumbling sheets. Presently I halted in a shaley hollow with a little overhang above me, and here I lingered, looking at the long twisting roots along the bank and listening to the wind. It took me back a lifetime. Just so had I crouched as a child listening to the wind; just so would others listen centuries hence, looking at the same ancient landscape. And who – and what – had listened here before me! If I had known it, one of these early inhabitants had been within twenty yards of me.

Just above the hollow I found a branching stream-bed which

was not smooth shale but ridged with ripple marks, like the water of a dam on a windy day. The others followed and we paced it up and down, exclaiming and marvelling. Two hundred million years ago shallow water running down this hill had formed those ripples in a muddy bed, and time had solidified them into rock. We knelt and stroked the surface. The current had worn the upper edges of the ripples smooth, but the undersides, like the under-side of a wave, were steep. Here and there were little dimples in the rock – 'fossil rain', the palaeontologists were later to call them. They had been made by raindrops 200 million years before!

A little way away in smooth shale Sita found a little fossil 'lizard'. It lay there delicately and beautifully outlined in white, every rib clearly showing in the blue shale, a little carnivorous reptile as old as the shale itself, the earliest creature that we knew of to have lived on Cranemere: as old as time, it seemed to us as we crowded round it. We moved between it and the ripple shale, loath to leave one or the other for more than a moment, until the light began to change and the winter evening to chill us.

We drove home thinking only of our shale bed and its treasures. Nothing then would have convinced us that we would return next day to a spot not five hundred yards away and spare them not one thought. Yet this was so.

Next morning we streamed back to Honey Mountain. A high cold wind blew and we were hungry, so before climbing to the ripples we decided to eat our dinner in the dry bed of the river that reached from Honey Mountain to the Plains below. We made a fire of sweet-thorn wood and sat around it on the sand, eating frikkadelle laced with rosemary and drinking coffee, talking of fossils, shale and reptiles, while the children ran up and down the river-bed hunting for dinosaur teeth.

Sita was leaning back, looking dreamily at a slice of the river bank with its limey soil, stones and twisted roots and thinking it looked like French nougat. Suddenly she gave a long moan. We gazed at her with astonishment. She was pointing with a trembling finger at the bank and there, not five feet from us, on the level of the sandy bed, something white protruded. As our eyes focused on it we saw other white shapes just showing through the silt and stones.

We none of us said a word. We did not even move, but all stared glassily at the bank, finished our frikkadelle, methodically wiped our fingers, and with one accord rose and hurled ourselves upon the objects. They were bones. There was no doubt about it, they were bone, but were they old? Were they new? Above them was five feet of soil and silt. Surely they *must* be old.

We began to dig. Jenks seized a screwdriver and a hammer and began to chip away the matrix. We seized on every possible tool and, the little boys arguing and squealing, we all began to dig and chip and dust and sort the bones. We realized at once that immense care was necessary, and we spent hours chipping out the first bone. It was the skull of a medium-sized animal, filled with soil and crumbling, and from it still projected the cores of two small horns. But the next bone was enormous and intact, and there followed bones of innumerable shapes and sizes, bulky fragments, entire bones, tiny flakes, small teeth, large teeth, and ostrich eggshell in quantity.

We kept the bones separate as far as we could, using every-thing at hand to house them. Every picnic plate, every cup, every bag was filled. A fine vertebra fitted neatly into my nylon cap. 'The vertebra plate', or 'the tusk plate', we would call, and gradually our pile increased. We worked in a frenzy of excite-ment until dusk closed around us. Then we sat back on our heels and looked at our haul. Even without any knowledge of anat-omy we knew that these bones did not come from one animal, but from a number, very different in size and shape. How had they possibly come here together, in one pile, in an area three feet by two? We argued endlessly, but at last concluded that this had been the lair of some wild animal, lion or hyena – 'Or a dinosaur's larder,' cried David.

Back at the farmhouse Maurice inspected the bones. 'Those

big ones look like ox,' he said, 'and the smaller ones like sheep. Somebody must have buried them there a couple of centuries ago.'

Like pricked balloons we crawled into bed. At dawn Jenks awoke. He stretched out his head slowly, and it was like a tortoise neck emerging from the bed-clothes, and croaked: 'They might have died of anthrax.' We considered this drearily and died a little in our beds.

Nevertheless we parcelled up the bones and took them back to Pretoria. A week later in the Bernard Price Institute of Palaeontology in Johannesburg we received the shock of our lives. Our bones had belonged to a number of antelope, wild cat, and to three species of animals now extinct on the Karoo – lion, buffalo, wildebeest: and they had been killed by Stone Age Man – probably Middle Stone Age – who among the bones had left a little fashioned bone tool that identified and dated him. What we had found was a Middle Stone Age slaughter-site.

James Kitching named them for us, vibrating with a passion of energy. We looked at him with interest, this tall dark lean man from the Karoo who had hunted fossils with Broom to emerge as one of the great 'bone' experts of the world.

'You've got the front ulna of a lion – the left foreleg,' he exclaimed; and beside it he placed the ulna of a modern lion, and we looked at the new bone, white and satin-smooth, and the ancient bone, coloured creamy-brown by thousands of years of time; one light in weight, one heavy; one bone, one mineralized. In shape they were identical.

'The skull is ribbok,' he said, 'and that's the tibia of a buffalo. And that a kudu metatarsal. Those are springbuck bones; those teeth are springbuck too, and those kudu, and those wild cat. That humerus and vertebra are wildebeest.'

'What killed them?' we asked. 'Was it human or animal?'

Kitching grinned. 'No small buck ever killed a lion,' he answered. 'Look,' and he held up a shattered wildebeest bone. 'There is not a tooth-mark on it but the bone has been broken and flaked. Only man did that. And look here.' He picked up a fragment of bone. 'It's a piece of wildebeest tibia. And also a tool. That was made and used, perhaps, to scrape the tissue from the skin.'

'By whom?' we chorused. 'When?'

'We don't know for sure,' he said slowly. 'Probably by Middle Stone Age Man, long before the Bushman. Perhaps it was a Florisbad Man.'

He looked at the little bone tool thoughtfully. 'Where you find one, you could find more. Surely there are other tools there. Will you look?'

We would! Dizzy with images, we fell into the nearest post-office and wired Sita and Maurice: 'Bones are Stone Age lion, buffalo, wildebeest, wild cat, ribbok, springbuck, kudu. Site may also contain prehistoric slaughter implements'. Three hours later we got a reply: 'Hip-hip-hoorah.'

As we lay in bed that night Jenks began to laugh. 'I know what Maurice is saying now,' he said. '"Those bloody kudu have been eating my mountain for a million years."'

We had urged Kitching to go down and investigate the site himself but he could not find the time. Who among our scientists could? Our bones were of passionate interest to us, but only of middling interest to them – unless, of course, we found something more. But – and this was one of the complexities we were now to encounter – it was illegal for *us* to dig. We must, the scientists insisted, remove no bones at all unless they were in danger of destruction.

Exactly how long, we wondered, would they remain there intact? We were sure they would not be there after the first storm of summer and those great walls of rushing, gouging water from the steep slopes of Honey Mountain just above. We had already picked up fragments of bone far below the Dig, washed down the river-bed in some storm and probably from this very site. Later Kitching was to decide that the greater part of the Dig had already been washed away and lost to us for good.

'Come and see,' wrote Sita. 'Come now. That old Florisbad Man lies waiting for us to find. The bones are on the surface. Don't let the rains wash him away.' In the spring we went.

This time we went armed with a little basic knowledge. Dates, of course, were the first things we had wanted, but dates, we had found, are something the experts still fight shy of, and well they may when they can differ not by centuries but by tens of thousands of years. Many scientists, however, agree that the Early Stone Age probably lasted some 400 000-500 000 years, the Middle some 40 000 years, and the Late Stone Age 8 000 years, and these approximate dates gave us some bearings.

We found Sita immersed in prehistory. Kneeling on the front stoep among a medley of bones and stones, she showed us what she and Alex, home from school for the holidays, had retrieved in the weeks that we had been away. Their prize was laid out in a long kitchen box, and she opened it carefully and took out a long, fashioned bone. We looked at it in silence.

It was a fifteen-inch weapon made from a wildebeest tibia, a stiletto with hilt and blade, carefully worked, precise, beautiful, lethal. Later when they examined it in Johannesburg through an electron-microscope, Professor Dart and Kitching were to see that this had been a stabbing weapon, used with a wicked underhand thrust and a killing twist, as shown by the minute scars upon the blade; and it had been used in preparing meat as well, for the blunt end of the haft had been worn into little scollops where its Stone Age owner had stripped muscles and tendons. It was polished with use, and upon the hilt Cranemere Stone Age Man had left the indent of his thumb, worn as he hunted lion and antelope round Honey Mountain.

It had been a skilfully made and much-loved tool; and it was one of the finest bone Stone Age weapons the palaeontologists had seen. For them it completed a sequence. Weapons similar to it but not so carefully fashioned, orange-brown, heavy as stone, had been found in an ape-man deposit, and Dart was certain that the ape-man had used them. As a type of weapon Cranemere stiletto was one million years old.

Close to the stiletto Sita and Alex had found a small curved piece of bone. This we found later had been broken off the stiletto to make a bone knife. A few inches away lay two bones which Dick, who had given up copying Bushman paintings for a few days to help us dig bones, later fitted together to form a dagger, not as beautiful as the stiletto but efficient.

Why, we asked ourselves, had three fine and treasured weapons been left here together by their Stone Age owner? The answer was obvious to us. Because he died. His skull, suitably crushed, was no doubt a foot away!

This time Sita and Alex had found more than bone: they had found stone as well.

A low koppie rises up from the slaughter-site. It is covered with no more than a thin skin of soil with the shale showing in many parts. Here, perhaps thirty yards from the Dig, Sita one day picked up a hand-axe. It was a stone shaped like an almond, eight inches long, and carefully and cleverly fashioned out of indurated shale. She knew as it lay at her feet that it was both old and worked by man. She did not then realize that she was looking at a shaped stone that had been the standard weapon and tool of man in Africa for nearly half a million years.

This was one of the very early tools dating from perhaps 500 000-50 000 years ago, after which it no longer seems to have been made. Not only an African tool, it was also made in Europe and Asia, for hand-axes from the three continents have been found, often identical in shape and pattern. Sita's was a 'formal' tool made over a period of half a million years by half the world.

Some archaeologists think it was used for everything – for killing, for cutting, for digging; others believe it was a tool for specialized use such as scraping and flensing, for the edges are seldom badly scarred. But it seems that it was not hafted, nor was it shaped like an axe as we know an axe today, but like an almond, and 'almond stone' the Afrikaners call it.

Our Cranemere hand-axe belongs, we later learned, to the Chelles-Acheul culture of the Early Stone Age, which takes part of its name from St Acheul in France, de Perthes's famous site where implements of this culture were first found. Some scientists believe this culture spread not from Europe to the Cape but from the Cape to Europe. 'So that Charlemagne,' said Jenks amid applause, 'was descended from Cranemere.'

If Florisbad Man made Cranemere stiletto, who shaped our almond stone? Nobody knows. The maker of the hand-axe preceded Florisbad Man, and apart from a jawbone from the Transvaal and the skull from Saldanha Bay – which *may* have belonged to the maker of the hand-axe – he, as a man, is little known in South Africa although his tools are plentiful. What if his bones too, we thrilled, lay somewhere on our veld, preserved by the same lime that had kept almost intact the stilettos of later man! We looked at Honey Mountain, at Cranemere, at the Plains of Camdeboo, with a new and ardent gaze.

'The title-deeds to Cranemere are half a million years old,' said Jenks, and with his words resounding in our ears we hastened back to our Mountain Dig. We stood on the koppie above it and looked about us with what we hoped were Stone Age eyes.

To the east was Honey Mountain. To the west was the Rooikop, jutting like a lonely beacon into the Plains. These Plains we knew in historic times as merciless, without water, shade and shelter – and we had often gloried in our hill which caught the great south-east winds and drank up the moisture so that even in drought it was clothed in succulence. Hordes of wild animals from elephant to kudu must once have browsed here.

The mountain bush had housed the first trek-farmers in hard and stormy weather, for the low dense crowns of the small trees had been a rain-proof roof. Surely it had protected a more ancient race as well.

Honey Mountain itself gave shelter from the tearing winds; and here between the two was our shallow valley sloping between them to the Plains below. High up in the neck of the valley, backed by a buttress of low hills, was the Dig, and the koppies beside it where Sita had found the hand-axe. Surely there had been water in this cup of shale about the Dig, a fountain, a water-hole, a vlei (a marshy place) perhaps which had attracted man and beast in numbers in a waterless world. Surely man had watched and plotted his hunt from the little koppie behind and had hidden here at the waterside to kill his beast, and had here skinned it and cut it up.

Kitching later was to bear this out, for the bones we brought him showed water cracks. The lime which had preserved them had been dissolved from the basic rock, borne upwards, and deposited by water, possibly from a fountain (spring). And when Maurice recalled that many years ago a fountain had burst out in this valley close by the Dig to run strongly for a while, we were certain. Here had been water, food and shelter for thousands upon thousands of years.

We started once again to dig. This time we had two helpers, Jack and Ou Boet, strong and filled with curiosity, and the work went quickly. We listened to their crowbars ringing and they rang with the sound of bells. Near the bones we worked with screwdrivers. Soon bone after bone lay before us, buffalo bones, tremendous, like the bones of giant animals, greyish-white, and as we touched them they clinked. They were no longer merely old bones. They had suffered a great change and they rang like the stones about them.

This time, warned by the scientists, we did not attempt to dig out anything but the bones which lay exposed, and, according to instructions, we did not burrow. We cut a portion of the bank from top to bottom, above and around the bones. The bank was five feet high and stretched downwards in layers, brown silty soil interlaced with fine roots on top; broken shale and silt impregnated with lime below; and this, at a point five feet down, held the bones intact. Below this again was a soft ochre-coloured soil where the bones crumbled at a touch, and below this boulders and blue shale.

As our soil profile grew before us we longed to see in it evidence, not of one slaughter-site but of two or more, one built upon the other through the ages.

There were no more bones above, but there was something

else. Two inches from the top the men unearthed a tiny object. It lay on a spadeful of soil in our sieve – an oldfashioned braided silk button. I knew where I had seen its mate. As children rummaging through Fanny Palmer's old clothes we had seen these buttons, perhaps on her riding-coat. Stone Age to Fanny Palmer! The perfect sequence! We were enraptured.

Back home we sorted the bones, trying to piece together those we had broken in digging. It was a tremendous job fitting piece into piece like a jig-saw puzzle. 'It's tricky,' Dick said. 'What if we do it wrong? Then there'll be another Piltdown do!'

These bones told us three more things. Our Middle Stone Age Man had known fire, for some bones were fire-marked. Here he had found 'horse', perhaps the extinct quagga that once roamed the Cape. And he had been a mighty hunter, for here in a heap a few feet across were bones of fourteen different species of animals, including lion. We can only guess how he had killed them, whether with bow and arrow, spear, traps, or by driving them into pits or mud and there knifing or spearing them. But it was clear he had been resourceful, strong, and brave.

In between digging for bones we tramped over the koppies and veld hunting for stones. At first we did not know for what stones to look. We picked up the round red-brown stones that strewed the veld and looked questioningly at them. They had not been shaped by men, but a few bore the marks of use, and wonderful missiles they must have been. We learned laboriously that many of the stones which appeared worked by hand had been shaped by weather. The fractures on their surface were convex, while the man-made fractures were concave. We learned to look for the percussion bulge, and tell-tale bulge on hand-worked flakes. We learned to examine with care the dark grey or brown indurated shales and sandstones which had been the favourite raw materials of Cranemere prehistoric man.

There were no books dealing with the stones and artefacts of the Karoo, but we carried with us Dr Revil Mason's splendidly illustrated *Prehistory of the Transvaal*, which became worn in those weeks.

119

No longer did we seek the stones at random across the farm. Stone Age Man's slaughter-site and our picnic spot were the same. His common sense was ours. Let us apply it, we thought. If game abounded still on Cranemere, where would we watch and hunt it? At the foot of the Rooikop, high yet not too high, where the bush merged with the veld? This could have been a vantage point. It had been. Here we picked up stones worn with use, the grinding stones of Late Stone Age, of the Bushmen or their ancestors; flakes, the cutting and scraping tools of that same people.

We climbed the koppies behind the dam. Through the narrow valley between these, game had once come to drink at the immemorial pools. Surely hunters had watched for it on these hills. Heavy perforated sandstone weights for digging sticks had once been found on one koppie across the valley. We stood on a koppie opposite, next to an old boerboon with a thick crooked trunk covered in lichen, and a crown bearing a few sparse dull green leaves, like a picture in a child's book of an old magical scene.

Jenks said, 'I bet the old Stone Age hunters watched from this koppie too. How could any hunter pass it by?' And as he spoke he bent and picked up an old worked stone which lay at the foot of the tree.

As we ranged further we found sites where the stones lay in quantities. There was hardly a bare spot, an eroded section round a sheep kraal or a gate, that did not yield its horde of artefacts. They lay, too, where the soil had been disturbed, around earth banks in the veld, and about the burrows of the ground squirrels, the meerkats and the ant-bears.

A schoolboy found a second Early Stone Age hand-axe. We found largish Middle Stone Age artefacts in sandstone, and tiny Late Stone Age tools of indurated shale; and of these we found not scores but thousands. Janette and Hilary Deacon had coached us. We no longer carried them away but set up a beacon at the site, and later at home marked the position on the farm map. The flags gradually spread across its surface.

So men had lived here, certainly for fifty thousand years, perhaps for many times as long. We saw our familiar world anew and it was a stirring time. Our red soil held history. And the stones that littered it told of the Adventure of Man. We picked them up on every side, not only shaped but with the marks of use upon them; and we knew that what we held in our hands was the first strategy of human kind, the first art, the first science; some of the first evidence that men could think, that they could destroy and build and shape the world and reach the stars.

When the first rains of summer fell on Cranemere, Sita walked up to the Dig, for the road was impassable by lorry, and as she looked at the river bank her flesh crept. The bank where we had worked had washed away entirely. Now a yellow-brown bone showed upon the new surface where two days before there had been nothing. She lifted it out. It was a stiletto made of lion bone.

At home she calmed herself with Beethoven. Maurice took a tranquillizer.

The moment had come when we all realized that it was time for science to take over from the Palmers. The site, the scientists now clamoured, might be rich; and we knew that we could not really deal with a Florisbad Man or the maker of the hand-axe, even if the law permitted it. Once we had pleaded for palaeontologists and archaeologists, and now they were ready to come. The stilettos had accomplished this.

Cranemere, lying in the immense plains athwart the vanishing highway, has its ancient memories of reptiles that were nearly mammals, perhaps of fabulous beasts and Man-Ape or Ape-Man, or only of their descendants. It is a memory that science must now interpret. As for us, we have guessed at 'this long, splendid, and laborious past', and in the guessing have found a new dimension.

8. Vanished Kings

It would have been exciting to have found the bones of some extinct prehistoric animal in Cranemere soil, a three-toed horse, or a giant pig, or giant buffalo, which lived thousands of years ago. We never have, for the bones we have so far unearthed have all been of 'modern' animals. Yet among our bones are those of animals we shall never see again. They are gone as surely as the three-toed horse.

We sat on the sand beside the Dig, sorting the bones and thinking of the animals that had once roamed here and now had vanished. Stone Age Man had hunted them – but so had the trekboers – and guns and hunting horses had done what neither axes nor arrows had. Here on our Plains they had snuffed out some dozen species of large animals, and although many of these are found in other parts of South Africa, two are everywhere extinct. Eland, gemsbok, hartebeest, black wildebeest, buffalo, hyena, wild dog, cheetah, warthog, hippo – once animals of the Karoo – still live, sometimes in numbers, farther afield, but the quagga and Cape lion have gone for ever.

We know from the early travellers that only two hundred years ago immense numbers of animals lived on the Karoo. All the deserts of the world have their own forms of life, and our eastern Karoo was only at its worst a desert; at its best it gave fine grazing. Here were all the desert buck, springbuck by the tens of thousands, eland, steenbok, and probably gemsbok, all animals which can live indefinitely without water where succulent plants are available, so that even when the pools and springs dried up across the Plains these buck still lived in numbers. In the good years there were surprising visitors (we presume they were only visitors) such as the buffalo which Pieter Cloete and his party hunted on the edge of Cranemere in 1776 and which, we had proved, Stone Age Man had known here thousands of years before.

When Van Riebeeck landed at the Cape in 1652 he found hippos in a swamp – later Church Square in Cape Town – and perhaps these 'first animals' once lived in the pools in the river beds on Cranemere. They certainly lived in many Karoo rivers. Le Vaillant killed one in the Great Fish River and ate its foot for breakfast! Today only place names remind us that Little Old Aunt Sea-Cow, as Laurens van der Post affectionately terms it, with its body like a barrel, its broad bottom, its wide mouth, its small brain, once floated in our pools, showing only the flat top of its head, decorated with eyes and nostrils, for curious eyes to see.

We wondered as we handled the Stone Age bones – would we find an elephant tusk? Had there ever been elephants on Cranemere? There could have been, for elephant remains have been found in the eastern Karoo. Some years ago a farmer found a tusk in the Melkrivier close to Cranemere. A Cradock farmer just north of us, ploughing a land, turned up a tusk, and Dr Rubidge has a fine tusk found by a farmer in the Aberdeen district when making a dam. Still another found the whole skull of an elephant – a modern elephant.

An arid land is not a common setting for an elephant so that these remains are tremendously interesting. We suppose the elephants wandered up the river valleys to the Karoo, perhaps from Sita's childhood home to the south. She remembers them well – small and vicious – in the Addo bush; and she remembers Major Jan Pretorius, of Konigsberg fame, shooting them; little Hottentots hacking off chunks of meat from the great white ribs with the blood running down their arms; and a vast woman in a big khaki hat measuring their ears. Now Sita hunts for a tusk of her old acquaintances on Cranemere.

We know there were once rhino here. Le Vaillant saw the spoor of a rhinoceros, presumably a black rhinoceros, on Cranemere. The red hartebeest was almost certainly here for it was once one of the commonest antelope in the Cape. I do not know of any written record of the gnu, the black wildebeest, on Cranemere, but the Dig showed us it had lived here once – the Cranemere stiletto was of wildebeest bone. There were possibly gemsbok; and definitely quagga, for Pieter Cloete had hunted them. Where there was game in such numbers there were also carnivorous beasts such as lions, cheetah, leopards, lynx, hyenas, jackals, wild cats, possibly wild dogs. We have records of most of them on Cranemere. Of these only the lynx, the wild cats, and jackals remain, and an occasional leopard in the mountains.

The great company of wild animals has gone. Their protective colouring did not help them, nor their speed and hearing and sense of smell; nothing availed once the huntsmen and their horses and guns arrived on the Karoo. Some, naturally enough, were killed because they were dangerous; some because of the destruction they caused to grazing or to crops. 'Buck make bad gardeners,' said the settlers of the hordes that devastated their lands. Many were killed for skins and for food, and meat drying on wagons and impaled on trees around the camps and farmhouses was a common sight in early days.

The Karoo was littered with bones. Even hunters from abroad were astonished at the number of skeletons and well-bleached skulls with which the plains were covered. Every farmhouse had beside it its great heap of skulls and horns, mainly of springbuck and black wildebeest.

Few even in a modern wild-life-conscious world would blame men for killing in order to live, but there were many who killed mainly for sport. They came from the Cape itself and from abroad, they killed not from need but for pleasure, and not in ones and twos but in huge numbers; they hunted in the heart of Southern Africa in the last century and killed a multitude of animals.

Sometimes such a hunter would race on horseback after a herd of buck, jump off while many hundred yards away, and fire into the moving mass of animals. 'Probably not one in ten of those mortally wounded was bagged,' an observer of such a massacre wrote. The number of cartridges carried by a man like this huntsman was generally fifty and he expected to use them all in a day.

Gordon Cumming, the young Scot who hunted in South Africa in the 1840s, left behind him a trail of maimed and dying animals, but although he had the means and opportunity to kill more than most men, his outlook was very general. He tells of his 'brilliant sport' with gusto, of how, for example, he shot his first ostrich on the Karoo, a fine old cock whose leg he broke, and of how in the act of dying it lashed out with its sound leg and laid him prostrate. Today, reading this, we can scarce forbear to cheer (the ostrich!), but back in Britain Cumming was a great man, his book *The Lion Hunters of South Africa* outselling Charles Dickens. A modern reader may wish that the Karoo sun which burnt the knees of this kilt-clad hero had struck him down entirely, but the shattered limbs and broken bones of his fleeing victims offended no public feeling in mid-nineteenth-century England.

Sportsmanship in the twentieth-century sense did not exist. In 1860 when the Graaff-Reinet Buck-hound Club was formed not a soul, apparently, raised a voice against its main object: the hunting down of the springbuck kids four to six weeks old by riders who boasted of their green and scarlet coats and top-hats. It was splendid sport and many kills could be made during one hunt!

Of course the animals dwindled. In 1782 Le Vaillant shot an eland on Cranemere and saw nine more. A decade later Barrow wrote that the number in the Cape was dwindling. Burchell found them becoming daily more scarce, and Harris in 1836 wrote that they were then extinct in the Cape Colony. It is not surprising: this huge, gentle creature has no weapons at all, in old age not even that of speed. Every man's hand has been against it since man began in Africa.

It was the favourite game of the Bushman and a young man was required to present the father of the girl he wished to marry with the breast and heart of an eland. 'My cattle', the Bushman called the eland and it provided him with a gargantuan meal in a desert land.

The colonists valued it for its bulk (it is the largest antelope in

South Africa), for its flesh and fat, and for its defencelessness. On horseback a man could easily ride down a heavy adult bull and it was a common thing for a hunter to turn a blown and exhausted animal and drive it back before him to camp as easily as he could a cow, and there kill it at his convenience. How many hunters in the past suffered even a passing pang as they killed these great, patient, gentle creatures with their soft dark eyes and long bristly eyelashes panting hopelessly and helplessly before them? Burchell witnessed such a scene, but he would not wait for the end and turned away so that he should not see the animal killed.

An eland bull can weigh up to 2 000 pounds. Its meat is extraordinarily good, as every hunter once knew. 'The venison fairly melts in the mouth: and as for the brisket, *that* is absolutely a cut for a monarch!' wrote Harris.

In the very early days there was a regular trade in salted eland tongues between the frontier farmers and the Cape. Most valuable of all, however, was the fat. None of the other antelopes, except possibly the gemsbok, were fat, and the eland was unique in yielding a vast quantity of fat which was particularly good for candle-making. Eland-fat candles lit the Cape by night for many years and hunters and explorers used the fat from the animals they killed to make their own, for most travellers carried candle-moulds. And it kept travellers dry! It furnished a good effective water-proofing for tents and wagon-covers.

The hide, too, was tremendously popular with the colonists. No other hide made such stout soles for boots, such traces and harness, or such thongs for binding a thatched roof; and the elegant spiral horns were used by the Hottentots for tobacco pipes.

Today few people of the Karoo have ever seen a wild eland. This means they have never seen a fine beast, for a mounted or even a zoo specimen is a sorry business, gross and dull, without even the good looks of a handsome ox. But in the wild – that is a different matter! We saw it once in numbers in the Kalahari Desert with its great frame scaled to the great desert about it, its light smooth coat glinting with an almost purple sheen, its thin elegant legs and its straight backward-pointing spiral horns; and we thought of them once galloping in single file across the Plains of Camdeboo and flying over the steepest hills with ease and vigour. They must have made one of the most gallant sights of the whole Karoo.

Once we had the most warlike and spectacular antelope of all – the gemsbok. I do not know that they ever lived on Cranemere, but they doubtless strayed across the Plains of Camdeboo, for they were found round Graaff-Reinet and to the west. Barrow saw them here and noted both their beauty and their courage. Gordon Cumming admired (and shot) them. 'The gemsbok is about the most beautiful and remarkable of all the antelope tribe,' he wrote. 'It possesses the erect mane, long sweeping black tail, and general appearance of the horse, with the head and hoofs of an antelope. It is robust in form, squarely and compactly built, and very noble in its bearing. Its height is about that of an ass and in colour it slightly resembles that animal.'

Cornwallis Harris wrote, and with felicity, of one he saw: 'There he stood, clad in half mourning, looming as large as a donkey, and scanning our party – his long taper toastingfork horns, like a pair of walking-sticks, standing out . . . He dropped his wild head, which looked exactly as if encased in a black patent leather headstall with nose-band and chinstrap complete.'

We saw them recently in the Gemsbok Reserve and I thought these two descriptions very good. There are few words that can suggest the thrill of seeing these antelope in the flesh, handsome and strange and wild, galloping – and they are then one of the sights of the world – muzzles outstretched and great horns lying back and long tails flying out straight behind.

Seen thus by the trekboers, they must have seemed rich and foreign creatures, and if a great legend grew from them that is only natural. They are, we are told, the unicorns of legend.

Our gemsbok is *Oryx gazella* and it is on animals of this genus, or so it is popularly believed today, that the fable of the unicorn is based. Traditionally the unicorn had the head and body of a horse, the hind legs of an antelope, the tail of a lion or a horse, and a single long sharp horn. It was sought for centuries and there were those who claimed to have seen it, including many people of the Cape. The colonists firmly believed that savage unicorns lived in the remote interior, almost on our doorstep I found from Sparrman, who was told that they had been seen near the present site of Somerset East. He planned an expedition to search for them, hoping to use their curiosity – which the colonists insisted was a characteristic – to trap them. His plan was simple. He was to mount a high rock and there make such a din that the inquisitive creatures would approach to see what made the noise, and he would then shoot them in safety.

This hunt never took place, but soon after Barrow was seeking unicorns near by. He had been assured by farmers that Bushman drawings of unicorns had been found on the frontier, which presupposed the existence of the animals, and this was supported by such a noteworthy explorer and naturalist as Colonel Gordon himself. Barrow *did* find a drawing but never a unicorn. In a cave in a high concealed kloof of the 'Tarka Mountains' he found upon a rock the drawing of an animal with a single horn projecting from its forehead. It was incomplete for the body and legs were concealed by the drawing of an elephant, but Barrow was exuberant. He was certain that the unicorn lived and was merely unknown because the interior was 'as yet untrodden ground', and he offered a reward of five thousand rix-dollars (about £375) to any man who would find a unicorn for him. Nobody did, but other travellers remained hopeful.

Burchell, who seems so modern a scientist in many ways, hoped to find a unicorn and make his fortune. Writing to his mother in 1811, he said that if he should be so fortunate as to discover one he was certain he could sell it for at least £7 500.

By the 1840s the myth was exploded. Gordon Cumming knew the gemsbok and the unicorn as one, and remarked that the gemsbok's long straight horns seen in profile so exactly covered one another as to give it the appearance of having but one.

Often, indeed, the gemsbok has but one horn, for the males are great fighters and frequently lose a horn in battle. This is true of its northern relations too. Pliny 1 900 years ago described the oryx as one-horned, so that it is true that one-horned beasts resembling both horse and antelope did indeed once live (and still do). It seems to me especially fitting that the ancient plains of the Karoo which had their dragons should also have had their unicorns.

We do not really regret the departure of the rhinos. They made very bad neighbours, and the colonists killed them because they were dangerous (and their killing was tremendous sport); and because their skin made the best whips in the Cape, of a beautiful horn colour, almost transparent, which took an even finer polish than those made of hippo hide.

The horns have for long been thought by the credulous to have medicinal properties. The colonists valued them also for a singular reason: they believed they 'would not endure the Touch of Poison' and so made marvellous drinking-cups in an age when poison was a neat way of eliminating an enemy. It was an old belief in Europe that a poisoned liquid would froth out of a rhino horn, and it seems to have been accepted as fact here too, many fashionable people of the early eighteenth-century Cape, Peter Kolben tells us, having their rhino horns set in silver or gold. 'If poison be put by itself into one of those cups, the cup, in an Instant, flies into Pieces.' And he adds, 'I have often been a witness to this!'

I was amused when I first read this tale. Then I paused to wonder if there could be any basis to the story, if certain chemicals could indeed react vigorously on touching rhino horn. But no; I am told by scientists that it is purely fable with no foundation whatsoever of fact; and this is a pity, for it is almost the only constructive story of a black rhinoceros that I know.

Among the animal bones excavated at the Dig were zebrine bones, and a zebrine skull that Janette and Hilary Deacon dug out in good condition. At first glance James Kitching thought that this was the skull of the extinct horse of the Cape, *Equus capensis*, although later he found it to be the skull of a very large Burchell's zebra – in itself of interest, for in historic times this zebra has never been seen so far south.

Some of the smaller bones may have belonged to its extinct relation, the quagga, and this is a fascinating possibility, for the last wild quagga was shot near Aberdeen, sixty miles west of Cranemere, just over a century ago, and the last quagga in the world died in 1883 in an Amsterdam menagerie.

It is almost as if it had never lived. In South Africa the only remains are a specimen of a foal from Beaufort West in the South African Museum, Cape Town, and a single skull in the Pretoria Museum. Overseas museums have several specimens; but in death the quagga is one of the rare animals of the world and scientists still ardently seek its relics. It was almost with veneration that we regarded our bones, for quagga had lived on Cranemere and had certainly died here too, so that these bones could well have been theirs.

Of all our vanished creatures we mourn these quaggas most of all. Scientists know them as *Equus quagga quagga*. Once they lived in great numbers in the Cape and Orange Free State and until the beginning of the nineteenth century they roamed the Karoo freely in herds with the white-tailed wildebeest and the ostrich, whose company they loved to share. Cornwallis Harris wrote of them: 'Moving slowly across the profile of the ocean-like horizon, uttering a shrill barking neigh . . . long files of Quaggas continually remind the early traveller of a rival caravan on its march.'

They must have been a wonderful sight. Like the zebras, they were startlingly handsome in form and colour and pattern, although in their case they were striped only on the head, neck and forequarters and the thighs and legs remained unbanded. They were a fine isabelline or chestnut colour and against this background the whitish stripes showed up distinctly. Barrow and other early observers noted their strong, well-shaped limbs and the fact that they always seemed in good condition. He believed them gentle and easily domesticated, and there are records of domesticated quaggas.

Some were driven in harness in the Cape; others were shipped to the Isle of France (Mauritius), where they were apparently frequently used to draw vehicles, and early in 1800 one pair was driven about the streets of London. A pair of quaggas bowling down Regent Street must indeed have been a sight!

For all their beauty and distinction, they were of more use to the colonists dead than alive. Although the farmers do not seem to have eaten quagga meat themselves, they killed them for their servants for they were an easy prey. One writer recorded that a precipice was pointed out to him over which the farmers were in the habit of driving troops of quaggas. They then simply gathered up the dead bodies below. The hides were used to make grain-sacks and the thicker parts for shoe soles – most excellent soles, the colonists said. In an age that valued wild-life for sport and use alone, the quaggas stood no chance at all.

The zebra of the Karoo is the mountain zebra, *Equus zebra zebra*, and it has escaped – but only just – the fate of the quagga. In the whole of South Africa, in the whole world, there are less than five hundred of them left, so that they are among the rarest of all living animals. They were killed for the same reasons as were the quaggas, but as a race they still survive because, whereas the quaggas loved the plains, they lived in the rocky and often inaccessible mountains.

They live here still, not fifty miles from Cranemere, and last winter we went to see them.

We travelled over the Swaershoek Mountains – the Brother-in-law's Corner Mountains – to the Mountain Zebra National Park near Cradock, where the National Parks Board is preserving two of the last herds on the rough mountain slopes of their natural home. Here are fifty-three zebras*, including two

In 1985 the park boasted 235 zebra, with a further 80 in the Karoo National Park near Beaufort West.

new foals that have been received with jubilation by the Parks Board. We watched seven of them, dozing and swishing their tails in the winter sun, against a background of Karoo rock and mountain, and with their plump small bodies, striped right down to their elegant hoofs, their big donkey ears, dewlaps and chestnut faces, we thought them delightful; and also immensely touching. They were among the last of a great race. But for these and a few other small herds in the Cape, they would be history only.

They are part of history. They were the first zebras the Dutch ever saw at the Cape. Five years after Van Riebeeck landed, a party of explorers near Paarl Mountain saw the tracks and droppings of what they took to be horses, and their amazement and curiosity can be imagined. In 1660 Van Riebeeck in his diary noted that Bushmen had brought him 'two or three stuffed heads, very beautifully striped but with ears as long as those of asses'. Rumours of these strange animals flew about among the settlers, some declaring they bore stripes of sky-blue!

By the middle of the eighteenth century the colonists knew them well and, at close quarters at any rate, respected them, for wildness was in their blood and they found that trying to tame a mountain zebra was often a very different thing from domesticating a quagga. Barrow tells the story of an English dragoon who mounted a little zebra mare. She tossed him into a river, dragged him, clinging to the bridle, to the shore and there quietly bit off his ear.

The zebras in the Karoo park are increasing and there is a chance the race will yet survive. Perhaps they may one day spread again throughout the Karoo. It gives me much pleasure to think that a Palmer in the year 2000 or later may see these wild, pretty, gay-looking creatures on the slopes of Honey Mountain.

Exciting as were the zebrine bones, they were nothing compared with those of the lion. The Cape lion has a part in our natural history that no other animal has, for not only is it extinct but today, a mere century after it disappeared, zoologists do not know for sure if it was the same as the surviving lion of our north, or a distinct sub-species, *Leo leo melanochaitus*, as some scientists believe. Nor are there sufficient relics of it left to determine the truth; it remains one of the great question marks of our natural history.

For me the bones had a special importance. The first story we have of Cranemere is of a lion that killed a traveller at the Gallows Tree. When I was a child, this lion held for me the allure and mystery of a creature from another age, of a beast of fable superimposed on a familiar land. I used to picture its yellow eyes gazing from the spekboom along the old road; or its big cat form lying in wait to make a kill near the pools that are now Cranemere dam. But I only half believed it.

The only other lion story of our Plains I knew did nothing to convince me that our lion had been a living beast. It was told by a man who was old when my father was a child. He was driving from Pearston to Graaff-Reinet, he said, and just before he reached the Gallows Tree he saw a great cloud of dust upon the veld.

'Hold the reins, Frikkie,' he told his Hottentot servant, and climbing out of his cart, he approached the dust cautiously.

'It was a truly wonderful sight,' he used to reminisce. 'There were two great lions and they were fighting – fighting with each other, and the dust they made reached the sky and their roars filled the world.'

He watched for an hour, then climbed back into the cart and drove on to Graaff-Reinet. The following week he returned along the same road and when he got to the place where the lions had fought he stopped, and again approached the scene of the battle. 'And what do you think I saw with my own eyes,' he would end triumphantly, 'but the two tips of the lions' tails fighting one another, *vroetel, vroetel, vroetel,* in a little-little dust no higher than a Karoo bush!' By tradition he was incensed if anyone at this point should laugh.

As I grew older I learned that our lion was fact. An old taxi-driver from Somerset East, driving me to the station to catch my train to boarding-school, used to tell me how his father, transport riding between Port Elizabeth and the Karoo, used to listen to the lions roaring by night – and the memory of these conversations helped to sustain me during the ten dreary weeks I was away from the farm.

Later still, I read of the travellers who had met lions on Cranemere itself and along the trek road. Le Vaillant claimed that the Plains of Camdeboo were the most dangerous lion country in the whole of the colony. A lion and lioness attacked his wagons as they were passing over Cranemere, stampeding the bellowing oxen and terrifying the party. He searched the sandy plains for his oxen with a flaming torch in one hand and a gun in the other, next morning finding traces of the lion almost next to his camp.

Lichtenstein's party passed this way through 'a wood full of lions', where seven had been seen the previous week. Only one had been killed, and this news did nothing to cheer the company, making a moonlight march to Graaff-Reinet to avoid the heat of the day. Their guide told them that this road was usually avoided by night because of the lions, at the very scent of which the oxen panicked and broke away, carrying the wagons with them.

Two of the most horrifying lion stories that I know were of Karoo lions. The Widow Wagenaar, who lived with her children near Graaff-Reinet, one day went out to frighten away a lion from her cattle. It seized her, bit off her arm, and when she fainted, devoured her head. A little Hottentot maid ran to her mistress's help – an act of courage that the Karoo has never, I am sure, seen equalled; and she too was killed. The children who had been locked into the house had watched their mother and nurse being killed through the crevices of the door. They dug themselves out through the earth under the back wall of the house and ran in terror to the nearest farm.

A Hottentot herdsman had an experience almost without parallel. Seeing a number of vultures soaring, and determining to share their prey, he came upon a dead hartebeest on which a lion had feasted. From behind a bush appeared the lion – happily replete – and circled the man, brushing him with its tail and growling softly. The Hottentot, pertrified, stood perfectly still. The lion withdrew a few paces and lay down: the Hottentot retreated a step and the lion, springing up, advanced; and so it continued, like a dog keeping watch over a thief. At length the man, grabbing a handful of dry grass, attempted to strike a light with his tinder-box, but when the lion heard the tapping of flint and steel he rose up and paced round the man, brushing him as before with his tail. Again the Hottentot was still and the lion retired. Again the man tried to strike a light and this time was lucky enough to set alight the grass beside him. The lion retreated and the Hottentot tottered homewards, doubtless to term himself for ever after 'the man who was stroked by the lion's tail'.

The lions did not belong only to the Karoo: they ranged the whole Cape. Van Riebeeck knew them and complained they seemed about to storm the fort for the sheep within. Farmers from the interior collecting salt from the Swartkops salt-pan near the present city of Port Elizabeth had many a close shave, for the bush about the edge of the pan teemed with lions. Every early traveller prepared himself to meet them, by day as well as by night, particularly when crossing tree- or bush-lined rivers. Coming in sight of a river, travellers would be torn by conflicting emotions – pure delight at the sight of water and terror at the lions that might be hiding near – and they never approached without cracking their whips furiously to frighten them off.

At night they tied the oxen to the wheels of the wagons, and the Hottentot servants would take up a stand on the leeward side of the wagons, knowing that lions – and Bushmen – never attacked from the windward side. Rainy nights were believed to be the most dangerous, for then, said travellers, the lions made no sound, the dogs could not as easily catch their scent, and the beasts could fall upon them without warning.

The people of the early Cape, in fact, knew lions very well indeed. Their knowledge was curiously compounded of fact, observation, and rioting imagination. Thunberg's advice on what to do when meeting a lion is a fine example. Never run away, he warned, 'but stand still, pluck up courage and look it stern in the face. If the lion is still without wagging its tail, there is no danger, but if it makes any motion with its tail then it is hungry and you are in great danger.'

Sparrman did not believe that lions are always courageous, and in this, at least, he appears correct. There are authenticated tales of a lion retreating from a branch, a paper, a feather. In parts native hunters attacking lions would sometimes plant a line of ostrich plumes in the ground, claiming that no lion would advance against these.

Sparrman added a fascinating tit-bit on lion behaviour. A lion which had missed its leap would never follow its prey any further, he claimed, but, ashamed of its failure, would return slowly step by step measuring the exact length between the two points of its jump to discover why it was short of, or beyond, the mark! It is extraordinarily refreshing to find Harris fifty years later describing a lion in the most unreverential terms as rougher than a French poodle and with eyes like round gooseberries.

I read all this, and more, with fascination. Then one day my lion-reading was given fresh impetus. I found a reference to the Cape lion by Colonel J. Stevenson-Hamilton, the famous warden of the Kruger National Park and one of our great authorities on wild animals, who wrote that he believed the extinct lion of the Cape had certain physical characteristics which entitled it to be regarded as a distinct type.

So our lion, with its terror and its might, had also been different! I was enthralled. I could not question Colonel Stevenson-Hamilton but I could see Dr Austin Roberts, then busy at the Transvaal Museum on his book *The Mammals of South Africa*. I did, and asked him for his opinion on the Cape lion. Without hesitation he replied that he believed it to have been a distinct sub-species.

Stevenson-Hamilton had commented on the great size of the Cape lion, adding a warning, however, that statistics regarding the size of lions were notoriously unreliable and that lion skins when fresh could be easily stretched. He thought the skull was relatively shorter between the eyes and nose than that of existing lions, and that it had had an almost retroussé nose. Moreover, it appeared to have had not only an unusually heavy black mane extending well over its back, but a fringe of black hair along the entire length of its belly.

Dr Roberts corroborated this and added a fascinating detail. He personally thought that the lions at the Dublin Zoo – which had been bred there for a very long time and had a luxuriant dark growth of mane – might not have developed this because they had been bred in captivity, as was generally thought. No, their ancestors might have been Cape lions, and this might have been an inherited trait. From here lions had gone to many zoos abroad, so that the Cape lion, he thought, might have populated zoos throughout the world.

When Dr Roberts died he was succeeded at the Transvaal Museum by the Swedish mammal expert, Dr B. Lundholm, who also was deeply interested in the Cape lion. But he, like Dr Roberts, was handicapped by lack of any material. When he arrived not a skull, not a skin, not a tuft of hair of any lion killed in the Cape was still known to exist in South Africa. In 1950, however, a farmer in the Murraysburg district, not far from Cranemere, found a lion skull in a river bank on his farm. It was of a fully grown lioness and was in very good condition with only a few teeth missing. The skull is now in the Port Elizabeth Museum.

Dr Lundholm, backing up Dr Roberts, believed that the skull showed sufficient difference from a living South African lion to warrant a sub-specific name, although he added that it was possible that other skulls of the Cape lion might show measurements approaching those of more northern races. None was found to examine.

I visited Dr Lundholm in my search for details of the lion, and he told me that he could get no further because there was no material to work on. I thought of the farmhouses of the Karoo and Eastern Cape with their lofts, their store-rooms, their cupboards, their skins and horns and mounted trophies, and I was certain that there must still be relics of the lions, for in any age a lion skin or skull would surely be treasured.

'I'm certain that I can raise you something,' I said, and I wrote off to one of the Cape daily papers and to the journal of the Wild Life Society appealing for any relics of lions killed in the Cape to be shown to Dr Lundholm. There was an immediate response but on paper only. A great many people were tremendously interested – but nobody had so much as a bone.

Dr Lundholm is one of the few people I have ever known who could consider the Cape lion impartially. Some enthusiasts accept completely Dr Roberts's theory that the Cape lion was a distinct race; and some refute it, pointing to the great hunter Selous, and others, who believed that dark and pale lions could come from the same litter and that the heavy manes of the Cape lions were no more than a protection against the cold. It is no academic affair to them and they argue for and against with passion; but they are never likely to know the truth for sure.

Today, as far as I know, there are only three mounted specimens of a Cape lion – and by that I mean any lion shot in the Cape – in the world: one in London, one in Paris, one in Leiden. There are no other certain remains at all, with the exception of the Murraysburg skull, one skull in England, and possibly two in Leiden. South Africa's only relic is the Murraysburg skull, and a fossilized lion skull of great size found – naturally enough – by Dr Broom.

Regretfully I turned back to the old books. They told me a lot, yet very little. The colonists and Hottentots had believed in two races of lions, a black and a blond: yet this proved nothing. Almost everyone who had seen or shot a lion thought it tremendous, but few ever recorded their measurements. Burchell saw a black-maned lion which seemed to him as big as an ox; Sparrman saw two lions while crossing the Little Fish River near Somerset East. Both, he reckoned, were considerably higher and longer than his saddle horse.

26 *The black wildebeest, once an animal of the Karoo, but now extinct there. From a painting by Dick Findlay.*

27 *The Cape lion, long since extinct, from a Bushman painting found in the mountains above Cranemere (Dick Findlay).*

28 One of the rarest animals in the world, the mountain zebra of the Karoo.

29 The quagga, now extinct, from a painting by Samuel Daniell.

30 Kudu among the thorn trees.

31 A graceful pose by springbuck.

32 Baboons are touchingly human in their care for their young.

33 A vervet monkey with her baby.

A shooting party including Thomas Pringle, the poet, shot a Cape lion near Pringle's home, Eildon, in the eastern Cape. Its head, wrote Pringle, seemed almost as large as that of an ordinary ox, and this he had boiled so as to preserve the skull. He sent this, together with the roughly tanned hide, to Sir Walter Scott, where they formed part of the ornaments of Scott's antique armoury at Abbotsford. I felt compensated for many days of research when I learned that the Cape lion, around which had centred so many tales of high adventure, had had so close a link with that great story-teller.

A lion's skull recently examined at the British Museum is said to have been taken to Scotland by Pringle. The odds are this is none other than Pringle's gift to Scott.

I found many assertions about size and colour and hairiness and ferocity of the old lions, but the more I read, the more I realized that the facts were few. Even the mounted specimen in the British Museum of Natural History is merely *supposed* to have been shot near Colesberg in the Cape in 1836 by Captain – later General – Copland-Crawford, who lent it to the Junior United Services Club in London, from where it was recently transferred to the British Museum. The last lion of all of which there is any certain record was shot in the Transkei in 1858. Perhaps there were others later. Nobody knows.

When James Kitching, in the Bernard Price Institute of Palaeontology, looked at our bones and said, 'That's lion,' I almost roared myself. What if they were too few to prove a thing? They were Cape lion! Heinrich Schliemann discovering the site of Troy knew no greater joy than mine.

Back on Cranemere we hunted for the skull. We have not found it yet but it could still be there and we shall never give up hope of finding it.

Meanwhile, we have seen our Cape lion again in the Bushman painting that Dick copied in our mountains. It is a lioness, so gives no clue as to the appearance of a Cape lion's mane: but this great golden cat is the embodiment of all the lions that once gave beauty and terror to the Karoo. Together with the lion

9. They Drink the Wind

Among the bones we found at the Dig were those of springbuck, and this was only to be expected for springbuck still live here in numbers and have since immemorial times.

They no longer exist in vast numbers nor are they free to roam as once they were. Here on Cranemere, as on all the farms around about, they are confined, but the fenced camps they range are often big and springbuck still number tens of thousands upon the Karoo.

In movement our springbuck are, quite simply, the most beautiful animals in the world. Many would doubtless disagree, but then few really know a springbuck at all. No one who has only seen a springbuck in a museum, a zoo, or even a paddock, has seen one at all. There they are pretty little creatures with neat small movements and their fawn and white and chocolate coats hardly hold the eye. But streaming across the plains, 'drinking the wind', as they fly, racing and bounding in their flight, they are one moment part of the veld and the next they are part of the sky.

They are one of my earliest memories. I have seen them in the far distance like white pin-points as the sun glinted on them, and from a few feet away, their isabelline coats glowing and their chocolate and white shining splendidly as they trotted in the winter sun. One sound, one movement, and they were away, sometimes swift and taut and hard as so many bullets, but sometimes running and springing with those fantastic leaps that make a springbuck for a moment half an animal and half a bird.

I do not think even hardened hunters have ever watched bounding springbuck unmoved. My father, out to shoot a buck, would often pause and murmur in admiration as he watched a herd crossing the track one after another with a single leap, or soaring up into the air, their hoofs bunched together, their backs arched like so many bucking horses, touching the ground for the space of a second and rocketing into the air again as if the veld they trod was a giant trampoline and they so many players upon it. And as they bucked and bounded they flaunted their white fans, the long snowy gossamer hairs upon their backs which they unfolded and hid at will, and they were for a space not only beautiful but brilliant with the brilliance of snow in sunlight.

It is their jumping and their strange white fans which have caused such interest and given fame – and a variety of names – to springbuck since they were first described in the eighteenth century. This famous fan is composed of very long white hairs from the rump to the shoulder-blades which lie flat within a fold of skin, usually seeming no more than a thin white line half-way along the back. This fold is opened at will, usually as the buck jumps, and the colour of the animal instantly appears to change. It has been said that when a herd shows its fans, it is as if a white sheet is swiftly drawn over it.

Many observers took the fold of skin upon the springbuck's back to be a pouch and in the first scientific account of it, in the *Histoire Naturelle* of Buffon, published at Amsterdam about 1778, it is called '*La Gazella à bourse sur le dos* – the gazelle with the pouch on its back'. The springbuck described was one of a dozen sent from the Cape by Colonel Gordon to the Prince of Orange. She alone survived the voyage to exist for a few months in Holland in the Menagerie of the Prince of Orange. M. Allamand, who described her, gave a sad little picture of her, beautiful, gentle, and perpetually frightened. The first scientific name of the springbuck, *Antilope marsupialis*, was established on Allamand's description of this little Karoo buck, so that although she had a very brief life in captivity she was, in her way, famous.

The springbuck has been known by other scientific names such as *Capra pygargus, Antilope euchore* (which was the name Burchell, for example, knew), *Gazella euchore, Antilope dorsata, Antilope saliens,* and others. Today it bears the name *Antidorcas marsupialis marsupialis,* from Greek words meaning a pouched wild goat or fawn. Its common names have been as many – the Jumping Goat, the Goat with the Fan, the Springer Antelope, the Gazelle with the Pouch on its Back, Gazelle de Parade, and the springbuck.

Early naturalists believed it to be a gazelle and it very nearly is, only its teeth and its fan separating it from the gazelles of northern Africa.

I do not think a traveller ever crossed the Karoo without mentioning the springbuck. They existed here in vast herds, and also on the upland, almost treeless plains of the Orange Free State and the Transvaal, both in well-watered and in desert country. Trees and bush were foreign to them, and if driven to their cover they were invariably back to their grass and karoo bush, sometimes within days, sometimes hours.

Some travellers writing of the dancing herds that speckled the broad plains were lyrical. Cornwallis Harris spoke almost in ecstasy of the lively cinnamon of the springbuck's back, the snowy whiteness of its lower parts, the intensely rich chestnut bands upon its flanks, its dark beaming eye, and its innocent and lamblike expression of face. His description of a buck 'pronking' – bucking and spreading its white fan – has never been bettered.

'Pricking their taper ears and elevating their graceful little heads upon the first appearance of any strange object, a dozen or more trot nimbly off to a distance,' he wrote, 'and having gazed impatiently for an instant to satisfy themselves of the actual presence of an enemy – putting their white noses to the ground they begin . . .to "pronken" or "make a show".

'Unfurling the snowy folds on their haunches so as to display around the elevated scut a broad white gossamer disc, shaped like the spread tail of a peacock, away they all go with a succession of strange perpendicular bounds, rising with curved loins high into the air, as if they had been struck with battledores – rebounding to the height of ten or twelve feet with the elasticity of corks thrown against a hard floor, vaulting over each other's backs with depressed heads and stiffened limbs, as if engaged in a game of leap-frog: and after appearing for a second as if suspended in the air, clearing at a single spring from ten to fifteen feet of ground without the smallest perceptible exertion – down come all four feet together with a single thump and, nimbly spurning the earth beneath, away they soar again as if about to take flight.'

Every hunter in the past had his theory as to why springbuck pronk, just as every Karoo farmer has today. Some believed they pronked when alarmed, or to get a better view over the countryside; or from excess of energy, or simply to show off. Cronwright-Schreiner, husband of the famous Olive Schreiner, who wrote a book on the springbuck and its migrations, believed that pronking was an instinctive act of protection on the one hand and a warning on the other. Its sudden and startling leap could carry a springbuck out of a leopard's claws, and its white fan at the same time blazed the danger to the herd. Even the little kids a day or two old, short-bodied, long-legged, exquisite things as Cronwright-Schreiner called them, spread their fans and danced in the sunny air, and this act was surely, he said, their safeguard in time of danger.

But I have seen springbuck when the veld was warm with winter sun but snow was in the air, pronking and showing their dazzling fans not – I am sure – because of danger but for pleasure alone.

A fully grown springbuck ram may weigh 80 pounds. The flesh is tender and delicious and the commonest and most popular venison of the Karoo: and also Cranemere's most famous dish. It has made many tons of biltong and on this, it is said, the Boer War was fought. In the droughts of the past when the sheep died of thirst, springbuck saved many people from starvation, for they, like the gazelles of the North African desert, can live with little water, and if there are many succulent plants, with none at all. In dry years, however, the kidding is always poor and in great drought the springbuck of today, confined by fences, die in numbers.

Even in death the springbuck has something rare for the white fan smells sweetly of honey. The scent, given off by a gland, disappears shortly after death.

The Hottentots called the springbuck their sheep. I do not know if the Bushmen had a special term of affection for them but it is likely, for greatly though they loved the eland, they used the springbuck even more. Springbuck must have been their mainstay in the Karoo.

Springbuck paunches were often their water-bags; springbuck skins roofed the frail huts, and clothed them; twisted fibres of the dorsal muscles were the strings for their bows; the skin of the thigh provided the surface of their drums; the dried inner skin of their ears filled with berries were their dancing rattles; springbuck sinews were their threads; springbuck horns, heated in the fire and straightened, were often the ends of their digging sticks. The springbuck provided food, protection, warmth and pleasure, and perhaps something more, for the Bushmen knew them and felt them in their blood – that 'springbuck sensation' within their bodies that had so fascinated the Bleeks, the tapping at their own ribs when they 'felt' the dark hair on the side of the buck, the sensation in their own faces when they felt the stripe on the face of the springbuck. It was their brother and sister of the veld; and, says one Bushman legend, the origin of man, for it was Mantis, the Hottentot God, who turned a springbuck into a human being.

Springbuck have always loved the Karoo. They have grown sleek on the pentzia bushes, on the succulents, on the flowers and leaves of the witgat trees, and the wild pomegranate of the koppies. Their small precise spoor was imprinted on the cinnamon earth long before that of sheep or goat, and they are as much a part of the veld as the bushes and grass themselves. They are likely to remain, for whatever their past, springbuck are now greatly valued, and the farmers who shoot them in the season count their numbers jealously none the less. In 1839 springbuck were sold on the Cradock market at $13\frac{1}{2}$d. each; they may now fetch nearly fifty times as much.

My father used to tell one of the oddest springbuck stories I know. He had at one time as manager on Cranemere a man afflicted with a nervous tremor, making his hands shake as if with palsy. Fanny Palmer, giving him his tea, would fill the cup not more than one-third full or the tea would land on the carpet. Yet this man was a first-class shot, his trembling hands losing every tremor when fastening round a rifle. In a land of keen eyesight he was distinguished by the fact that even when a springbuck was no more than a speck in the distance he knew if it were a ram or a ewe. Most huntsmen, from the size of the animal, the size of the horns and thickness of the neck, can guess at the sex of a buck within the sights of their guns, but this man did not guess. He knew. In all his stay upon the Karoo he *never* shot a ewe – and he sometimes shot from a great distance. The ewes in their turn knew. Wild as the wind, and as fast, they had no fear at all of this one man. My father would tell how, when the wind carried his scent towards them, the rams would streak away, running hard and smoothly, but the ewes would trot by him within yards, turning their little horned heads and soft alert eyes towards him and showing not one sign of fear.

'Nobody ever believed it until they saw,' said my father, 'and even when they'd seen it they could only shake their heads.'

On a farm close to Cranemere some white springbuck live, and to the north of us on a farm in the Murraysburg district some black buck caused a good deal of interest recently when it was claimed that they were a completely new race of springbuck. They are not so much black as a gun-metal colour, showing black in the sunlight, and they are recorded here as far back as 1888. Many scientists believe that these buck show no more than a colour variation, but something so strange among our familiar springbuck has naturally caused much talk.

Early one winter morning, driving to Graaff-Reinet, Sita saw what for a moment appeared an enchanted animal, a springbuck ram leaning fast asleep against the fence beside the road. It was covered in a coat of frost, and as she passed it woke and sprang away, the frost cracking and flying from its body like shooting diamonds.

The strangest of all things about the springbuck was first recorded by an eyewitness on the Plains of Camdeboo of buck that had probably drunk dry the brown pools on Cranemere. This was a springbuck migration which Le Vaillant described in 1782.

The springbuck migrations, when vast herds numbering not thousands but millions moved steadily and inexorably across the plains, trampling all before them and shaking the earth as if with a tremor, are something we shall never see ourselves. But they have fascinated naturalists since they were first recorded, for they occurred fairly frequently on a stupendous scale, they changed the face of the country, and the reason for them was never established.

Whatever the cause or causes, springbuck in the north of what is today the Cape Province would start to assemble in herds, wandering uneasily and aimlessly, until – obeying the same strange impulse – they would all begin to move in a mass, sometimes north, sometimes south, sometimes west. In some years they crossed the mountains of Namaqualand to the Atlantic Ocean; in others they pushed through Prieska southwards towards the Karoo, reaching from Somerset East far westward into near-desert country.

Colonists called them 'trekbokke' or 'travelling buck', and likened them to the locusts in the hopping stage, one of the terrible recurring curses of Africa.

Thunberg and Sparrman both knew of the trekbokke, but the first eyewitness account I have found is that of Le Vaillant in 1782 near Cranemere itself. He rode through the trekbokke filling the Plains of Camdeboo, and he could see neither the beginning nor the end of the moving mass. Pringle also saw them many years later near Somerset East. The Graaff-Reinet district often lay in the path of the buck and was continually ravaged by them. Stockenstrom at the beginning of the nineteenth century bewailed the damage the springbuck caused, the pasture and the crops destroyed, and the flocks of sheep swept away by the marching herds. Frantic farmers piled dry manure about their lands and lit it, hoping that the smoke would deflect the buck. It never did and the crops were invariably 'reaped level with the ground'. Others described how the very ground itself was loosened and scored and the bushes torn by the countless hoofs. Sometimes even people were killed when they were knocked down and trampled by the buck.

In 1849 the trekbokke poured across the Karoo again and were seen by a little boy of nine years old in the village of Beaufort West. He was John Fraser, later Sir John, and he described them years afterwards. A travelling hawker arriving from the north one day told the villagers the trekbokke were pouring southward. He owned stock himself and was a frightened man, bent only on hastening on to escape the buck. Hardly anyone in Beaufort West remembered a great migration, but they were soon to know one. One early morning they were wakened by the sound as of a strong wind, and suddenly the town was filled with animals, springbuck and the creatures borne along with them, wildebeest, blesbok, quagga, eland, and they filled the streets and gardens and the whole world within view, devouring every leaf and blade of grass and drinking from the fountains and dams and furrows in the streets. The herd, moving continuously, took three days to pass and when it was gone it looked as if a fire had passed over the Karoo.

Gordon Cumming, travelling between Cradock and Colesberg in the 1840s, saw a springbuck migration and rode into the midst of the animals, firing into the ranks until even he was satisfied and cried 'enough'. A few days later he saw yet another trek which infinitely surpassed the first. He saw 'the plains and even the hillsides, which stretched away on every side, thickly covered, not with herds, but with one vast mass of springboks; as far as the eye could strain, the landscape was alive with them, until they softened down to a dim mass of moving creatures'. He was seeing before his eyes some hundreds of thousands of buck, or so he reckoned, but the Boer with him told him this sight was nothing and that he had ridden for a long day over a countryside as thick with springbuck as sheep in a fold.

Those who saw these treks were struck by the fact that the springbuck never ran or trotted. They went at a steady plodding march, and if the front ranks could not ford a stream, they were pushed in by the buck behind and their bodies formed a bridge for the multitude that followed.

The springbuck is usually an alert and nervous creature, but on occasions not even its enemies will divert it from its course. What then possesses it nobody knows but it is an uncanny thing to see. As a child on horseback I once watched a herd of springbuck which came pouring towards me, startled by a shot on the flats below. Normally one glimpse of my pony and me would have sent them flying over the rise like a flash of fawn and white, but not this time. They came past, parting on either side of us, and I leaned down and touched their backs with my riding-switch, and I remember the fixed unseeing look in their eyes as they flew past my pony's legs.

Trekking buck always seemed to have this strange unawareness of their enemies. There are stories of lions that were swept along, powerless to escape, in a great herd of migrating buck that heeded them not one jot. The buck would come to a house filled with people, or a wagon or cart, part momentarily, and close their ranks beyond them. Hunters on foot could go among them killing them with a stick, or seizing their hind legs in their hands and breaking them. They often shot them with a pistol and from a cart, against the very wheels of which the buck would brush. Le Vaillant marched in the midst of them and they did not even notice him. They were slaughtered as easily as sheep and the whole of the Karoo turned out for a mighty kill. Wagons were strung out along the trek route and were piled high with bodies. While the men shot, the women cut up the meat to make biltong for the years to come. Every farmhouse was surrounded by skins pegged out upon the ground, and drying meat.

It was not only men who followed the trekbokke but wild animals, lions, leopards, wild dogs, hyenas, jackals, 'beast of the burrow and bird of the air', and even these ancient enemies went seemingly unnoticed.

Between 1887 and 1895 there were four big treks. The last one was seen and recorded by Cronwright-Schreiner himself, who described the offal, the heads, the bones of the dead buck that littered the plains in their wake. The buck he saw were distributed over a vast glittering plain, giving it a whitish tinge as if there had been a very light fall of snow, and he and his friends, all farmers used to counting stock, estimated that in their sight at one moment were half a million buck. The whole trek covered at least one hundred and thirty miles, in a band of some fifteen miles, so that the buck literally marched by the million.

They were, on the whole, a silent host. On trek they were known to make a peculiar noise, half whistle and half snort, but nobody ever seems to have recorded among trekbokke that quick 'ppfft' of surprise or alarm of the buck ranging the veld freely, or the small gentle noises a ewe makes to her kid. A traveller, outspanning one night among the trekbokke, noticed that the sound of the curious short grunts and the movements of the tens of thousands of animals was almost exactly like the breaking of the sea upon distant rocks. Another remembered that the earth not only sounded but shuddered with the stamping of the hoofs.

It is one of the most extraordinary things of the whole extraordinary business that often no one knew how a trek ended. In a single night the host could disappear. Sometimes the buck were stopped by the sea, but at other times no one knew what halted them. Even their homeward route was not clearly known, for they never seem to have returned in vast numbers. Sparrman was told they returned by the same route; Gordon Cumming believed they marched in a vast oval or square, always returning by a different route. Some farmers in the path of a trek declared they had never seen returning trekbokke, while others swore they had often seen them returning at a tremendous pace, covering one hundred miles in a single day.

Many, it is certain, never returned. About the year 1860 millions surged across Bushmanland and Namaqualand, crossed the mountains and dashed into the sea. They perished by the tens of thousands and it was said that their bodies lay in a continuous pile along the shore for over thirty miles.

The majority of the colonists were certain of the reason for the great treks. They, whose lives were ordered by the weather, were sure that rain and drought governed the movements of the buck, and that they would flee from drought to better pastures, returning only when rain had fallen in their own districts. Le Vaillant, who saw the first recorded trek over the Plains of Camdeboo, was certain the buck were moving away from drought. Pringle, Stockenstrom, and Sir John Fraser were all equally sure, and apparently voiced the opinion of the time.

The author and poet W. C. Scully, who was a magistrate in Namaqualand and saw the travelling buck, had no doubt that they trekked across Namaqualand before the kidding season started to the western fringe of the desert, which received winter rainfall and was green when the rest of the country was parched. Here was fresh green food which the ewes, and later the kids, needed. The fawning season over, 'the head', he wrote, 'melts slowly and flows gradually westward, until some night distant flashes of lightning on the cloudless horizon indicate where – perhaps hundreds of miles away – the first thunderstorm of the season is labouring down . . . Next morning not a single buck will be visible – all will have vanished like ghosts, making for the distant track of rain.' This migration of springbuck across the desert was, he thought, of immemorial antiquity.

Some believed that if no rain fell in their home lands the buck would stay in their new territory; but that if the drought broke they would know it, even hundreds of miles away, and would return at once.

Some of the early scientists seem to have considered that instinct might have played a part. Dr Andrew Smith, who made a famous zoological and collecting expedition into Southern Africa early in the last century, felt that often such movements and migrations were the result of some imperative impulse, rather than the exercise of free will. In considering migrations he thought that two different impulses operated: one the result of will as seen in elephants, rhinos and hippos, and one the result of uncontrollable instinct, and it was this that forced the springbuck hordes to trek.

Some who upheld the instinct theory pointed out that at times the trekking buck were not thin and drought-stricken but fat and sleek, and there was no reason why they should trek merely to get better grazing. Others, however, argued that since the migrations never occurred regularly and the animals did not always move in the same direction every time, instinct could not be the motive. They pointed out also that however many buck migrated, there were always some that did not – the '*houbokke*' or 'stay-at-homes', the farmers used to call them, and they divided them into a completely different category from the travelling buck.

Cronwright-Schreiner came near to modern theories when he wrote that the treks seemed to him erratic movements in search of food and possibly water, but that some obscure phenomena of an instinctive kind might also have been at work.

Biologists today tend to discount the theory of pure instinct. Lack of water, lack of grazing, lack of palatable food, may all have played a part, but considering the nature of these strange long-distance treks, of the reports of buck seemingly obsessed, so too, they think, may instinct. One modern biologist suggests that the instinct may have been based on the need of some form of natural population control.

A South African biologist, A. M. Brynard, who made a study of game migration, believes that no single factor is responsible for migration but rather a combination; and that when all conditions are favourable the buck trek, and that when they are not, the buck remain in their own country.

Naturally enough, the migrations have often been compared with the famous migrations of the lemmings in Sweden. Nearly two hundred years ago Thunberg compared the two. But paging through the accounts of the extraordinary migrations of living things throughout the world, I feel that the creatures that compare most nearly to migrating springbuck are not animals at all but *butterflies*, the big chestnut-brown Monarchs of North America, the *Danaus*, that begin at the coming of autumn to join together in twos and threes; then, like the buck, in larger groups;

and finally sometimes in swarms that stretch for miles. They move slowly southwards, resting when necessary as they go, but turned aside by nothing, and, like the trekking buck again, they forget to fear their enemies and may be lifted onto a finger and stroked. They fly until they reach their winter homes, and here for months they settle – in parts the same trees have been chosen as resting homes for more than half a century – and then in the spring activity begins, the great swarms break up, and the butterflies are off, often separately, to the north again.

Remembering the fate of the migrating springbuck, it is worth recording that in parts of California those who disturb a butterfly on its tree may be fined five hundred dollars.

Such insect migrations still occur regularly. Not so with the springbuck. Migratory movements – used in the layman's sense of large and definite movements from one area to another – are possible now only in the Kalahari Desert, in the Gemsbok Reserve, for example, where some trekking can still be noted but in small numbers. The springbuck treks of the Karoo are over; the great hordes will never again drink dry the Cranemere waters; and now we will never know for certain what sent a buck travelling or what made it stay at home.

10. Twilight Souls

Many people, seeing the Karoo for the first time, swear that there is no wild life here at all and – bitterly – that even the sheep and goats are seldom visible.

The Karoo is, in fact, filled with a teeming and exuberant life but it is true that it is not easily seen. The plains enfold the animals; the tawny skins are one with the bush and ground and rock and shadows. The great bustards in speckled brown, the little larks and chats, are equally invisible; the cobras basking on the yellow soil in a pale sunshine, the puff-adders asleep among the rocks, the grey-brown lizards among the koppie stones, the brown and yellow tortoises, the great horde of brown or khaki insects, are seldom visible.

To any but the zoologist our animals can be neatly divided into two groups: those we see and those we do not; and the second is by far the larger. But how rewarding are the ones we know.

What most people remember vividly on Cranemere are the ground squirrels. One still morning last winter, after days of winds, we drove out into the veld. The birds and mammals were abroad in numbers, making the most of the mildness, and we stopped to watch a party of ground squirrels near their burrows.

Most Karoo people know them as meerkats, a comprehensive name for the meerkats (our prettiest little carnivores) and the ground squirrels, which are rodents, and it is true that when we see them in the distance, sitting up like so many ninepins at the mouths of their burrows, sometimes whole colonies of them together, they look very much alike. We discovered, however, that – like the animals of the game reserves – they do not associate motor-cars with people, so that it is possible to drive close to them and watch them as they gather their food and play, quite unperturbed, and then their species is obvious.

That morning we stopped a few feet away from them. Fat little creatures some eight or nine inches long with coats like polished biscuits and a side stripe from shoulder to flank, they whisked around their holes with quick, neat little movements, rearing up on their hind legs to nibble at a bulb or root in their forepaws, their dark handsome speckled tails, outlined in white, waving behind them, not from side to side but – surprisingly – up and down with a sinuous slinky motion like that of a snake.

They spent a great deal of time upright, surveying us and the world with bright inquisitive eyes. At rest they sat upon their haunches with their tails flat on the ground behind them, and their paws crossed upon their chests in a meek devotional attitude, but on the alert they rose up on their toes, their tails acting as fine third legs, their forepaws dangling and quivering before them. One little pair that had watched us thus for minutes relaxed to touch noses together, and in the space of twenty minutes they paused to do this a dozen times, an extraordinarily confiding, pretty gesture to watch, although we did not know the significance of it.

When we opened the door they vanished in a flash down their burrows, but only seconds later their heads slowly emerged and they peered at us cautiously; and finding all was still, shot out and started to whisk about us once again. I remembered with pleasure that Barrow had seen these on the Plains of Camdeboo nearly 170 years ago and had thought them beautiful.

I remembered, too, how as a child they had been a constant amusement to me. On a summer morning I often went riding with Rob. We would start at four o'clock in the morning while it was still dark, feeling for our horses in the stable – and I recall that at the sound of their hoofs on the cobbles I shivered in the darkness with purest joy. For the most part we rode in silence, looking and listening. By the time we had reached the main road the east was red, and at the Rooikop the sun was up. The spider-webs were gleaming in the bushes, the geese on the veld dams calling, and sometimes a troop of cranes would be dancing in the pale sun. And the ground squirrels and slender-tailed meerkats would be sunning themselves in little colonies beside the road.

The striped meerkats, neat as little birds, with tremendous finish from their tiny feet to their precise ears and little pointed snouts, emitted staccato puppy barks that sent the dogs crazy with excitement. The two are traditional enemies yet I once heard of a Karoo meerkat reared as a pet which became the inseparable companion of the farm dogs. When it was later taken to England it confounded English dogs – which apparently thought it was a kind of rat – by trotting happily up to them hoping for a frolic.

'Pretty!' Rob would say looking at the little animals, 'But, man, they can *bite*.' They can. Like their kinsman, the mongoose, they can kill a cobra.

Sometimes we saw a little mongoose; or sometimes the red meerkat with its squirrel-like tail tipped with white – a mighty hunter of all small creatures and even adult snakes. Once one set us laughing until our sides ached. It was playing with our fox-terrier, which was pursuing it with hysterical hunting howls. As the dog was upon it, the meerkat would leap off at an angle, flaunting its bushy tail in the very face of the terrier, and this continued for some time until the meerkat had had enough and suddenly disappeared down its hole. Only then did we realize it had darted to and fro over its burrow. It had not been escaping at all but baiting its pursuer.

We always saw hares sheltering in the grass or bushes, crouching with their large ears flat along their backs. They would start up at the horses' hoofs and be gone in a flash of grey and buff and pink, leaving their small shelters shaped to their very forms. Sometimes I could not resist dismounting to feel these and they were warm with life.

There were always steenbok, among the smallest antelope in Africa. Walt Disney might have imagined them with their amber-red coats, their delicate legs and large ears; and little duiker, not much bigger, with their little quiffs of hair between their horns, leaping and diving as they fled away from us. Rob had long ago seen klipspringer, beautiful little mountain buck, on Cranemere, but they had disappeared.

Sometimes we saw a polecat – a *muishond* to all on the farm – a black-and-white flash. We never paused to think it was beautiful but urged on our horses and prayed the dogs were too far afield to scent it. Not for nothing is it a virile relation of the skunk! Stink-breeches, the colonists once called it, and a fine descriptive name it is.

There were dassies – rock rabbits – on the mountain and as we reached the foot we would see their furry brown forms running up and down perpendicular rock faces. I never knew which was the more extraordinary: the black soles of their small neat feet that make airtight cups against the rocks, or the fact that they are related to the elephant.

The thorn trees along the dry stream-beds nearly always housed monkeys and we would see them, like the meerkats, sunning their bellies. They were the vervet or blue monkeys, small, grizzled, white-bellied, with the black faces of tiny ancient human beings. They were familiar friends, for when the prickly pear jungles enclosed the roads we would see them on every journey, feasting on the fruit and darting to and fro across the road in parties, the mothers with their very young babies clinging to the long hair on their breasts.

Once my father and I saw a sight we never forgot. We had been driving through the tall prickly pears and had passed a gang of men fencing the road. As we turned the corner my father hooted. A troop of monkeys which had crossed the road and were eating fruit in the tall prickly pears beyond were startled at the noise and streamed back to reach their homes. In their absence the stretch of road across their path had been fenced and they collided with the unfamiliar wire, falling abruptly on their backs. It was a huge troop, and the monkeys behind paid no attention to their fallen brothers, but, leaping upon their prostrate bodies, themselves bounded against the fence, only to fall backwards in their turn. They lay in a struggling pile three feet deep, and when they finally disentangled themselves, all unhurt in limb, their rage and chagrin were heard far around. For the moment they were not little wild animals but little people, screwing up their faces, dancing and screaming and gesticulating. Almost, they shook their fists at us.

We never saw them near the farmhouse but we always looked for them in the well-bushed parts of the farm and found them perennially interesting.

In the mountains there were baboons. We often saw them on the krantz above, and we always heard them, hoching and grunting and the babies squealing, following good maternal slaps that rang across the valley, and we always reined in our horses to listen. I would strain my eyes to see them but we seldom saw them closely. Yet, like all Karoo people, we knew them well and the fantastic stories that had grown around them.

'Some Hottentots are of opinion that baboons can speak,' wrote Kolben two centuries ago, 'but that they avoid it for fear men should lay 'em by the heels and make 'em work for their living.' So a century before Darwin, men here in the Cape were suggesting a baboon's affinity with man. For myself, I have never doubted it. A baboon wearing a hibiscus flower showed me more eloquently than ever science could that he and I were kin.

He lived in a cage in the old garden of the Grand Hotel in Port Elizabeth. I was four years old when I met him and I remember still the impact of the meeting. Lolling back, his arms embracing the bars, a flower-stalk between his teeth, the bloom red against his hairy cheek, he was plainly no mere animal but a cousin, a fascinating cousin. I considered him with curiosity and esteem.

We have many stories of the likenesses of baboon to man; these are sometimes funny, sometimes sad, but always enthralling. There are the tales of baboons that have stolen away human children and reared them as their own; of young baboons that – like children – loved everything small: goats, lambs, piglets, puppies, goslings. Eugene Marais, who wrote *My Friends the Baboons*, one of the best true animal stories ever written, once saw African children and young baboons playing together at a water-hole, digging pot clay with their hands, laughing, struggling and jostling one another in perfect accord.

For three years Eugene Marais lived in close touch with a troop of baboons – Chacma baboons which range over all South Africa. As Marais watched them he marvelled, for he found that in their ways they were at times almost human, with a well-marked social life, every single one in a troop having a well-defined status. They fell in love, he maintained, and a husband always protected and fed his mate. They had strict rules concerning the privacy of birth. They rallied to a comrade in danger, and saved the babies of a troop, not necessarily their own, at the risk of their lives. He thought that their great advantage over other animals was that – like man – their environment could suddenly be changed and they could yet survive.

On the Karoo we had learnt this lesson bitterly. By nature baboons are plant- and insect-eaters. They had adored the fruit of the prickly pears when they grew on the Karoo; and when these were exterminated they fed on the luscious white grubs of the cacto-blastis that killed the prickly pear. When these too disappeared they raided lands and gardens and sometimes learned to tear open the stomachs of lambs to drink the curdled milk; or to rip open the udders of living ewes.

Farmers found them the most formidable opponents, claiming that they *thought*. They knew what a gun was; and they soon learned to avoid traps. Once near the mountain my father installed a large wire cage with a drop door into which he hoped to lure the baboons with mealies. He never caught one.

One Karoo farmer once sent a native armed with a shot-gun to inspect such a trap, and when he had not returned by nightfall went himself to look for him. He found the man alive – but only just. He had shot an adult baboon in the cage, and seeing a baby with it he had crept in to seize it for a pet. The baby began to cry and instantly the old males from its troops had rallied to it from the mountainside: some had tried to squeeze into the cage, others stretched their arms through the netting to tear at him. His ammunition was finished and when help arrived he was torn and bleeding and half insane.

South of Cranemere lies a valley known as Baviaanskloof –

the Valley of the Baboons. Old Landman, the carpenter from Pearston, has a tale of this valley which he told us one day.

About thirty years ago, he said, there lived here a man called Pieter Slaght. There are many of that name there but Pieter and his sons were known as being wild and rough. Old Slaght believed in nothing – 'No God, no nothing,' said Landman. One day Pieter sat on his stoep and called his younger son.

'Take your horse and gun,' he said. 'Go and shoot the baboons in the pen.'

Up got the younger son and rode away while the old man waited on the stoep. He heard one shot and then all was still. Presently his son returned, sitting on his horse and hanging his head.

'Well,' said the old man, 'was there only one?'

'No,' said the son dejectedly, 'there were two. But, Father, I didn't see my way to shoot the second.'

'What!' roard his father. 'You lily-livered bastard! You go,' he said, turning to his elder son. But presently he too returned drooping in his saddle.

'No, Father, I too did not see my way to shoot the baboon,' he said.

The old man was speechless. Seizing his own gun, he mounted his horse and rode off in fury. He dismounted, crept round a clump of bushes to the side of the pen, and saw what his sons had seen. Lying in the cage, dead and spattered with blood, was the *jong wyfie* – the young wife, and caressing her, hugging her, and crying in anguish was a young male baboon. As the old man watched he took her in his arms and held her to him, moaning softly, and embraced her until he too was covered in her blood.

Pieter did not shoot but stood and stared. Presently he turned, mounted his horse, and rode away. The Slaght family had gathered on the stoep to await his return. He climbed heavily up the steps and flung down his gun.

'Go and open the pen,' he said. 'While I have breath in my body, so help me God, I will never kill another baboon.'

'And that,' said Landman, 'was the first time he had ever used God's name not in vain.'

Old Slaght crept into his room and shut the door. After a long time his wife peeped through a crack and saw her husband kneeling on the floor praying for forgiveness.

'And that,' ended Landman, 'was how Slaght was brought to God – and by a baboon!'

There are many stories of baboons acting not as enemies but as friends to men. Eugene Marais knew of one woman who allowed a baboon to care for her baby!

In the last century a man adopted a young baboon and made it his shepherd. It took its duties very seriously, remaining all day with the goats and driving them home at night, riding behind them on the back of one of them. It was allowed to drink the milk of one goat and never cheated, sucking from that goat alone, and guarding the milk of the others from the children. It was a trustworthy shepherd for a whole year, when it was tragically killed by a leopard.

There was a good deal of interest recently when another baboon was discovered acting in a similar way. Her name is Ahla and she is a goat-herd too, caring for her flock of goats, removing their ticks, guarding them, and, it is claimed, counting them. She is the third baboon goat-herd on the same farm, but one tippled, one knocked over every milk-can on sight, and Ahla is the only one to be truly reliable.

The first baboon I know of to work for a man in South Africa was Kees, and he belonged to Le Vaillant. He acted as a watchdog for the ornithologist on his trip through the Karoo; and more important, as his 'taster', sampling all unknown roots and fruits before Le Vaillant would try them. If Kees refused anything Le Vaillant judged it either unpleasant or poisonous and threw it away. He was of particular value in the Karoo where water was scarce, for he knew every succulent root, which he would tear up by his own ingenious method. He would take a tuft of leaves in his teeth, press his forepaws firmly on the earth and jerk his head backwards, sometimes turning somersault, but he always succeeded in pulling out the root.

161

Kees's favourite root – and his master's too – was the juicy kambro, shaped like a very large radish. It grows on the Karoo – and here on Cranemere – and has saved many lives, animal and human. Kees could find this even when the small leaves were withered and there was nothing of it visible above the surface of the soil, and he would lead Le Vaillant to it and they would dig it up together, he with his paws and Le Vailliant with his poniard. They then shared the root between them.

Once when they were extremely thirsty Le Vaillant saw Kees stop suddenly, turn his nose towards the wind, and begin to run with all the dogs running silently behind him. He followed them and found them all collected round a beautiful spring three hundred paces from their course. He named the spring Keesfontein.

'My dear Kees', as Le Vaillant called him, was his inseparable companion, sleeping with him, riding in the wagon, and hunting with him. Kees was particularly fond of gum and of honey and would search diligently for these. Le Vaillant shared everything he ate and drank with Kees, and if he forgot him Kees would soon remind him of his obligations by smacking his lips or patting Le Vaillant's hand.

He greatly loved milk, but was equally fond of brandy, which, however, he was not allowed to drink from a glass for he choked himself in his eagerness to take it and coughed and sneezed for hours afterwards. He drank his liquor from a plate, but waited his turn, following with his eyes the bottle which was passed from Hottentot to Hottentot. 'How strongly did he express by his motions and looks that he feared the cruel bottle would be emptied too soon and would not reach him,' wrote his master.

Once when Kees was preparing to taste his brandy Le Vaillant lit a flip of paper and set light to it. Kees gave a shrill cry and leapt into the air. He would have nothing more to do with his master that evening but put himself to bed. He would never again touch a drop of brandy, but would mutter between his teeth when he saw the bottle, and sometimes hit out at it with his paw.

Kees had a great dread of lions and fellow baboons. When a lion was in the neighbourhood he started at the least sound and moaned like a sick person. The sound of the wild baboons and monkeys in the mountains sent him crazy with terror, although he always replied to them. If they approached he fled with horrified cries and ran between Le Vaillant's legs, imploring protection. When Le Vaillant shot four monkeys, however, Kees showed deep interest in them, turning them over and over, finally feeling their cheeks. Here were riches and he opened their mouths and plundered their cheek-pouches in which baboons and monkeys stow their treasures, removing the little fruits he found there and transferring them to his own mouth!

He was a better guard than the watch-dogs, which always went to sleep, apparently feeling perfectly secure when Kees was near. They listened for his voice, and when he had given the alarm watched for his signal, the least motion of his eyes or shake of his head, and would then all rush in whatever direction Kees was looking.

He had a working arrangement with Le Vaillant's dogs, for when he got tired he simply mounted one and rode it. The largest and strongest dog was, however, also the most intelligent, and outwitted even Kees. When the baboon jumped upon his back he simply stopped in his tracks and stood motionless, allowing the caravan to pass him by. He was not afraid of losing sight of people but he knew Kees was. As the wagons disappeared in the distance Kees would lose his nerve and jump off the dog, and the two of them would then run side by side with all their might to overtake the wagons.

All adult baboons are terrified of snakes. One pet baboon reared on the Karoo fainted, it is said, when she unwrapped a parcel which had been given her to find within it a dead snake. She was revived with brandy. Le Vaillant played the cruellest trick possible upon Kees when he tied a dead cobra to his tail so as to enjoy the baboon's anguished attempts to rid himself of it. Reading Le Vaillant's adventures with Kees on the Karoo, it is easy enough to understand why Le Vaillant found the baboon attractive but not always so easy to see why Kees should have loved the man.

Kees remains one of the most engaging and interesting visitors Cranemere has ever had. I hope he did not find the baboons in the mountains or the lions and cobras on the Plains of Camdeboo too unnerving an experience.

Kees is not the only baboon to have been used to locate juicy bulbs and water in the veld. Farmers once used them frequently to find water, leading them by a long cord and noting where the thirsty baboons dug. Perhaps some trekboer used them so on Cranemere long ago.

There are stories of young baboons trained to lead a team of oxen and to pull the reins to halt them. All baboons seem to love to ride and to enjoy the company of horses, making good jockeys. Tame baboons, in fact, ride anything they can from dogs to goats. A female baboon called Mrs Bett once lived not far from Cranemere and used regularly to take the horses to water, riding on the back of one. She went camping with her master but her curiosity was a problem, for – like Kees – she would inspect and try everything, even devouring the candles. Once her master and a friend found, in the morning, that although their spectacle-frames were intact the lenses had vanished from them. They seized Mrs Bett. Her cheeks were not soft to the touch but hard, and forcing open her mouth, they found in her cheek-pouches their lenses still intact.

The most famous baboon of all was Jack, the baboon signalman of Uitenhage. His story is remarkable on several levels and its implications have left many ill at ease. 'Twilight souls', Eugene Marais called the baboon people; but having heard Jack's tale some might question the 'twilight'.

Among those who told the story was F. W. FitzSimons, for many years the director of the Port Elizabeth museum and snake park, in his *Natural History of South Africa*. He did not know Jack himself but he questioned many who did and he believed all the details of the story to be correct, and this lends weight to a very strange tale.

Uitenhage is a small, hot town eighty miles south of Crane-mere on one of the main routes from the Karoo to the sea. One day an elderly cripple, James Wide, employed on the railways as a signalman, was in the Uitenhage market when he saw a team of oxen passing along the road. It was led by a young baboon.

Wide was immensely interested. He questioned the driver of the wagon, who told him that he had captured the animal when it was very young, and that it was intelligent and had quickly learned to lead the oxen. Wide bought the baboon and took it home with him. Here Jack settled down in one of the oddest associations that any animal has ever had with man. He was not only a loving companion and protector – many animals of many kinds have been that – but he became a general assistant in Wide's house and garden and at work – and a capable, trust-worthy assistant.

Except on Sundays, when he slept the day through after his Saturday ration of brandy, Jack arose early, pumped the water, carried it to the house, fetched the wood, and did a variety of household jobs. He was a strong animal, which was as well, for the firewood was often old track-sleepers weighing up to 150 pounds which he collected regularly from the stores depot and carried to a trolley two hundred yards away. He would then push the trolley home, roll the sleepers off, and take them to the wood-pile.

FitzSimons describes how Jack and Wide had an early break-fast together and then set off to work. Wide had made a light trolley for himself consisting of a wooden platform and two sets of wheels which ran on rails, and he used this to get from his cottage to the signal-box. He had originally used a large mongrel dog to pull the trolley, but when it was run over by a train Jack took over its duties.

He would seat himself at the side of the track, work first one wheel, then the other into position, and finally lift the platform on top. Wide would then clamber in; Jack would lock the front door of the cottage, hand Wide the key, and would begin either to push him, or to pull him along by a riem which Wide held in his hands. When the track sloped downwards Jack would leap onto the back of the trolley and, filled with obvious joy, would take a ride with his master.

Wide operated the train signals controlling traffic on the Uitenhage to Port Elizabeth and the Uitenhage to Graaff-Reinet lines. Soon Jack was not content to watch Wide at work but began to work as well. He did more than imitate his master; he learned the job. He knew every signal and every lever to pull, and was able to associate the number of blasts from a train whistle with the correct lever to pull. He always looked to Wide for confirmation. Wide would hold up one finger or two, and Jack would then pull the correct lever. Once when Wide hurt his arm Jack managed all the work himself under supervision.

Naturally enough, passengers by train were not always happy at knowing their safety lay in the hands of a baboon. Jack never made a mistake in his nine years' work and gradually the alarm died down. At the end of his life he was the pride of the district.

Jack and Wide were devoted friends and everybody who saw them together remarked the deep bond of confidence and love between them. Jack used to sit with one arm round Wide's neck and the other stroking his face or his hand, chattering to him incessantly as he did so. Once a fellow railwayman quarrelled with Wide in Jack's presence. Jack pushed him off the platform with loud and furious cries and the man retreated.

Jack finally died of tuberculosis, caused, it was thought, by overstrain, for nothing could stop him from working for Wide, pulling, pushing, pumping, lifting until he dropped from exhaustion, to lie still for a minute before starting again. His death was the tragedy of Wide's life. More than twenty years later he burst into tears when telling FitzSimons the story of Jack, declaring the time with his baboon had been the happiest in his whole life.

Wide eventually returned to Wales, where he died. Jack's skull is in the Albany Museum in Grahamstown. But Wide and Jack are remembered all over the Cape and children are still reared upon their story. It remains one of the great animal tales of the world.

One winter day we set out to look for kudu. Our kudu may be counted a triumph for they are the only big animals completely destroyed in our countryside to have returned in numbers. Stone Age Man knew them on Cranemere, but my father never did, nor did we as children. Some years ago they began to drift back from the south, leaping the fences and living with apparent satisfaction in our mountain bush. I had never seen them and determined to do so.

It had rained and all the birds and beasts of the veld had left their imprints criss-crossing one another in the soil. There were the tiny neat hoof-marks of the steenbok and duiker, spoors of springbuck, ant-bear, cranes, guineafowl, geese. But it was the big triangular hoof-marks of the kudu that we wanted and we followed them with ardour.

They led us from the flats and the karoo bush to the mountain slopes and a gorge, dry now and coloured silver with wild buddleia, through which the wind funnelled and roared like rushing water. Wild pelargoniums with big heads of mauve flowers scrambled in the bushes and we crushed the leaves in our hands and their strong aromatic smell travelled with us. Every now and again the bush was too thick and we had to turn back and force a new path between the spekboom, the wild plum and the klapper, now bright with colour. Once when we paused a little dark scorpion crept from under a rock and moved slowly at our feet.

As we climbed the spur of the mountain, the wind caught us, tearing at our clothes and hair and whipping away our voices; but there were kudu spoors and fresh droppings to urge us on, and we scrambled over the crest and down past euphorbia in clumps of elongated thorny thumbs, and – surprisingly – through a flight of butterflies. Suddenly before us, running easily and well up the mountain slope, was a kudu bull and we all cried out, and a spurt of wind carrying away voices and butterflies together, we were left breathless from wind and pleasure.

The kudu was a prince among animals. As big as a small horse, banded in white with noble spiral horns, it flew up the mountainside like a great bird. Seeing it move, I knew why farmers argue endlessly the height a kudu fence should be, for what could contain such an animal? I remembered that Stevenson-Hamilton had found they would clear his eight-foot fence to eat his zinnias.

Maurice saw it with pride and gloom, pride for its beauty, gloom for its appetite. 'It eats as much as an ox,' he said, 'and it *always* picks the best.' As a farmer in a semi-desert, he wonders how many such treasures he can afford.

We trekked home in a glow of pleasure. As we went, I thought not only of the animals we had seen that day, but of all those beneath our feet, yards down below the surface of the soil, that we seldom or never know – rats, mice, elephant shrews, moles, porcupines, springhares, badgers, wild cats, genets, jackals, maanhaarjakkals. Here they were below us, given shelter and life by the soil itself: cool in the fierce summer, warm in winter when the pools above them froze, safe – or safe as wild animals might be.

Here were golden moles, different structurally from all other animals, without eyes or ears or tails, their very nostrils hidden in a leathery pad. Purely African, they were the first creatures that Broom collected in South Africa, a steppingstone, as it were, to the Missing Link. Here were hedgehogs. None of us, I thought, would ever have known of their existence but for the fact that George Palmer had found a baby one years ago and reared it as a pet. Here were porcupines. We knew they were here because they strewed the farm with their handsome banded quills. In all my time on Cranemere I had seen only two. All around us in their roomy burrows were springhares, those kangaroo-like creatures with their enormous hind legs that go hoppity-hoppity over the veld at night and whose eyes, reflecting a torch or the headlights of a car, rise and fall like bright stars.

Somewhere about us lived the elegant little bat-eared or desert foxes, with the keening cry, that people sometimes saw in the headlights of their cars. Charming innocents living largely upon insects, bulbs and berries, they are captivating with their long silver fur, thin delicate legs and big round ears. We had never seen one by day on Cranemere.

There were the silver jackals. Sometimes we almost walk on one hiding in an ant-bear hole. A pair live in the Pomegranate Camp not far from the house, and Sita and Maurice sometimes hear their long, weird, blood-curdling cries. They were probably all about us, their silent silver forms hidden below the ground. Cranemere has waged an endless war not on them but on their red, black-backed cousins – fast, hardy, cunning killers of the veld. We could have passed these too, hidden in thickets or bush, for they never go for good. Eighty years after George set his first jackal trap Maurice is still battling with them. Biologists, talking of the balance of nature, say they must never be eliminated. They are not likely to be: dogs, poison, traps – they elude them all.

FitzSimons believed that even the cubs were super-animals, scratching small side-tunnels off the main ant-bear burrow in which they often lived, blocking up the entrance and hiding here from pursuing dogs; or escaping from the dogs through small 'back doors' – holes just big enough for them to squeeze through but too small for adult dogs; and sometimes sharing burrows with porcupines which they deliberately use as weapons of defence.

Jackals often refuse poisoned bait and their scent is so keen that they are difficult to trap. Maurice once learned of an infallible concoction for wiping out the smell of man about a jackal trap, one which at the same time was guaranteed irresistible to jackals. It was a mixture of high meat, bad sardines, donkey fat, glycerine and jackal entrails, to be buried in a container for several weeks before using. Maurice kept a large choice piece of meat until the required odour and when Sita's back was turned took her mincing-machine – one of Cranemere's pre-Boer War heirlooms – to mince it. He broke it on the meat and a crisis arose a week later when Sita looked for her mincer and found it gone. Nor was that the end of the story, for Maurice lost his fine brew. He buried it in Sita's flower-garden 'to ripen it' and forgot its hiding-place, so that for months to follow Sita was afraid to dig.

There is one man in our countryside who always manages to catch his jackal. He is a young Xhosa who – for a price – will visit a farm, live in the veld, and trap the jackals about. How he does it is his own secret, but Maurice is sure he is part human, part jackal – in mind, at least. Of a morning when Maurice visits him, during his stays on Cranemere, he tells the story of the movements of all the animals at night – here ran a maanhaar-jakkal, here a silver jackal, there hunted a red jackal, there cried a desert fox. About him accumulate the bones of all the little animals of the veld, picked clean and white, until Maurice can bear it no longer and chooses to live with the live jackals rather than their hunter.

One of Cranemere's best stories is a jackal story. Many years ago Vardy, a young manager on Cranemere, saw a red jackal in the veld and gave chase until to his chagrin it bolted down an ant-bear hole. He searched for something with which to stop the mouth of the burrow but there was nothing, not even a stone, in the vicinity. His blood was up, and, stripping off his trousers, he stuffed them into the hole and rushed home for help. Fanny Palmer was holding an unexpected tea-party, and before the eyes of her incredulous guests who were sipping tea on the front stoep out of thinnest Japanese tea-cups, there appeared on the dam wall in fine silhouette the form of Vardy hastening home for help. So intent was he on his jackal catch that he was among the ladies before he was aware of the rustle of a petticoat.

There could have been lynx or red cats in the mountain behind us and probably many a litter had been raised in the ant-bear holes we passed. Even in a zoo these animals are wonderful, the size of a small leopard, not spotted but brick red with jet-black pointed ears and emerald eyes. Last year Maurice caught

34 *The brilliant coloured lynx or rooikat – rich red with jet-black ear tufts – is one of the most feared killers of the veld.*

35 These little meerkats, which live on Cranemere in great numbers, can kill a cobra.

36 Ground squirrels are among the most attractive of the smaller Cranemere animals.

37 A Karoo elephant shrew – a timid creature that is seldom seen.

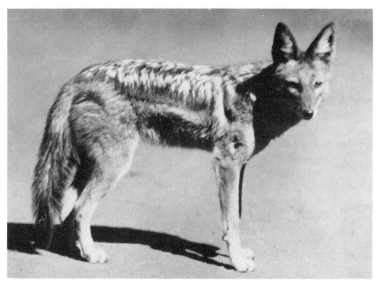

38 The black-backed or red jackal, the great killer of the Karoo.

39 The harmless maanhaarjakkals, or aardwolf, was described for the first time by Sparrman, who found it near what is now Cranemere.

one that had been taking lambs and even in death it was brilliant and beautiful. If Sita had lived a hundred years before she would have kept the skin in her medicine-cupboard as a cure for gout, lumbago and rheumatics.

Presently as we tramped an animal flashed across our path, a big mongoose, long, sleek, grey. We remembered all at once Sita's mystery animal which she had seen years before and around which had grown a perennial family argument. Very early one morning she had looked out of her window to see a strange darkish animal of medium size on the stoep breakfasting on the dogs' meat. Sita swore it was an otter, Maurice a honey badger, and others this grey mongoose, or perhaps even a water-mongoose. Whichever it was, it had been an interesting visitor.

The large grey mongoose is nocturnal and rarely seen, and as for the water-mongoose with its foxy face and small bright eyes, it is reputed to live in the Karoo but we had never seen one. Dick had. He had once looked after a tame water-mongoose for a friend and told us that it was filled with cleverness. Like a pet dog, it had demanded constant attention, waiting at his knees to be scratched, setting off on a brief perambulation, and returning again and again for more attention. It played with water with a commotion of movement and delight. In the wild these little animals feed on freshwater mussels and such things, feeling for them in the mud with their paws, and Dick watched this one stealing an electric light plug, rearing up on its hind legs with the plug in its forepaws and hurling it against a stone to crack it. Once it had put its paw under the flap of a visitor's bag and searched tentatively and delicately within, without ever *looking* at what it touched. It had found a lipstick which it had promptly carried off to crack. We listened to his story with pleasure, but regretfully dismissed the likelihood that the water-mongoose had been Sita's visitor.

We longed for it to have been an otter, for Jenks and I had once seen an otter playing a fantastic game and we would have welcomed a creature with this sense of heroic comedy. It had been teasing two crocodiles which were sunning themselves on a

171

sandbank in a Transvaal river, nipping out of the water, darting at the crocodiles, and as they lunged at him, flipping back into the water and advancing again from the other side, to disappear finally in a triumphant swirl. The Cape otter is known in Karoo rivers and does wander on land, so – like the water-mongoose – it was a possibility, but only just.

But, allowing for the tricks light could play, it could have been a honey badger or ratel, for they have been seen on Cranemere. If so, Sita had had a famous guest.

This strong, stocky, black-and-white relation of the otter is unique: for its courage (Colonel Stevenson-Hamilton thought it the most absolutely courageous animal in the world); for its colour, for unlike most animals its back is lighter-coloured than its belly; for its skin, which enfolds it like a loose rubber coat and through which no teeth or fangs or stings can penetrate; and for its strange association with a bird.

An efficient business arrangement is said to exist between it and a small bird known as the honey-guide, which is reputed to lead people to bees' nests. It is claimed that the honey badger has learnt the bird's signal and will follow it, like a man, to the nest, which it will then rifle, always – being an untidy eater – leaving some of the comb for the bird. Colonel Stevenson-Hamilton in *Wild Life in South Africa* described a honey badger following a honey-guide, a little grey-black form moving at a steady jog-trot; with the tail carried above the back and the head a little low, the bird calling to it and the animal answering with a hissing and chuckling sound. We occasionally see or hear a honey-guide on Cranemere, and we know that the honey badger lives here, so that some day we may see what Stevenson-Hamilton saw: and what a sight to remember for ever.

One of the earliest descriptions of the honey badger was given by Sparrman, who saw one on his way to Bruintjeshoogte, perhaps a score of miles from Cranemere. He said that as a sailor at the masthead could best see a sail at sunset, so this was the best time for the honey badger to look out for his supper. He would therefore sit looking towards the sun, but holding one paw before his eyes so that they might not be hurt by the sun's rays, and peering first round one side of his paw and then the other, he would note the direction in which the bees flew and immediately follow them to rifle their nests. This is the most charming animal fantasy I know, the stocky and intent badger peering from behind its paw across the Plains of Camdeboo towards the sun setting behind the Mountain of Teeth, and the bees, a golden trail, in the evening light.

And there were the ant-bears. We saw the great gaping mouths of their burrows everywhere, those roomy burrows dug at an angle that give such hospitality to so many wild animals; and we crossed ant-bear spoors again and again.

'Can there be anything more annoying,' I complained to Maurice. 'Here they are, and they leave the most positive evidence that they live among us and in numbers. They must have great termite orgies almost every night from the number of tracks they leave behind them. But I've never seen one here in the flesh.'

Maurice had. One night he and the children had seen, in the headlights of the car, the ant-bear that lived above the house and whose tracks we saw every day on the farm road, if we cared to look. It had appeared like a pale plump ghost in the circle of light, and for the children it had been the event of the year.

We know the ant-bear – this purely African creature – with its stout, pig-like body, its kangaroo-like tail, its elongated snout and large dark eyes, usually only from museums. There can be very few who have seen it at work licking up termites with its long sticky tongue which, it is said, it can stretch out a full eighteen inches. This is as well, for it is a great creature and its fatty flesh a delicacy, so that it has always been hunted by Bantu and Hottentot, and probably by the Bushmen too. It owes its survival to its nocturnal habits, its flair for evading traps, its keen hearing, and above all to its digging powers.

They are, in sober fact, fantastic. When in danger an ant-bear always starts to dig and it is then usually impossible to stop. Shortridge claimed that nothing less powerful than a lion-trap would hold it, and it is said that at least four oxen are needed to pull a digging ant-bear out of its hole.

Our day had a perfect ending. When we got back there was old Mr Landman and if we were full of ant-bear stories, so was he. He told us of a native herdsman who, seeing an ant-bear on the veld, tied a rope round its hind legs and the other round his waist, presumably to halt it until someone arrived to help him kill it. That night the farmer waited in vain for his cattle to return, and next morning he went out to look for them. He found them: and also the dead body of the herdsman wedged into the ant-bear burrow. He had apparently been unable to cut the rope that joined him to the animal and had died frightfully in the hole.

It was true, said Landman soberly, and we thought it could be.

He talked on and on and we listened with delight as he told us his version of the famous story of the man who tied an ant-bear to his horse's tail. He caught it, said Landman with appropriate action, in the veld near Pearston. The animal began immediately to dig and the man was soon exhausted by trying to keep it above ground. Finally he tied a riem round the ant-bear's hindquarters and, fastening the other end to the long tail of his horse, he hastened to find help. On returning he found the horse was sitting erect upon the ground, its bottom filling the mouth of the hole, its back legs straight out in front of it on the surface of the soil and its forelegs waving up and down.

'I don't know what happened to the ant-bear,' ended Landman, 'but the horse's tail was never the same again.'

Perhaps one day we shall see Gerald Durrell hunting a Karoo ant-bear for a modern zoo. Then indeed Landman should have material for a great new epic.

11. Cranemere's Bird

It is the blue crane, *Tetrapteryx paradisea,* that remains above all others Cranemere's bird.

Fanny, when she gave its name to her home, thought it a bird of distinction – and so had the Bushmen before her. They believed it to be 'a person of an early race', and this showed the most perceptive imagination, for among all the birds they knew this one alone has a ghostly elegance not wholly bird.

See its smoky feathers and smooth proud lines merging with the dim waters it loves by night and it is not real at all: a bird or a spirit or a branch in the night air – it could be all or none until it moves and the air is filled with clamour.

Scientists know cranes as a very old group of birds. Some of the species are almost extinct; others, it is feared, on their way to extinction. Oliver L. Austin in his *Birds of the World* says they are nowhere common except in some Buddhist countries where they are protected by religious beliefs. But Austin cannot have known the blue cranes of the Karoo and other high places of South Africa.

Here, then, is one of their last strongholds; and in all this crane-filled land I do not believe that such vast numbers were ever found in one spot as they are about Cranemere dam. Forty or more years ago, when this was the only big stretch of water in the Plains of Camdeboo and one of the largest in the whole Karoo, water-birds flocked to it from far away, and in particular the cranes. By day these spread out over the whole countryside, but at dusk they returned to the water, and as the light began to fade the first troops would appear, black against the darkening sky.

They did not come by the hundred but by the thousand, and standing on the wall of the dam at sunset and gazing upwards into a sky part luminous and part filled with shadow, we sometimes had the feeling that the very sky was moving as we looked.

The birds flew sometimes in small groups, but mostly in great troops in V-formation one behind the other, their elongated necks and their long legs stretched out in one thin line and their wings a black moving bar, each wing-beat seeming slow but carrying the birds swiftly by us.

We counted thousands of birds of an evening although we never saw but a tenth of them. But those troops we saw we learned to know, for they apparently kept to the same company and the individual flocks would number the same night by night.

As the sun sank the first cries of the cranes would be heard miles distant, until gradually the whole dark world was roaring with them. It is a sound familiar to every Karoo-born, harsh, strong and rich, and an evening filled with these wild cries is splendid and unforgettable.

When George and Fanny first saw the farm the cranes were there in even greater numbers, and of a night they made a huge solid band of birds the far side of the dam. They were wonderful guards. All through the Anglo-Boer War when scattered forces of Boers and British troops roved the countryside, alike commandeering food, horses, and sometimes other things that took their fancy, the cranes gave warning. A great burst of angry crane cries from the water, and every person on Cranemere sprang from bed to hide his valuables.

The cranes, my father used to say, never returned in such fantastic numbers after the great drought at the beginning of the century. Today they come only by the score, but this, oddly enough, is not because of drought but because of abundance of water. There are now dams throughout the Karoo, and each draws its flocks of cranes so that they are widely dispersed. But in drought time they always come back to Cranemere, for here the dam often holds water longer than those round about.

The birds sleep knee-deep in the water, standing upon one leg. They must have considerable stamina for the water sometimes freezes around them! On such nights they always call more loudly, complaining – Sita is sure – of their discomforts.

What is probably the first account of the blue crane was that of Kolben two hundred years ago. He had noted the crane's habit of roosting upon one leg and his imagination had seized on this. Cranes, he stated categorically, planted sentries while they slept; these stood upon their left legs and each one held up in the right claw a stone, so that if they should be overcome by sleep the falling of the stone, and the consequent splash, would awake them to their duties.

By day the cranes usually take to the veld and we see them, sometimes in numbers, sometimes in couples or family groups, the young ones without the drooping plumes of the adults, hunting for insects and roots among the Karoo bushes. Sometimes they may be found in the lands pecking out the germinating plants – when they cease abruptly to be birds of grace.

They lay their large brown eggs on the ground in the open veld, and these, blotched with darker brown or purple, are very difficult to see. The chicks are guarded carefully by the parents which, like the ostrich, will feign an injury to lead an enemy away from their young. I have seen a crane, drooping one wing upon the ground, run within a few feet of me to divert me from my course too near its chicks.

Our blue crane is also known as the Stanley crane. It belongs only to South Africa, although it resembles its northern relations in its graceful form and movements. I think in outline it is the most beautiful bird in Southern Africa, from its smooth elegant head to its long dark drooping plumes, and its colour – like the smoke from a wood fire – is exquisite. The crown of its head is white and the Bleeks recorded that the Bushmen, who loved to paint it, thought the head was stone-shaped and that every blue crane sang a song about it:

> 'A splinter which is white,
> A splinter which is white,
> A splinter which is white,'

and as it walked slowly away in a 'walk of peace' it sang,

> 'A white stone splinter,
> A white stone splinter.'

To the Xhosa people it was a proud bird, a warrior's bird. They commonly called it *inDwe*, but it was also once known by a name meaning 'the bird revered by the maidens'. Its plumes were held in great honour and were worn on special occasions only, when a chief's daughter came to woman's estate, or as emblems of bravery worn by tried warriors in time of war. It was deemed unworthy for a warrior bearing blue crane feathers in his headband to fight another who had not this badge of seasoned skill, and today when I pick up a feather near the water I think of it as one of the great heroic emblems.

Very little has ever been written about what is one of the strangest and most beautiful performances of any bird: the dancing of the cranes. There are seasoned ornithologists who have never seen it, yet every one of us on Cranemere must have watched it scores of times. Out on the veld, often in the early morning or towards evening, the cranes assemble, not from far and wide but apparently only in their own troops, and they join together in a dance.

It has an oddly human quality about it – and perhaps this is why some ornithologists have found it comic; but comedy is notably absent. Among a big flock of birds it is a grave, dignified and beautiful performance, danced by each individual bird with grace and solemnity. The dancing varies. The birds usually face one another, sometimes in a rough circle, sometimes in a long line or lines, and they often appear to dance in couples, probably a male and a female for the one is usually bigger than the other. One rises slightly off the ground, opening and fanning its wings, and the other bends its head in a bow, both moving with dancing steps and, some observers maintain, with rhythm. Often as a child, out on horseback in the very early summer morning, I would see a great flock of cranes dancing, themselves the colour of the pearly sky, and would rein in my pony and watch, for this is something one can see with delight a thousand times.

Cranes are said to dance only in courting time, but in fact they dance throughout the year. At midday one winter day Sita and I watched them dance, and we have seen them at all times of the day during every calendar month. In captivity they are said to dance even by themselves; so it seems that although it may be a courting rite, they dance also for pleasure.

The crane upon the five-cent coin is a Cranemere bird. Dick Findlay, who did the design, sketched it upon the farm, so our cranes are now shared by all South Africa.

In the early dawn before the veld birds are awake we are sometimes roused by the water-birds, and even louder than the cranes are the wild geese. We lie in bed before the farm noises have begun and listen to a clamour rising to a crescendo of noise, with sometimes the hooting of an owl in the foreground – sounds of the Karoo from immemorial times. And immemorial they are. These water-birds are of an ancient lineage; the Bushman in his cave, the Stone Age Man of Honey Mountain, listened at dawn to such cries as these, and millions upon millions of years before them lived the ancestors of crane, heron, duck, goose and ibis. The pelican that sometimes visits Cranemere dam is much the same as the one whose fossil bones date back forty million years. I know of little that so reduces vanity and fear as to lie in the first dawn listening to the water-birds and thinking of these things.

Our wild geese are the Egyptian geese, or the Nile geese, which once figured on monuments of ancient Egypt four thousand miles away. They are biggish, handsome birds, white, chestnut, grey and black, touched with metallic green and purple, but we seldom get close enough to see them in detail for they are shy. Once as a child I tied a large ragged bush upon my head and, swimming very carefully and quietly, peering through the trailing leaves, I swam into the midst of a family party on the dam. It is the only time I have ever seen wild geese face to face, and I still remember the alarm and fury their round eyes registered before they took off with angry squawks.

Ornithologists have for long been puzzled over the nesting habits of our geese. Every farm boy on the Karoo, however, knows them as the most adaptable birds possible, making do with what they can get, for when their favourite nesting-spots – rocky ledges, hollow trees, thick rushes – are absent, as they so often are on the Karoo, they nest perfectly happily in the thorn trees around the dams. Once Maurice found a nest on the top of a tall aloe. But their favourite nesting-place in the bare Karoo is a triumph of common sense: it is not above ground but below, in an ant-bear burrow. Shelduck nest in holes, but the fact that our geese do too is little known. One professional ornithologist refused to credit it, maintaining that a bird would never so depart from its normal habits. But what indeed is normal? Sita, collecting facts from the farmers around, found one who confessed that until he was a grown man he did not know that geese *ever* nested elsewhere but in holes in the ground. Rob Rafferty, our old manager, confirmed this nesting habit.

'Have you ever dug out a nest?' asked Sita, putting the question science would pose.

Rob answered crossly, 'What for, man? If you *see* the spoor of the geese and chicks coming out of an ant-bear hole and going back, and then you *see* the geese and chicks going in and out, you mean you don't believe it?' And his moustache quivered. Science! Bah!

The ancient Greeks might have noted that these geese nested in burrows. They called them 'fox geese', surely because of their nesting habits.

Shelduck, well-known for making their nests in holes, often choose ant-bear burrows. It is recorded that a farmer, Gurth Edelston, opening up an earth out of which his shepherd had seen a shelduck emerge, found – twenty-seven feet away from the opening of the hole – a beautiful nest of down containing ten white eggs. It took many hours of work to reach the nest, and it must have been a dramatic moment when he found the eggs by the light of a torch. The story gave me a new respect for the shelduck – and for the ant-bear.

Shelduck frequent the dams on Cranemere. I long to see the newly-hatched young carried down to the water on the backs of the females. This improbable story is supposed to be true, and I like to think it is.

There are no indigenous swans in South Africa but two birds destined for Cranemere dam have become a legend in the Eastern Province. They were a pair of white swans which were sent to George Palmer many years ago from England. George had coveted a pair for years and was elated at the thought of seeing them sailing over Cranemere dam, but when their ship was passing the mouth of the Kromme River not far from Port Elizabeth the swans broke their cage and flew ashore.

The Palmers lamented them and for years heard no more of them, until a small flock of wild swans was reported on the Kromme River. Our elation knew no bounds. They could not, we were sure, be any but the descendants of the Cranemere swans.

There has, of course, been much general speculation about the origin of the birds, for they are a sight in an otherwise swanless countryside. Our version is possibly correct – at any rate the only certain thing in the whole swan story is that the Cranemere pair did once escape near here.

The swans have now been accepted into South African avifauna. According to Mr C. J. Skead, field officer for the Percy FitzPatrick Institute of African Ornithology, there are now over sixty birds on the Kromme and neighbouring rivers. 'So you see,' says he, 'what happens when a cage breaks open.'

Often we see grey herons standing motionless for hours in the dam, or rising with slow, deep, flapping movements to fly away, their necks drawn back in an 'S' and their legs trailing away behind them.

One of these herons caused a Cranemere drama. Sita had a fine new hen-house below her garden and was reaping the benefit in scores of eggs. Suddenly these began to disappear at the rate of twenty or more a day, and finally eight small chickens as well were taken in a few hours. The hens would always give the alarm and at their wild squawking everyone would drop tools and rush for the hen-house, but always too late. The eggs were gone and not a fragment of shell or a paw-print in the dust remained to tell of the culprit.

The thief grew not only bolder but more cunning. It learned to wait for the farm bell to ring for meals and the garden to empty before making a raid.

The family was sitting at breakfast one morning when pandemonium broke out. It was the gardener having hysterics.

'*Reier, reier* – heron, heron,' he screeched. 'Come, come, it's swallowing the eggs, it's eating the chickens.'

And it was. For once it had misjudged its time and had a witness to its felony. It saw the family streaming towards it and gobbled wildly. Down its throat went one egg, then another, and another, and with yet one more in its beak it flew off beyond the range of a gun, swallowing this one too as it went. It was Sita's first rogue heron, but probably not her last.

Recently a large number of white storks, famous and legendary birds, assembled on the far side of the dam, and they came, as far as we knew, from Europe for a ringed bird found north of us at Cradock had travelled from Rumania, and two at Colesberg had come from Germany and Poland. They took off again on an autumn day, presumably for the chimneystacks and farm roofs of their northern homes.

The sacred ibis is a rare visitor to Cranemere, occasionally seen flying across the farm, presumbly from river to river and halting at the dam – another touch of ancient Egypt in our land. Several times pelicans have appeared and it is easy, looking at their strange outline, to believe they are survivors from another age. Sometimes small parties of spoonbills appear, purest white with great red flattened bills. They keep to the far end of the dam where they wade with half-open bills, swinging their heads from side to side in great sweeping motions. They are often seen and always an interest.

The most beautiful of the water-birds to Sita are the avocets. They often come flying over the dam in flocks of twenty to thirty with a swift streaming flight, wheeling and turning back with the whistling cry of sea-birds. Last spring there were over two hundred. They waded on long legs in the shallow water, their black-and-white plumage incredibly brilliant, their thin, immaculately chiselled, recurved beaks giving them an air of delicate curiosity. We watched them for hours on end.

To me the most fascinating visitors of all are the flamingoes. The first that I know of to visit Cranemere arrived some twenty years ago. From across the dam I one day saw three white birds, with incredibly long legs and necks, at the edge of the water. They were too far to distinguish clearly, but I was certain they were foreign and at evening I determined to see them closely. The nearer I approached, the more curious I grew. My dog was with me and suddenly he bounded forward and the birds rose, showing their splendid crimson wings. These have been likened to pink roses or cyclamen buds or rosy clouds, but I could compare them with nothing for I had seen nothing to match them. I still remember the scene: the water with its first touch of evening colour, the big black Newfoundland dog, and the astonishing black and white and crimson brilliance of the birds.

Since then they have – to Maurice and Sita's great pleasure – become regular visitors to the dam. They have never bred here; indeed, it is only recently that they have been known to breed anywhere in South Africa, and when a few years ago the raised, oddly-shaped mud nests of the greater flamingo were found near Bredasdorp in the south, ornithologists were jubilant.

They only come to Cranemere when the dam is low. They never venture far in, but move along the edge of the water, feeding steadily, curving their long necks and dipping their heads below the water in a half circle so that the tops of their bills are bottom-most, and in this extraordinary posture they strain up the rich brew of dam water. We look at them and marvel that anything so immaculately elegant could live on mud!

But how do they know when the water becomes shallow? They never visit Cranemere when the dam is full but always when the water shrinks. To Sita this is a flamingo mystery. Perhaps they fly for miles to inspect the water and when it is low pass on the news to one another.

Sometimes the big white-breasted cormorants and the coots

come to the dam. The long-legged waders with their piping calls are here too in numbers. The little plovers, native to South Africa, scurrying among the stones at the edge of the water, are pretty, gay little creatures, and their tiny speckled chicks a marvellous example of natural camouflage. Their eggs, too, laid on the bare ground among the stones, are invisible. Once I used to play a game with myself. After a swim I would lie quietly sunning myself among the stones at the edge of the dam: if I saw nothing I had lost the game, but if my eyes at length picked out chicks or eggs I had won. It was surprising how often I won.

Sometimes our plovers are joined by the waders from the northern hemisphere, and it is a fascinating sight to see a little stint, bred perhaps in the Arctic, or a greenshank or curlew, hobnobbing with the Karoo birds around our hot brown water.

For many years a pair of *hamerkoppe* or hammerheads lived near a pool beyond Cranemere gates, a weird couple with their brown plumage lit with purple gloss, and their thick crests streaming backwards giving them the look of always facing a high wind. Sometimes we would see them dancing together and would smile at their ungainliness, but at dusk nobody smiled at the hamerkops, for they were then always faintly sinister.

Once I saw one of them kill a snake by seizing it by its neck, flying upwards with it, and dropping it upon the cement-hard ground.

They nested near by in a tree and their home was a sight – a gigantic rubbish-heap of bones, old clothing, grass, reeds, twigs, stuck together with mud and of remarkable strength.

We never saw the hamerkop in numbers. I do not think that anybody ever does. Yet in spite of this it is one of the best-known birds, not only of the Karoo but of Africa, for it attaches itself to a particular pool or stream where it may be seen, as the years go by, hunting for frogs and tadpoles and, say some Xhosas, admiring its reflection in the water. 'You are a hamerkop,' one Xhosa says with derision to another who is preening himself before a looking-glass.

In parts it is held to be a rain bird foretelling rain by its cry and therefore seldom harmed, and to have magical powers which it stores in its crest. Long ago it was a special bird for the Bushmen, foretelling death when it flew over them. 'It comes to tell us our person is dead,' they grieved.

When I was a child I thought it was related to a witch. Today I would never willingly kill any bird: and never, never would I kill a hamerkop, stocky, strong, dark and still, beside its glimmering pool.

12. Birds of the Veld

One winter morning I walked down to the big garden below the house. As I passed the stable a dull-coloured little sparrow flew out of a swallow's nest built against the eaves. It was a true English house sparrow. This most forward little bird, introduced at East London more than thirty years ago, has pushed and pushed its way southwards and inland ever since until here it is on Cranemere, occupying the traditional homes of the swallows, ousting our own Cape sparrows from their old territory about the house, and stealing the dogs' food – flying down and pecking their bread from between their paws.

In the garden, however, our own sparrows – bright, friendly, noisy and established friends – flew and twittered in numbers, and I was glad to see them. I looked about and thought how rich this corner of the garden was in birds, even in midwinter. Freddie the gardener was leading water, and a little egret, sparkling white, standing beside a bed of cabbages, was reflected in the slowly spreading pool between them.

Innumerable wagtails bobbed about and I saw the long tails of several mousebirds as they flew about a tree. A three-banded plover was paddling in the furrow, there was a band of starlings, and the thorn trees were full of laughing doves: a pied barbet was eating berries in the kruisbessie bush near by, and a pair of brown-hooded kingfishers flew past showing their brilliant tail and wing feathers.

In the summer I knew that the whole garden would be alive with bird movement, colour and sound. One summer some years ago our friend Reg Doe, who is a noted amateur ornithologist, spent a weekend on Cranemere. In less than two days he counted seventy-five different species of bird within a few hundred yards of the house and along one farm road, and these were only a part of the bird life upon the farm.

Here soon would be shrikes in numbers, the yellow, green and black bokmakierie with its clear, melodious calls, and that shocking little cannibal, the butcher bird or fiscal shrike. '*Xa, xa, xa! Mxhome, mxhome* – Ha, ha, ha! Pin him up! Pin him up!' the Xhosas say he chuckles. I guessed that his larder would be spiked on the long white thorns of the sweet-thorn trees around. Here would be weaver birds, and seed-eaters, and pigeons and doves of various kinds, and dozens of other species, and the air would be filled with the calls of the turtle doves which to Cranemere people are the sound of summer.

Here would be red bishop birds in summer plumage, the grenadier of Barrow, or as the French once called them, the cardinals of the Cape of Good Hope. Picking fruit in the garden one summer, Sita saw a bird like a jewel sail past her. She stopped in delight: it was a red bishop bird, black and glowing scarlet, on its way to the reeds with its drab-coloured harem. It marked the day for Sita. For months she remembered it as the day of the first bishop bird.

The male malachite sunbirds would be flashing their astonishing green and gold – colours, I have always thought, more fitted to tropical lushness than to our arid plains, but in our setting they are perhaps more splendid still. With their colour, neatness, and elegant, long, curved beaks, they are some of the most beautiful birds in the world and it seems singularly appropriate that they should live mainly on nectar. That the other half of their diet should be spiders gives them a robust Jekyll-and-Hyde quality which I find very pleasing.

Seventy years ago, my father used to say, these were not the only sunbirds here; other species also frequented the flowers. As a boy, he went riding one spring day in the veld and, feeling the sun hot, he dismounted, hitched his horse to a branch, and lay down under an old boerboon tree covered in flowers. As he slept he dreamed he heard the cries of countless birds. He opened his eyes slowly and found he was not dreaming but awake, and that the tree above was alive with sound and colour, for over the mantle of red nectar-filled blossom hovered sunbirds by the hundred, green and scarlet and orange with blue and golden lights, flashing and glowing in the sun. It was a sight he talked of all his life.

Above all else on Cranemere there would be swallows. Swallows are beloved. It seems that mankind is truly sentimental about these birds alone and offers them a respect and protection it grants to no others. Here on the Plains of Camdeboo they are literally a part of our lives, and if the peasant farmers in various parts of the world nail shelves for them below the eaves of their roofs, so do the farmers of the Plains. Barrow, travelling here nearly two centuries ago, remarked that here the farmers nailed small shelves against the beams of their houses to help the swallows nest in comfort. Today the swallows still nest in colonies on these same farms, packing their mud nests close together under the eaves of a building, and sometimes covering the whole wall as if with a great honeycomb.

We have noted at least four different species of swallow on Cranemere, not counting their relations the rock martins, but it is the cliff swallow that covers the stable walls with these round, tightly packed nests that we know the best, either shooting through the air like a long dark bullet touched with blue or clinging to the entrance to its nest.

Unlike the martins which stay throughout the year, these swallows are migrants, wintering, it is believed, in the southern Congo and returning to South Africa in the spring. Barrow thought they returned to the same place for many years and generally on the same day, while some have gone further, maintaining that the swallows return not only to the old locality but to their former nests. Sita has noticed that on Cranemere the swallows sometimes arrive back on Maurice's birthday, September 21, whether to their old nest or not nobody knows.

Every spring this ancient mystery of how and why and whence is enacted again on Cranemere in the gleaming bodies, not six inches long, not one ounce in weight. 'The swallows are back,' say the children and they know that before them for many months stretch shimmering heat, earth too hot for bare feet, evenings when the brown waters lie cooling and the air is filled with swallows, and nights when the south-easters howl across the plains and the big red spiders streak out of the darkness towards the bright house-lights. There is hardly anything so evocative as the coming of the swallows.

Even here, where no human hurts a swallow, they do not find complete sanctuary, for Karoo weather, which they fly across half Africa to find, can be a bitter enemy. One hot summer when the nests were filled with twittering young, a snow storm swept across the mountains and a piercing wind shrieked round the buildings, whipping nests from walls and flinging fledglings and adults to the ground. My father was out all night frantically collecting the birds. He brought them in by the hundred, frozen and apparently lifeless, and laid them in tiers around the kitchen until every shelf, every table and chair and corner of the stove was covered with swallows; and he set the farm to catching flies for them. Many of the birds lived. The servants still remember it. 'The Christmas when the Seur warmed the swallows,' they say.

These are the birds around the house and gardens that we see. But there are birds that – like the animals – escape our notice, and these are the birds of the open veld that tend to merge into their sober background. In drought time many of them vanish altogether, unlike the water-birds that then come in numbers to the dam. Like the bees, they simply disappear, perhaps to the mountains to the north, leaving as a rule no dead but returning to the plains when the rains fall, full of life and familiar song.

Even in good seasons strangers find it difficult to see many of these birds, for their natural camouflage is perfect. I am sure that most people who watch the veld birds are struck by this camouflage, for although now and then they may see a glint of colour – a brilliant Didrik cuckoo or Klaas's cuckoo, a male weaver in summer plumage of black and yellow, the sunbirds or bishop birds – they are glimpses only. Even the ostriches become part of the karoo bush, and I have often marvelled that birds as enormous as these should be so hard to see. By day the drab-coloured hen, sitting on her nest – no more than a bare depression in the veld – is almost impossible to detect, and when she lays her neck flat upon the ground, she is invisible. So, too, the cock, sitting upon the eggs at night, is one with the darkness.

For a long time as a child I never thought of the ostriches as birds, and they are indeed most un-birdlike. Years later I was gratified to discover that Aristotle had considered the ostrich part bird, part quadruped. He was not the first, nor indeed the last, to think it was partly mammal, a link, in fact, between birds and mammals. But it takes a modern scientist to relate it to a dinosaur.

Today many scientists believe that birds and dinosaurs had a common ancestor and that birds' feathers are simply modified reptilian scales. When I look at the leg of an ostrich this does not seem fanciful at all, and I can readily believe those who claim that the hind leg of a carnivorous dinosaur was much like this huge primitive limb covered with lizard-like skin. Nor could the dinosaur have looked much stranger than a cock ostrich, eight feet tall and weighing perhaps several hundredweight, with its big feathered body and its elongated neck, topped with a mean little head, pale-eyed, with ridiculous filmstar lashes, and long raking legs ending in frightful two-toed, two-clawed feet.

Ostriches originally ran wild over most of South Africa, including the Karoo. Van Riebeeck knew them. Several times tame ostriches were sent from the Cape to the Indies as unusual gifts for Eastern potentates. Van Riebeeck, in fact, suggested the taming of ostriches, merely as useful gifts. No Europeans in Africa, apparently, then thought their feathers of much value. The main use for these seemed to be to brush away flies; and slaves armed with ostrich feathers stood at the tables throughout the Colony and drove away flies at meals.

Some of the native peoples seem to have prized feathers for the most unexpected reasons – lions feared them and cattle could be taught to respect them. Herdsmen taught their cattle to feed and lie down around a 'plume' containing a number of ostrich feathers. They would plant the 'plume' in the ground and depart, knowing that the cattle would not move far from the feathers which they regarded 'as the herdsman's representative'. A great many feathers were used to make such a 'plume' and its value was considered equal to that of an ox.

It is not certain who was the first man to guess that ostrich feathers could make a fortune. One of the first was a Karoo farmer by the name of Booysen. He caught wild ostrich chicks on the veld not far from Cranemere and bred from them, and the first truly domesticated ostrich chicks hatched out two years later.

What a thing he set in motion! Soon ostrich feathers were selling for £100 a pound. Eighteen years after he had caught his first wild chicks George and Fanny Palmer were paying £190 for one pair of ostriches – a big sum in 1880 – and I note with amusement from the old Cash and Day Book that they bought the birds six months before they bought themselves any bedroom furniture, for which they paid altogether £21 12s. 6d.

Ostriches were naturally the most important birds that Cranemere has ever known and the farm activities centred round them for years. We never knew this period, for the feather boom had ended before we were born and my father kept ostriches mainly in the hope that such times would return. They never have, although the feathers have always been regularly clipped.

In the old days the incubator room, where the eggs were artificially hatched, was the hub of the farm. My father loved to tell the story of the day the incubator broke down just as a batch of eggs from selected birds had been laid, and the farm was thrown into turmoil.

'Do you want a fine holiday?' he said to the young manager. 'All you have to do is to go to bed with the eggs – and hatch 'em.'

The youth obliged. He climbed into bed and twenty-one eggs were packed around him.

He hatched all twenty-one.

We grew up with batches of young ostrich chicks and only in their extreme youth did we find them pleasing, and then only to the eye, for they were spiky to the touch and an acute anxiety to their guardians since at this stage they died with celerity and ease. Pretty in infancy, they were horrible in adolescence. Then they would peck their ungainly way round the farmyard, swallowing everything possible – litter, stones, bottles, fowls, kittens. The only really attractive thing about them then were their swallows, which we would watch with passionate interest descending down the length of their necks.

Out on the veld the chicks can be delightful. They are born with a ready-made escape mechanism – immobility. When an enemy is near they will scatter and squat upon the ground. Often on horseback we have searched for them, having seen a flurry of movement and then nothing, and sometimes when we were lucky we saw them, little mottled feathery forms squatting immobile among the bushes, sometimes with their necks stretched out along the ground. At such times we felt a warmth even for the parents, often enough pretending an injury, falling and fluttering, feigning a broken leg or wing, to lead us away from the chicks; or one parent dancing and hissing and ruffling its feathers while the other attempted to hustle the chicks away.

A really vicious ostrich is a horrifying opponent. Those immense dinosaur legs kick with ferocious power, sending a man spinning, and the clawed feet rip flesh from bones with ease. Sometimes an ostrich will kneel and roll upon a prostrate body, scrunching the bones as it does so. One old lady in the district had all her ribs broken by an ostrich but yet survived.

On Cranemere the dangers of an angry ostrich were bred into our bones. One bitter winter day, when the mountains were coated with snow and an ice-laden wind streamed across the plains, my mother and a friend set out to warm their blood with a quick walk across the veld. Not half a mile away they heard, between them and the safety of a clump of trees, the pounding of feet on the ice-hard earth, and saw a great cock ostrich, black and white with flaring red legs, charging down upon them.

'Run,' screamed my mother, 'run!' And they ran. Their only safety lay before them, the icy waters of the dam, and into this they plunged, cowering up to their waists behind an old thorn tree that the water had encircled. My mother's companion had a weak heart, and my mother, supporting her, watched her face turn blue.

They screamed, but no one heard save the cock ostrich marching up and down on the shore. My mother strained her eyes towards the homestead. The nursemaid was due to bring me, then an infant, to meet her on her walk. She shuddered.

My father, returning from a shoot, saw across the dam an odd sight. It was too far to see accurately and as he drew nearer he became puzzled. Then the figures became clear, the human and the ostrich; and he raced towards the house, throwing out children, bellowing for brandy and hot-water bottles. He roared towards the dam and the ostrich, but so angry was he that he could not shoot the bird – every shot was wide. The two women, in a state of collapse, were rescued. They had a life-and-death story to tell for the rest of their lives; and for many years the 'ostrich' tree which had saved my mother was shown to all comers with pride. It disintegrated only a few years ago.

Our ostriches seldom attack anyone on horseback, but when I was a child they could fill my ride with terror. Some cocks, obviously longing for our blood but too nervous to close in, would drop a few yards behind the horses and keep this distance, stopping only to 'roll', when they dropped upon their knees, opened and swung their wings with their long necks and heads swinging and their feathers on end, hissing viciously. On these memorable rides I was always torn with doubt as to whether it was better to turn my face, or conventionally my back, upon the bird. It was a harrowing choice.

Our traditional weapon against such an ostrich was a branch of the common thorn tree, for the birds knew the long straight white thorns like miniature swords and usually kept their distance from them.

I have never tried but I am told that it is quite useless hitting an ostrich on its body: it simply does not feel a blow at all. Its breastbone is tremendously thick and strong, making, in effect, a sort of live battering-ram. Cronwright-Schreiner, who wrote of the migrating springbuck, once saw an eighteen-month-old chick run against a two-foot-thick stone wall and break a gap through it, without the slightest harm to itself, and an adult ostrich snap a thick pole of sneezewood, one of the toughest woods in Africa. A guard on a goods train once told him that a cock had charged his train. It saw the train rattling towards it down a steep hill and sprang fearlessly to fight the monster. This seems one of the few occasions when an ostrich had the worst of the battle.

Not many Europeans relish ostrich meat or biltong, but the soft yellow fat was – and probably in parts still is – prized for soap, guns and saddles. I do not know if any South Africans have ever eaten ostrich brains but the Romans did. Heliogabalus, Roman emperor and notorious glutton, had six hundred ostrich brains served to him at a single meal!

We have all of us, however, enjoyed the eggs, and I know of no more epicurean breakfast than a slice of hard-boiled ostrich egg mashed with butter, pepper and salt, and eaten piping hot with fresh farm bread. An egg is supposed to be equal to about twenty-four fowls' eggs, and its takes just under an hour to be boiled hard. The Hottentots used to scramble the egg in its shell, placing it in hot ashes and stirring the contents with a stick through a small hole in the shell. This is a foolproof method which survives today.

Robbing an ostrich nest in the veld is not always easy, for a cock defending its nest can be a terrifying antagonist. I have often seen a cock advancing with fury to guard its nest, and remember the thrill of fear it caused us as children; and the astonishment at finding that its belligerence would cease abruptly as we reached its nest. It would sooner see the eggs removed than indulge in a rough-house near these precious objects.

Today the ostriches on Cranemere are little more than ornaments. In the long past, however, they must have been an integral part of the lives of the people who lived here. In the Mountain Dig we found quantities of ostrich egg-shell among the animal bones. Our Middle Stone Age Man had probably eaten both eggs and flesh. We know that the Bushmen did this and more. They used ostrich feathers as a hunting disguise, holding before them a stick to imitate an ostrich neck, and this may be seen in many rock paintings, including the paintings in the mountain above Cranemere.

They used the breastbone as a dish, and from the egg-shell they made the most beautiful beads, symmetrical and shining, which they used in girdles and ornaments. The making of these beads is now known as one of the very old Bushman crafts.

One of the great Bushman stories was of an ostrich. It was a tale of rebirth and was told thus to William Bleek and his sister-in-law Lucy, who recorded it in *Bushman Folklore*.

A Bushman killed an ostrich.

'A little whirlwind comes to them: it blows up the ostrich feathers. A little ostrich feather that has blood upon it, it blows up, the little feather, into the sky. The little feather falls down out of the sky, it having whirled round falls down, it goes into the water, it becomes wet in the water, it is conscious, it lies in the water, it becomes ostrich flesh; it gets feathers, it puts on its wings, it gets its legs, while it lies in the water.

'It walks out of the water, it basks in the sun upon the water's edge, because it is still a young ostrich. Its feathers are young feathers. They are black; for a little male ostrich it is. He dries his feathers lying upon the water's bank . . .

'While he walks strengthening his feet, he lies down, he hardens his breast, that his breastbone may become bone. He walks away, he eats young bushes because a young ostrich he is . . . His little feather it was which became the ostrich, it was that the wind blew up, while the wind was a little whirlwind.'

And he grew larger still and stronger, to return at last with glory, roaring mightily, to his wives.

The Bushmen painted very few birds. The ostrich and the blue crane are exceptions and their likenesses appear in many rock shelters. Perhaps this is not merely because they were both common birds but because they had a special meaning in the life of the Bushmen – the crane as a member of the 'early race', the ostrich as a creature of flesh and blood which could die and yet be reborn.

If the ostrich is the mightiest bird of the veld, the handsomest must surely be the secretary bird, standing over four feet high and striding about on its long legs in its dark feathered pantaloons, with orange cheeks and eagle's bill, its light grey plumage shining white in the sun. Even these contrasting colours are not easily seen and, as with other birds of prey, it is movement that most often reveals its presence.

Its gait reminded early ornithologists of a bowman about to shoot his arrows and so they named it the Archer (Sagittarius), while its crest of long feathers standing out at the back of its head looked like the quill pens that clerks once stuck behind their ears, and gave it its common name of secretary bird.

This purely African bird was once a source of delighted speculation to early scientists. Nearly two hundred years ago one was sent from the Cape to the Prince of Orange, and created a furore for no one could decide for sure what it was. Sparrman, watching one on the African veld, thought it was part eagle and part crane, and he was nearly right for it is now known to be related to vultures or eagles. Dr Leonard Gill, a modern ornithologist, calls it 'a sort of long-legged marching eagle'.

It has a tremendous reputation as a killer of snakes. Le Vaillant called it the Serpent Eater and was full of rather naïve praise for it. We have several times on Cranemere watched a secretary bird killing a snake, a tremendous sight with its wings spread like a great dark shield and its strong clawed feet striking viciously. At such a moment it is one of the most formidable sights of the Karoo.

Snakes are not its only diet. It devours small animals, tortoises, and insects of all kinds, and it has its own recognized hunting-grounds, a pair of these birds driving off all intruders with fury.

A few years ago a pair of secretary birds built a huge nest right

196

on top of a thorn tree near Honey Mountain. Bertram Allan, the manager, climbed up a bank to look down on the nest and found it an impressive sight, almost five feet across. Nobody saw the eggs hatch, or the chicks feeding, thrusting their beaks into their parents' open bills for the regurgitated food, but this would be a sight worth patient planning to see.

A relation of the secretary bird sometimes visits Cranemere. It is the Cape vulture, with its massive body, predatory beak, and long naked blue neck. In the air, sailing on those tremendous wings, it is a magnificent sight.

My father remembered seeing it often as a boy, but it had last made an appearance in 1905. Maurice has never seen it until it made a fearful reappearance forty-five years later. A shepherd, frantic with haste and panic, rushed in from the veld shouting that 'the big birds' were killing the sheep. Maurice seized his gun, leapt into the lorry, and raced for the spot. In the distance he saw a number of huge birds upon the ground, and as he fired they rose up sluggishly and flew heavily away. The veld for some thirty yards had been trampled bare as a board and was soaked with blood, and on it were lying sixteen dead and dying Persian ewes, some already only skeletons. They had been lambing and had been torn apart while still alive.

Some ornithologists of the time, who knew the vulture as a scavenger only, found this story difficult to credit. In the end however, they accepted evidence that under certain unusual circumstances vultures could kill. In the 1980s whether the Cape vulture kills or not is by the way – it is now a threatened species and is to be guarded and respected.

Nobody knew where the vultures had come from or where they went, but they have often reappeared since then in the lambing season. We sometimes see their droppings in the veld, a brilliant white on the lichened rocks. Presumably they nest on some inaccessible rock ledge in the mountains to the north, but where they die is not known for nobody ever sees a dead body.

Many years ago a Karoo boy from Beaufort West, Alfred Jackson, found a vultures' cemetery, and he told the story in his book *Manna in the Desert*. Where, he had wondered as he roamed the veld, did the vultures go to die? There came to him the thought that when death was upon them they might return to their breeding-places, to perish on the same rocky ledge where they had hatched, their bodies falling to the foot of the precipices below. The ledge where the vultures bred in his countryside was white against the face of the rocks and could be seen from thirty miles away, but no one had ventured near for the base of the precipice was guarded by almost impenetrable scrub. Through this Jackson one day forced his way to burst upon a fantastic scene: the dead bodies and bones of generations of vultures, not by the score but by the hundred, piled along the base of the great rock.

Last winter we saw from the top of the mountain a black eagle circling above us on its long pointed wings, showing its jet-black plumage marked with brilliant white. There can be few sights so memorable as one of these birds soaring above the precipices and we watched an unsurpassed show of speed and power and rushing beauty. It seemed, as it soared and swooped, to be the fastest creature of the air, and indeed it is held to be the swiftest of all our eagles, the famed dassie-catcher. A pair of black eagles such as this will, it is said, devour up to four hundred dassies in a year – and this perhaps, will save its life.

Once all stock farmers in South Africa made war on every eagle to protect their lambs and kids. The black and martial and tawny eagles dwindled, and the lammergeyer vanished from our mountains; and as they went, in a great exuberant unthreatened burst of life, the animals they had preyed upon appeared. Rats, mice and other small animals flourished and grew fat. The dassies left the mountains and descended to the plains; and farmers in astonishment saw these little animals of the rocks for the first time in their cultivated lands. One Karoo farmer found them stripping the peach trees in his orchard and thought they were possessed.

They were not. They were celebrating the death of the eagles.

Gradually first one worried farmer and then another,

watching this 'new vermin' taking form and life, began to re-value the eagle and to protect it. As I watched the black eagle on Honey Mountain I thought of this and wished our fierce ally long life, good hunting (and few lambs).

We still probably have nine or ten species of eagle and hawk on Cranemere, although they are obvious only on the wing or in silhouette on a tree or pole. But one of the common sights in the countryside are the lesser kestrels or locust birds perched upon the telephone poles. They are some of the first birds I remember, little sentinels, I thought them, strung across the plains. These smallish bright chestnut birds have become a feature of the life of Pearston, for here every spring they arrive in numbers to take over certain trees as their summer homes. At dawn they are off, flying far and wide searching for insects, and we see them swooping over Cranemere or sometimes perching motionless along the roads.

Every evening they fly back to the village to their individual trees, but so like humans are they, says Maurice, that they never choose the large but lonely trees in the park but the trees in the main street, or some other equally companionable spot. Here they roost, to the townspeople's fury, with their raucous voices and their liberal droppings, until at the coming of autumn they take off, probably for northern Africa or southern Europe.

Cranemere has, often in numbers, what I think must be the heaviest of all flying birds. It is the Kori bustard, a dweller of the desert or semi-desert, a gigantic creature weighing up to fifty pounds or more, heavier than the great bustard of Eurasia which is usually held to be the heaviest bird of the air. It has a wing span of up to eight feet, and it stands nearly five feet high. When it springs into the air the sound of its beating wings is like the rising of a high wind.

It might be thought that because of its great size it would be seen easily among the low karoo bushes, but it is not. Its chest-nut-coloured back finely lined with black, its black head and black and white throat, are once again the colours of the veld. Like an elephant in low mopani country, it is an invisible giant.

Usually it is the movement of the long neck and patrician crested head that discloses it.

Its common name is the *gompou* – the gum pou – for it loves to eat the gum from thorn trees, and I have always thought this touching, like a giant with a taste for sweets.

In the Karoo it was once considered a sign of marksmanship if a man could shoot a pou through the head at a distance of 200 yards, but those days are past for the pous are now protected birds.

They are superlative eating, as every hunter knew – brown-breasted, white-legged. Fanny Palmer's pous, pot-roasted with home-cured bacon and herbs and a glass of brandy, are glorious memories. I have no doubt she dished one up for Cecil Rhodes.

Le Vaillant said that the pous made a noise like a toad, but on the whole we find them silent birds. They have, however, the noisiest possible relations, the korhaans. These, the black and the vaal (dun), rising up at the approach of any person with strong resounding cries of 'koork, koork', have always been a tribulation to hunters. These cries must be the commonest of our open veld, and in spite of their harshness, one of the loveliest.

Just as noisy are the guineafowl, 'the farmers' watchdogs'. These handsome black birds, speckled with white, have naked blue necks vaguely suggestive of a vulture, but they are far more agreeable characters. The bushy parts of Cranemere abound with them, and it is always a pleasure to watch them, round and rather garish, scuttling furiously among the thickets. They are easily domesticated, as the Greeks and Romans knew, and they can become very much part of a household. A tame guineafowl we saw recently on a nearby farm, brought up in company with the dogs, fancied itself a dog, too, demanding all their privileges and riding with them in the back of the farm lorry.

Sometimes, walking between Honey Mountain and the Rooikop, we disturb the partridges – the real partridge, the greywing, and the Namaqua partridge which is a sand-grouse – and occasionally we see quail. These fat little birds have all the glamour of great history, for their brethren fed the Children of Israel in the desert: 'And the Lord spake unto Moses saying ". . . At even ye shall eat flesh . . ." And it came to pass that at even the quails came up and covered the camp.'

Many of the small veld birds are undistinguished in appearance, such as the familiar chat and the pipits, or the little brown larks of the open country that lay their eggs upon the ground. These have been called the feathered policemen of the Karoo, for they keep the insect hordes in check. It is said that once these larks inhabited the Karoo in millions but that they have died off little by little through every drought. Nevertheless, we see and hear them often.

One of these larks, a little brown speckled bird, remains for me one of those extraordinarily sweet and clear-cut pictures that last perhaps a lifetime. It was a Cape clapper lark on a late spring day on Cranemere. It rose up from the ground, straight up like a bullet, almost too swift for the eye to follow in flight, until it hung far above me beating its wings with a far-away clapping in the empty sky, and falling to earth again with a single long-drawn-out 'pheeuw'.

Everyone on Cranemere with ears attuned to the sounds of birds knows the clapper lark. Sometimes on a still day its clapping wings may be heard when the bird itself is too far away to be seen, an unmistakable sound carrying for a great distance. Le Vaillant saw this lark on the Karoo and noted that for two hours on end it would rise up, flap its wings, drop down, and rise again.

One morning when we had risen with the dawn to reach the Dig a large owl flew down the river-bed before us like a big pale quiet ghost. We often see them at dusk in the veld or round the house, and their hooting is one of the common sounds of night. 'Hoo-hoo, hoo-hoo,' they call. All over the world since man began he has heard and interpreted this eerie cry. Do any other people hear in it a wife and husband bickering, I wonder? The male, say the Xhosa people, is moaning, 'The mouse is not getting up,' and the female hoots in reply, 'It's your fault, Jujuju, for you're sitting on it!' – a pretty piece of conjugal dialogue recounted by the Rev. Robert Godfrey in his *Bird-Lore of the Eastern Cape*.

Occasionally there appears on Cranemere after a good season a bird famous in Cape history. It is the wattled starling or locust bird, and apart from the honey-guide, it was probably more often described in early journals than any other bird in South Africa.

Ordinarily a rather insignificant buff-coloured bird with darker wings and tail and a pale abdomen and rump, the male sometimes and the female occasionally develops an extraordinary appearance: It loses the feathers on its face and the top of its head, a unique characteristic.

What made these birds unusual to the early naturalists was not their appearance, however, but their habits – the timing of their breeding, how they built their homes and caught their food, traditionally locusts, and the seemingly miraculous way they could materialize in numbers out of the blue in country where they had not been known for many years.

Barrow saw them nesting in the country north of Cranemere. He thought they were thrushes and marvelled that birds so small could build nests fit for 'the vultures that hovered around'. When he drew closer he saw that the nests he had thought so enormous consisted of 'a number of cells, each of which was a separate nest with a tube that led into it through the side. Of such cells each clump contained from six to twenty and one roof of interwoven twigs covered the whole.' But the starlings can do even better than this: they have been known to build thousands and thousands of nests together, covering hundreds of yards.

On Cranemere they always choose thorn trees in which to build their nests, large untidy affairs down the sides of which, and the trunks of the trees, pour streams of droppings. Sometimes the weight of their nests pulls the trees askew and the droppings burn off the foliage. These droppings are to Maurice evidence of the quantity of noxious insects the birds consume, but to Sita the birds are no more than an ugly crowd of trippers

40 A Karoo porcupine, showing its handsome, ferocious quills.

41 The Karoo's strangest, commonest, least-known animal – the ant-bear.

42 *Two illustrations from Le Vaillant's great book on birds: the Cape eagle owl, resident on Cranemere, and the locust bird or wattled starling, one of the most famous birds of early Cape history.*

One of the very first illustrations of a Cape pelican, the strangest visitor to Cranemere dam, from A Natural History of Birds *(1745) by George Edwards.*

43 Cranemere's bird – the blue crane.

44 An ostrich chick camouflages itself against sand and stone.

45 Spoonbills at the far end of Cranemere dam.

with no anti-litter ideas, dumping themselves in the quietness of the veld and filling it with ghastly noise.

These birds come and go and for years they may not be seen at all. Gill calls them roving birds, appearing almost anywhere for a time in flocks and disappearing again. When vast swarms of locusts were one of the hazards of the Colony these starlings used to follow the swarms, existing almost entirely on them, and nesting in huge numbers where the locusts bred.

The breeding of the starlings coincided most wonderfully with the mass hatchings of the locusts, and this sometimes seemed a miracle from heaven to the early settlers, for birds were then their only protection against this scourge. Once, however, the starlings' timing went wrong and the calamity that followed was recorded by one of the great naturalists of the Cape, Mary Elizabeth Barber.

The starlings had followed the locust flights from the interior of the Cape to the valleys near the Fish River where the locusts had laid their eggs, and here the following spring the birds built their nests. They were late, however, the young locusts appearing while the birds were still making their nests, so that when the starling young were hatching, the locusts – hoppers, and those which had grown to the winged stage – were leaving the neighbourhood.

The distance between the nests and the swarms of locusts grew day by day, and although the parent starlings worked hard, flying constantly between the locusts and their young, they could not collect enough food for them. Soon the locusts were twenty miles from the nests and the starlings faced a choice: to perish with their young or to abandon them and follow the locusts. They followed the locusts. The young were left to perish, not one old starling remaining behind, and 'the thorn tree valley with its countless thousands of nests became the valley of the shadow of death.'

The gigantic locust swarms that once devastated the Cape Colony are probably gone for ever, so we shall not see a host of wattled starlings doing battle with the hoppers. It is said that they advanced 'in long lines three or four deep, the rear-most birds constantly jumping over those in front of them', and that in the air, pursuing the winged locusts, they performed most beautiful acrobatics.

Nearly four hundred years ago a Portuguese priest at Sofala in Mozambique noted that in his new country was a little bird that led men to honey, and which would fly into his wooden church to eat the pieces of wax left in the candlesticks. In later years, far to the south in the Cape of Good Hope, other men wrote of these strange birds, like sparrows said some, like cuckoos said others, which deliberately led men to the nests of bees, to be rewarded by ancient custom with a portion of the comb. There is probably no bird that has so seized the imagination of men, and the little honey-guide remains the most described bird of Africa.

Its scientific name is *Indicator indicator*. We know it as the greater honey-guide, although it was once called Sparrman's honey-guide, for Sparrman was one of the first to describe it, claiming that it had led him to honey many times in the 'deserts' of the Cape. His description of its habits has been repeated over and over again for, strange as it is, it is considered accurate.

The Hottentots, Kaffirs, and also the honey badger, he claimed, followed the drab little bird, which flew before them with an alluring '*cherr-cherr-cherr*' until it reached the bees' nest over which it hovered for a few seconds. The persons following would speak to it every now and then with a soft and very gentle whistle. If they were unable to keep up with it, it flew back to meet them and with redoubled cries upbraided them for being so tardy. Such a bird was always rewarded: but Sparrman was told that it was bad policy to be too grateful to it but instead to leave it only so much comb as would stimulate its appetite to seach for another nest.

Sparrman promised beads and tobacco to his Hottentots if they would shoot a honey-guide for him, but they would not. Perhaps they looked on it as a valued friend, or perhaps they feared if they killed one they would never again be led to a bees' nest.

Le Vaillant wondered at the skin of the bird, so thick and tough that it could hardly be penetrated by a pin – or the sting of a bee – and at the ingenuity of nature which had given it so efficient an armour. Barrow thought there was someting in the conduct of the honey-guide that placed it above the 'brute part of creation', and there have probably been many others who agreed with him.

Occasionally we see the honey-guides on Cranemere, hopping from tree to tree and uttering their urgent calls, and Petrus, our old gardener and honey gatherer, used to follow them. Once Sita and I followed one for miles through the mountain bush but we found no honey. I have not given up hope that some day I shall see for myself how this strange story works.

Ornithologists are interested in the honey-guides for yet another reason. They do not rear their young themselves but lay their eggs in the nests of other birds, so that as fledglings they receive only the food their foster-parents bring them. And this is never wax. Yet as adults it is wax they eat, and from generation to generation they solicit the help of man and animal to gain it; and this is surely a most fascinating and curious thing.

It is not only the honey-guides on Cranemere that use other birds' nests. We have our cuckoos, with the same labour-saving habits, at least three species of which we sometimes see on Cranemere. There is the pretty metallic green Didrik cuckoo, and Klaas's cuckoo that Le Vaillant named after the Hottentot servant who travelled with him. He found this cuckoo for the first time on the Platrivier, a few miles fron Cranemere, so that this is this cuckoo's type-locality.

A cuckoo of even greater interest entranced Le Vaillant near the Little Fish River. This was the red-chested cuckoo, which Le Vaillant described as a blackbird with an orange-coloured belly, known across South Africa as the *Piet-my-vrou* (Piet-my-wife), which words almost exactly reproduce its call.

Le Vaillant had among his servants a Hottentot called Piet, who shot a female cuckoo which he brought to his master. Le Vaillant ordered him to return at once to the spot where he had killed it and shoot, if possible, the male. But Piet refused and, lamenting, told his story. He had scarcely killed the female when the male began to pursue him with great fury crying, '*Piet-my-vrou, Piet-my-vrou.*' Piet fled in horror from this bird seeking its mate with human words, and thereafter nothing would ever induce him to fire on another cuckoo.

Sometimes in the bush we hear – but seldom see – the Piet-my-vrou, and its call is unmistakable. Listening to it, it is indeed astonishing, for it is as if human words in the cadences of a bird are fluting across the veld.

13. Consider the Cobras

For eighty years a colony of cobras has lived under Cranemere house. Perhaps they have lived there even longer, for their sleek and ghostly ancestors may have frequented the reed-roofed cottage more than a century ago.

Lying in bed of a night, I used often as a child to think of them moving below me with only a row of flooring boards between us, and strained my ears to hear their sounds. The naturalist W. H. Hudson used as a boy in his home on the plains of South America to lie awake on summer evenings and listen to the snakes below *his* floor holding a ghostly hissing conversation, 'death-watch and flutter and hiss', and would listen and tremble. But although I waited to hear them I never did.

They are there, however, and perhaps in numbers. It is an uneasy partnership, that of the Palmers and the cobras, filled with mutual suspicion, and it is one we would be happy to end. Not so the cobras. They fear us, perhaps as much as we fear them, but they cannot do without us or the joys we offer: the broad stoep with its warm glow, a reptilian delight on a chilly day; those foundations with the lovely cracks and holes, those sheltering flooring boards; and above all the dim high rooms forty degrees cooler than the summer world without. Not for food but for these comforts our cobras bear with us.

Like all snakes, they tolerate extreme heat no better than extreme cold. In winter they hibernate below the floors, and on those aching summer days when it hurts to breathe and the mud, where there is moisture, bubbles with heat, a snake will die unless it finds shelter. Men may live in the open in a temperature of 110 degrees, but snakes cannot. So with common sense they make use of the coolness we offer. There is now wire mesh before every opening to the house but still they try to enter. Twice at least as I have opened a door on to the stoep on a hot summer day a cobra has slipped over my feet and into the coolness beyond. Once a cobra spent a probably terrifying afternoon beneath my mother's easy-chair until, visitors gone, it slid tentatively from under the frills that had concealed it. 'Never leave a wire door open,' was a command we learned from infancy.

Usually the cobras avoid us. They have no ear openings and cannot hear us, but they feel the vibrations of our feet and are gone in a yellow-brown flash before we near them. Not always, of course. The first Christmas David spent on Cranemere I heard Sita admonish him. 'Never run lightly with bare feet,' she said. 'Stamp. Then the cobras get out of your way. Maurice would be very angry if he had to shoot one of his cobras because it bit you because *you* forgot to stamp and trod on it.' The point was well taken.

Some cobra stories have become Cranemere history. We grew up with the tale of Chrissie and the cobra – Chrissie, the little coloured maid who, pushing open a door between two stoeps, found her neck encircled by a cobra. It had been lying asleep along the top of the half-opened door and the push had jerked it down upon her. Chrissie, it is recorded, had hysterics.

When Alex was a baby he slept on the stoep in a large perambulator. One day, soon after he had been taken indoors, a little barefooted girl ran up to the pram to find within not a baby but a big yellow cobra fast asleep. 'We killed it,' said Sita. 'Turn and turn about did not suit me.'

But had it indeed been turn and turn about or a cosier arrangement? There are very few records of snakes biting babies, perhaps because babies are not aggressive, and the snake could have found Alex tolerable company.

Only once have I ever laughed at a cobra. It was a young one, possibly not a foot long, and only two inches of it were visible. Its head protruded through a crack against a wall and it was investigating a half-grown spaniel, in her turn delighted by this novelty. The puppy was one long extended line of curiosity, tail to nose, and the little cobra's neck appeared elongated in equal interest, its tongue flicking round the puppy's nose, its round eyes holding, I am sure, an expression of identical wonder. It

208

was a ridiculous and enchanting moment of youth and curiosity.

Even when young, a cobra is dangerous and a newly hatched babe can kill. Once Sita found a maid agitatedly sweeping up 'worms' on the stoep. They were eleven baby cobras.

All those reared on the tale of Kipling's Rikki-Tikki know a cobra as wily and vindictive, plotting vengeance and fearful death. Yet this is not so: it is timid, stupid – and sometimes very beautiful. Not at any time in their strange association have the Cranemere cobras killed a Palmer, but often enough we have killed the cobras. They hide from us when they can, and when the heat becomes insupportable and they slide into the house with a quick furtive glide, they ask only to be left alone in the coolness. When the family close the house and go down to the sea in midsummer, the cobras come out for their annual holiday to live in the window-boxes and flower-garden and in the cool corners of the stoep until the family returns, when they slither smartly back to their foundations.

Out on the veld they cool themselves in the cement tanks which hold water for the sheep. These are entirely roofed except for a small opening, through which the cobras slip to lie almost entirely submerged in the water, their heads protected from the heat by the boards above. Several times as Maurice has reached down to the ball-valves which control the water supply he has almost put his hand on a cobra. Now he has learnt to stop and look for the small unwinking eyes above the water. Once Sita watched such a snake emerge, its great body reaching the whole height of the reservoir, and she found it the most terrifying thing she had ever seen.

Many of them are huge. The size of snakes is often exaggerated but we have measured many cobras, newly killed, of five and six feet and over. They can be beautiful. Recently we saw a great glowing red-gold pair slide into the bushes on the mountain road. A brilliant ripple in the veld and they were gone. They must just have sloughed their old skins, for they shone as if fresh minted. Often they are brown or yellow, sometimes a guinea-gold or this handsome red-gold, and their movement among the bushes is a sight to see, the same fluidity as running water, and there are few things that can so delight and terrify as one of these richly-coloured snakes flowing over the dun Karoo.

At bay, I do not think anyone thinks of a cobra's beauty at all: then it is pure horror. When it rears up to almost half its length with that tremendous flattened hood, that fearful sway, to and fro, to and fro, that murderous lunge, it is all the evil in the world. And it is deadly. Brought up as we are in South Africa on tales of the potency of mamba venom, it is a shock to know that drop for drop the venom of our common Cape cobra is more potent. Here on Cranemere we live in a cobra world: a small prayer of gratitude for their timidity would not come amiss.

Sometimes we see a long, graceful, chinless snake in the veld, with a dark muscular body shining as if carefully polished. This is the mole snake and is harmless to man, killing its prey by constriction. Like all snakes, it is the constant enemy of rats and mice and other small animals. It must be the only snake in South Africa to have thwarted a big official scheme. Once an attempt was made to stock Robben Island near Cape Town with rabbits as food for passing ships, but the authorities had not reckoned with the mole snakes which abounded there and devoured the rabbit young. We may think rabbits are prolific but mole snake families are no mean affairs. A single litter of ninety-five was once recorded! No wonder the rabbits did not increase.

George Palmer was held to be slightly mad because – in a day when such things were not thought of – he offered five pounds for every pair of mole snakes brought unharmed onto the farm. Maurice still welcomes them but with reservations. It is not always easy for the layman to tell a brownish mole snake from a dark-coloured cobra, and the sight of the neat neck of an apparently harmless snake flaring before one's eyes into the cobra's frightful hood is a memory for life.

Once, tramping over a koppie with my father, we stepped onto a puff-adder, a bloated creature with a broad triangular head, the colour of the stones. It lashed at us with unexpected speed, and I thought of it afterwards, fat, obscene and deadly, as a creature with no single redeeming feature. But I was wrong. One day I saw the open mouth of a puff-adder with those jutting fangs and it was lined with skin shining gently like mother-of-pearl.

This is the great killer in South Africa, and its venom is one of nature's most ruthless and efficient devices. It has a double action, both neurotoxic and haematoxic. It is the former which kills – most rapidly and satisfactorily for a hungry adder – the small animals on which it preys; and the latter which slowly but often surely kills man, unless prompt action is taken.

The loud angry hiss of a puff-adder is a ghastly sound. I do not believe any country-born South African, wherever he may later be, hears a hiss near by without quite simply and instantly springing a yard into the air. It is a bit of knowledge we never lose.

One hot February, when picking yellow peaches at the top of an old tree on the farm, a young coloured boy came face to face with a boomslang, the long green tree snake with the short head and large eyes, that is so elegant, colourful and deadly.

'Snake, snake, snake,' he screamed, sticking fast to the nearest branch.

'Jump, man, jump,' bellowed Maurice.

'Snake, snake,' screeched Jan, not moving an inch.

'Jump,' roared Maurice, and so it went on until suddenly Jan, in a limp bundle, hurtled to the ground quite grey with fear but also quite untouched. Some might believe the boomslang had hypnotized the boy, but in fact it seems he was rigid with shock. The snake may have been also.

If Jan had been deeply bitten he would almost certainly have died, for only in the last few months has an antidote to the venom been available.

The fangs of the boomslang are very far back and to the side of the mouth, so that they do not penetrate a surface easily: and the snakes are timid. Naturally there have been very few casualties. Once, indeed, boomslangs were believed harmless. We remember with awe that our great-grandfather, Thomas, conceived a tenderness for the breed and kept a number in his home, making especially thick curtain rods for them to twine about in imitation of branches. Visitors must have wondered, perhaps verbally, perhaps in silence, at the snakes' heads weaving among the sitting-room curtains.

I wonder what Thomas would have felt had he known that his pets could kill. But he never did. Nobody was ever bitten. Perhaps the snakes grew used to him, or perhaps the whole family was slow and gentle in its movements. Telling the story one day to Dr Vivian FitzSimons, the great authority on reptiles, he told me how snakes seldom strike unless frightened by quick movement, and described an old lady whom he knew who kept a number of poisonous snakes. She handled them very slowly, and quietly, stroking them 'like Persian kittens'. They never bit her.

Other colonists besides Thomas admired the 'tree-serpents'. They once used to send them preserved in spirits to their friends in Holland. Some melted down their fat which they used in making candles. This, said one old Cape historian, had a very surprising effect, for such a candle in the night time 'makes the room it burns in appear to be full of serpents'.

Even today odd tales about these snakes linger that may be legend, or may equally be fact. A local and aggressive breed, said to be fully nine feet long and to prefer tall grass to trees, is reputed to live in the mountains about Somerset East and eastwards. This sounds unlikely, yet Dr FitzSimons says that foresters and other trustworthy observers have reported the existence of these giants. He has offered a reward for one but fruitlessly.

Sometimes snakes kill stock in the veld; occasionally a dog. Once a woman on Cranemere was bitten on the foot when she stepped on a snake in the dark, but my mother injected anti-snake-bite serum and she lived. It is remarkable that, in spite of their great numbers, the incidents are so few. But what a life the snakes lead, for the world is their enemy. Man; all the quick sharp-toothed creatures of the veld such as mongoose, meerkat, honey badger, wild cat; warthogs where they exist; birds in number; all these hunt the snake with ferocity, and many more hunt their eggs. Some of these, moreover, have their own peculiar defences against the snake, such as the mongoose and meerkat which are apparently highly resistant to cobra venom.

The small birds, while they do not tackle a snake themselves, are often responsible for its death. Many times, on a hot, still, summer afternoon, we have heard a sudden tumult of twittering, of squeaking and chittering, from a mob of little birds collected together in fury and fear and screaming the news that an enemy is there. Occasionally it is only a cat, but more often it is a snake.

It is natural, I suppose, that anything as interesting as a snake should evoke a crop of odd stories. We have our own local brands, although nothing as dramatic as the great serpent of the Orange River. There is, for instance, a neighbour's claim to have seen, here on our plains, a snake with legs. Such a story turns up from time to time all over the country, causing a frenzy of speculation. The legs are, in fact, the two penes of the male snake extruding from the exit holes at the base of the tail. They may be up to one and a half inches long and hooked, and look remarkably like two little legs with toes. Newspapers are often asked to comment but never do: they believe the explanation to be indelicate.

When we think of reptiles we think first of snakes, and yet the lizards outnumber them by millions. They live in great numbers all over the farm, gay little creatures animating the rocks and veld, sometimes dark, sleek and graceful; sometimes in courting time the colours of an angry sunset. We see them sunning themselves on the rocks and in the heat darting from shade to shade, for, like the snakes, they cannot stand extremes of temperatures. They are far more fascinating co-dwellers than the snakes; and have recently become of great interest to scientists.

Reptiles have no means of regulating their temperatures, no built-in thermostats, so to say, as have mammals, and so their temperatures vary according to their surroundings. They must seek warmth and coolness not merely for comfort but for life, and lizards manage this in an odd way. Once when looking at Dr Rubidge's fossils, I examined the great and apparently three-eyed head of a *Platycyclops*. The 'third eye' was plain to see – not truly an eye, Dr Broom had said long ago, but more likely an additional sense. He was right – as he so often was – for this was the 'third eye', the parietal eye, which exists even in modern lizards and has brought to South Africa curious scientists from across the world. This third eye, scientists claim, is the lizard's thermostat: here is housed the sense that tells it enough is enough and sends it out of the sun back into the shade.

Sometimes our lizards find shade in unlikely places. Trap-door spiders make long dark tunnels shut off from the weather and enemies by silken lid-like doors, and these a species of gecko sometimes uses for shelter. They do so without harming those delicate doors, and this I find fascinating. How did a gecko learn to open and shut a door? How long did it take to learn?

And those eyes! Not all our lizards, but some of those that live in sand, have what is one of the most remarkable adaptations in the world – windows in their lower eyelids – so that they can close their eyes against the sand and still see!

My favourite lizards are the little house geckos, armed not against sand but against gravity, for their feet have adhesive pads beneath them. Sometimes a visitor will flinch to see a small form moving up a wall and across the ceiling. It is a gecko on its nocturnal hunt for moths and other insects. Such a visitor may count himself favoured, for the geckos which live between the double wall of the living-room are timid. They come out readily to hunt when Sita and Maurice are alone but seldom when there are strangers. Presumably they peep with their wide gentle eyes before they venture out, or perhaps they are warned by un-familiar voices.

Once a gecko had a brush with Maurice. What happened to its adhesive equipment I do not know but it fell from the ceiling upon his head. He sprang to his feet with a shout, beating wildly with his hands, and the gecko was catapulted to the floor where its body parted neatly from its tail, the legs carrying it to freedom and the tail spinning in a macabre little dance on its own. Maurice, like so many others seeing this phenomenon, gave not a thought to the body but only to the dancing tail. As an escape mechanism, it is unparalleled in simplicity and brilliance.

The chameleon does not lose its tail; it uses it to grip. We find it sometimes – as it is found all through Africa in garden and veld and bush – clasping a branch or twig with its tail, its legs at an angle to its body, its incredible feet, like nightmare prehistoric hands, two toes on one side, three on the other, anchoring it firmly; or perhaps creeping along a branch, lifting one foot at a time and setting it down, all with a swaying motion more leisurely than a snail.

I do think it is a frightening little creature in appearance. Its very gait is not of this world; nor are those eyes which look backwards and forwards and sideways, swivelling as they please quite independently of one another; nor its ridged reptilian back, nor its colour that changes under the eye; nor its tongue lying there like a squashed concertina in its mouth to emerge in a murderous flash. When it is angry, when it swells itself up and darkens, and opens its jaws to bare an orange cavity within, hissing the while, it is a little ancient monster. All the Bantu dread it. I believe all those on Cranemere would rather face a cobra. Poor dragon, it is defenceless except for its looks.

Last spring the koggelmannetjies were abroad in greater numbers than I ever recall. They are rather thick-set, lively lizards which have the amusing habit – as they lie on the rocks in the sun – of raising and lowering the fore parts of their bodies and moving their heads, so that they appear to be nodding or shaking their heads, and this has given them their popular name of 'little mockers'.

Our common one has a blue head – bloukop, it is called – and in breeding-time the male is a gorgeous sight, blue and yellow and orange. That spring we saw them everywhere, not only on the rocks but perched on the tops of bushes from which they sprang in great sailing leaps. On the roads we had to slow down to avoid them and they darted across in front of us like miniature dachshunds with their tails at an angle and a cocky dachshund gait.

Some of our prettiest lizards are the skinks, streamlined and shining, found in sand, on the koppies, and about the house, and like all our lizards they are quite harmless and are said to be easily tamed. It is touching that lizards, and surely there is nothing naturally wilder or freer than they, should yet sometimes show a liking for men who so delight in persecuting them.

There is one lizard on Cranemere we all respect, the leguaan – the monitor of other lands – a hunter and stealer of eggs and chickens, with a great whipping tail. Like the crocodile, it looks timeless and its genus, *Veranus*, is very properly an ancient one. I saw one once perhaps six feet long straddling the farm road and defying the motor-car, moving not one inch and hissing frightfully, and if a pair of wings had sprouted from its scaly back it would have been the dragon in flesh of a child's story.

Occasionally in the winter we find a hibernating tortoise in a bush or a shallow hole. Once, hunting for stapelias, we found a large mound in the shelter of a spreading karoo bush, and when we scratched the surface the pattern of a tortoise shell showed through the sand. In the spring the tortoises come out of these hibernating quarters and roam the veld in numbers. There is no country in the world so rich in them as ours, and here on Cranemere they are a familiar and delightful sight. However many we see, we still pause to look at them, and visitors find them seductive.

We have four common species, all interesting and sometimes beautiful. Even a normally drab species like the padloper or road traveller with its flattish, dull-coloured carapace can sometimes be gorgeous, like the two we saw recently, not shades of brown but of lime-green and gold. The one that is most generally admired is the tent or geometric tortoise, and it is a little beauty. Smaller than the padloper, its rounded carapace has raised plates like little brown pyramids gaudily and gaily striped with yellow.

It is a lover of dry hot places and is very decorative moving slowly across the sandy ground. Once it was exported abroad in numbers and hawked through the streets of great cities. I do not suppose that anywhere it would look commonplace, but how odd it must have appeared, and – if a tortoise can feel – how desolate it must have been, in a London street instead of in the sands and sun of Africa.

Our star is the mountain or leopard tortoise, a fifty-pounder more or less, two feet over the curve of its back and of an age as great or greater than any animal on the farm. It is an aggressive, domineering, independent creature and thinks little of dogs and nothing of men, and this it has indicated to us clearly. One October Sita and a group of visitors were picnicking in the lands when a great tortoise came trundling towards them through the wheat along a track which it had worn quite flat. They were obviously sitting in its usual line of march and waited to see what it would do. It looked belligerently at them but never hesitated, marching on with that swimming motion slap through the middle of the picnickers, upsetting the plates as it marched. One such tortoise devoured a whole plantation of young spineless cactus which Maurice was nursing carefully. It would meet him, thrust out its horny face as if on purpose to annoy, and bite a leaf beneath his furious gaze.

I once tried to stop one from entering a dam by clinging on to its carapace with both hands. Its strong scaly legs, pigeon-toed in front, worked away steadily, and apart from a hiss it took no notice of me at all, sliding into the water triumphantly and leaving me alone upon the bank.

The Bushmen told a story of how a mountain tortoise persuaded a 'man of an earlier race' to rub its neck with fat. Drawing in its neck suddenly, it caught his hands under its carapace and held them so until the skin and nails decayed, leaving only the bones. I cannot even smile at this story; it could so easily be true.

The first time we brought our city dachshund to Cranemere he jumped over a giant tortoise, obviously thinking it was a stone, but in mid-spring the tortoise stretched out its neck and began to walk. The dog never forgave it. Ever after when he saw a tortoise he walked delicately past, averting his face, and this we thought a very sophisticated attitude.

Mountain tortoises are said to have a great homing instinct, returning to the same spot to hibernate, and even swimming rivers (or crossing by bridge) to get back to their homes. What they want to do, they *do*. There must be many stories of these self-willed giants.

Although our mountain tortoises manage without water in drought they love it when it is there, and we always find them around the veld dams. One day Sita and I saw one emerging from a pool with something on its back. It was a water tortoise which fell off with a loud splash. I was glad to see a water tortoise at a disadvantage, for they had spoilt many a swim for me as a child. Somebody had once told me that they snapped at toes in the water, and as they are notorious for seizing the legs of young water birds, dragging them below, and devouring them, it seemed to me quite possible that they also favoured toes.

Their habits are bad, their appearance – green and slimy – poor, and they smell. Yet the brown dam water without their protruding heads like so many corks above the surface, or a sunny dam bank without their flat forms, would be incomplete.

One winter we had passed a small veld dam every day for a week without seeing a tortoise. On the seventh day we saw that for the first time water tortoises were moving slowly about the bank.

'Look at them,' said Sita. 'Now the weather is going to change.'

Sita's words were in good Cape tradition. I remembered with amusement that the early colonists had once used water tortoises as barometers. They had kept them in their houses in big glass bowls, claiming that at the approach of rainy weather the tortoises rose higher in the bowls.

When the dams dry up the water tortoises leave and bury themselves in some soft place until the rains come. There is no mystery about them. But the bull-frogs! That is another matter.

One year when I was about ten years old all the dams and pools filled and overflowed. Above the big dam stretched a string of pools and in these I came one evening on a crowd of bull-frogs. I had never seen them before and was transfixed. I know today they were probably not more than six or seven inches long, but to me they appeared as big as half-grown terriers, yellow and green: and they roared.

When my father heard of them he rushed to see them, and we walked up and down for a long time examining them with the greatest pleasure and curiosity. As we moved towards them they sprang at us with snapping jaws, and it was clear that they were defending their pool with courage.

'Where do they come from?' I asked, and my father, looking at them thoughtfully, answered, 'I haven't an idea.' It was, he reckoned, nearly ten years since he had last seen bull-frogs on Cranemere, and although we did not guess it then, they were not to be seen again for almost another decade. Since then they have often appeared at intervals of years. I think it is fact that they do not come regularly, for their size and colour and noise make the bull-frogs conspicuous, and if they had appeared, certainly in the populated parts of the farm, they would have been noted at once.

Where do they come from? Where do they go? And where do they exist all those years when they live unseen? Years later Dr FitzSimons, authority on amphibia as well as reptiles, answered the questions and told me their story, and what a curious story it is.

All creatures in South Africa completely dependent on water have a risky time, but the danger to the bull-frogs is minimized because the first part of their life cycle is unusually quick – the stages from egg to tadpole to frog – giving the frogs time to develop before the water disappears. Before the ground is dry the frogs dig their holes in the soft soil, far below the surface, and here they aestivate, perhaps for many years, in neat, home-made, plastic bags composed of a skin secretion which hardens and envelops them completely. One day when every condition, or combination of conditions, is right, they burst forth again to bellow and brag in their pools.

'Once,' said Dr FitzSimons, 'I saw one turned over by a plough. It was encased in its plastic covering and seemed quite dead. "Look, we've got a mummy," someone said. We put it in water. Within fifteen minutes one eye opened, then shut; and then the other opened. One leg stretched, and kicked; then another. It soon came to life completely and swam happily about.'

This was not the end of the story of the frogs. Those angry rushes and those snapping jaws that had so amused us at the frog pool were not empty gestures – the frogs were guarding their tadpoles and eggs, or so some scientists affirm – and this sets our bull-frogs, our baby-sitting bull-frogs, apart from most of the amphibia of the world.

14. The Red Men

Under the rocks and stones and old wood on the veld, and in burrows in the ground, live the scorpions. There are those who like them, believing their shapes to be not sinister but picturesque, and their habits fascinating. For myself, I considered them a singularly unrewarding race until the day I learned that our modern scorpion, claws, tail and all, is almost the same as its ancestor that lived millions upon millions of years ago. I thought of it then with sudden interest. What had it, this little scorpion, to bring it through the ages so little changed to live on triumphantly today under almost every stone on Cranemere?

I needed, I felt, to inspect it more closely, and offered to pay one penny for every scorpion brought me. Rather rashly, I added a penny for spiders and for anything else of interest. Instantly an animated flow began between the native homes and the big house and long files of African children stood waiting throughout the day for Sita and me, clutching tins filled with scorpions, spiders, centipedes, crabs. Those who brought nothing came to see the fun – the transference of these very lively spoils from the tins to the bottles of spirits. For an entomologist or a zoologist this might have been commonplace but for us it proved an agonizing process.

We were usually so much in haste that we had no time to examine our live captives, and once as we tipped a scorpion out we saw too late that it was not one but many, a large burrowing mother scorpion with her young clinging in the most neat and organized manner upon her back. Later that scorpion was to weigh upon my conscience when I found I had pickled a loving mother that – mammal-like – had nourished her babes within her body and given birth to them, helped them upon her back, guarded them; a creature, as Eugene Marais maintained, that even suffered birth-pangs!

She had probably already devoured her mate, but this was by

the way. She had acquired a personality, and I wished I had known more of her, of her courting days when she and her mate had danced together, claw clasping claw, tails intertwined, in what must have been the most bizarre love-making in the world. I was not fortunate enough that year to see the scorpion waltz, but our pickled specimens brought Cranemere a new interest and a most valued friend.

Back in Pretoria, David and I visited the Transvaal Museum with a large scorpion in a cigarette-box and a jar of arachnids in spirits. We were fortunate: working here for a few days was South Africa's greatest authority on scorpions and spiders, Dr R. F. Lawrence, then director of the Pietermaritzburg Museum, and he named our specimens for us.

'Where do these come from?' he asked, politely handing them back.

'Pearston,' I said.

'Do you live there?' he asked; and I had the lively impression of a dog pointing.

'No,' I answered, 'but my brother does.'

Dr Lawrence glowed. 'Ask him if I may come and stay with him,' he said.

Sita and Maurice were delighted. Soon after he arrived, plus his caravan and a huge wooden box filled with equipment, and a new excitement suddenly blossomed on the farm. He was hunting not only the usual scorpions, spiders, and centipedes, but a species of Solpuga, a desert spider, the very existence of which was uncertain.

Solpugas, or Sun-spiders, are not true spiders at all for their bodies have three main divisions and their jaws are most horridly armed with great teeth. They infest the Karoo, and here in the Pearston mountains sixty years ago Dr Broom – how many trails lead back to him! – had discovered a Solpuga (named *Broomiella* after him) with a particular oddity in its leg structure, and ever since scientists had wondered whether it was a freak or indeed a new species.

For years Pearston had been for Dr Lawrence a sort of Mecca.

He longed to find another *Broomiella* himself: and here on Crane-mere he did. He found a single specimen – a female – which in itself was a great thrill but not enough to decide if it is truly a new species. Some time he will return to hunt the twenty males and twenty females he needs and perhaps he will find them here.

I was not surprised that a newsworthy Solpuga had been found on Cranemere. As a race, they have always been for me of the utmost importance, the most alarming things I ever expect to encounter, ferocious, brilliant, and the fastest spiders in the world. Lawrie – for by this time he had become this to us all – told us something of their history, how they had routed a people more surely than an army could have done, and how Pliny had recorded this strange event in Ethiopia centuries ago when great numbers of Solpugas appeared and the inhabitants of a whole countryside left their homes and fled. And Lawrie added wryly that they were harmless!

South Africa, according to his estimate, has at least two hundred different species, which makes it a plum for Solpuga hunters. Most of them inhabit the hot dry parts of the country, and here on Cranemere we must have tens of thousands of them of various species. On the farm we know most of the diurnal species as jagspinnekoppe or hunting spiders, and the nocturnal species as Rooimans or Red Men, and of these latter I can neither think nor speak except in capitals.

By day we see the hunting spiders rushing about erratically on the blazing soil between the little bushes hunting their prey – grasshoppers, crickets, beetles, small insects of many kinds – and often they are too swift for the eye to follow. It is difficult to examine them as they run, for if cornered they double back at a breakneck pace, sometimes darting endlessly about in one bush from one side to the other. Last summer I followed one with persistence and for an instant saw it clearly and not merely as a flicker of colour. It was dark-coloured with a long black oval mark down the middle of its back, and its back legs were a glory, crimson fringed with long white hairs; as these caught the light it looked as if it were clothed in ornamental pantaloons.

It was a variety of *Solpuga chelicornis*, one of the most colourful of the Solpugas. Cronwright-Schreiner – the same who wrote of the migrating springbuck, and the ostriches of the Karoo – thought it a splendid creature. He began his farming career not far from Cranemere in the Pearston district, and perhaps his interest in our desert spiders began here. Later, helped by the children of the countryside, he was to collect several thousand specimens of Karoo spiders and scorpions, and he said of our *Solpuga chelicornis*: 'A most brilliant yellow with a heavy black band down the back of the abdomen, while the legs are covered with long golden hair which in the male becomes a distinct mane and is iridescent. As it lies on the sand on a hot day, sparkling in the sunshine, it is a most exquisite creature.'

'You see,' says Lawrie, quoting him, 'others besides zoologists admire them!'

The people on the farm call the hunting spider Sissiewolle – Little Woolly Sister – and to me this is the only endearing thing about them.

Most of them have a woolly covering of greyish hairs. 'Sometimes they are so thick on the back legs,' said Lawrie, 'that we specialists call it a mane. These hairs are a wonderful way of breaking up the outlines of the body so that it is impossible to say not only what order of beast it belongs to but even if it is a beast at all. It might be the seed of a plant, for instance.'

I saw one recently, black and silver, and as it swept over the ground it appeared to be flying. 'It's a wasp,' somebody cried. 'That thing doesn't move on legs. It's flying.' But it was not.

When my father was courting my mother in the days of carts and horses, she heard a story of these spiders that, he declared, almost prejudiced her against the farm for good. With terrible precision they were supposed to jump upon the flicking whips of the drivers, up which they ran like striped lightning, and so into the carts where they routed the occupants in hysterics.

This had always seemed to us the most improbable story in the world and over the years we had laughed uproariously at it. Lawrie killed our mockery. 'Oh yes,' he said mildly, 'I can well believe they run up whips. They are *quite* quick enough to get on to a whiplash, and they can hold on to vertical surfaces with the sucker-like organ at the tip of the palps – the feelers, you know.'

Lawrie is filled with the most improbable knowledge about them. He is the only person I have ever met who has *heard* the footsteps of these spiders. They cannot weigh more than a feather and I would not have believed their movement could be heard at all, but one hot day Lawrie, sitting quietly on the edge of a lowveld forest, watched them rushing about with incredible speed and heard the pattering of their tiny feet on the thin dry leaves of the forest carpet.

Our Woolly Sisters do not really disturb us for they stay out on the veld, but their nocturnal relations, the Red Men, come into the house at night – invade would at times be a better word – for they are attracted by lights. They are monstrous. Of medium size – perhaps three inches with the legs fully spread, although they can be larger – orange-red, hairy, fast, with great snapping beak-like jaws which, most horrifyingly, they move at the same time up and down and from side to side, they can flatten themselves to a nothing to creep under a door or through a crack, and they can rear up inches high to fight when provoked.

'They are not poisonous,' a naturalist once assured me, 'but nasty, very nasty, if you tease them.' *Tease* a Red Man! The things that scientists do!

The Red Man's body, like that of all Solpugas, is divided into three portions, but like ordinary spiders, it has four pairs of legs. Inspired by Lawrie, we inspected our pickled corpses intently: there, below the fourth pair of legs, was a row of little growths like minute mushrooms and these, and that delicate frosting of hairs, are organs of touch – the spider's radar – and give our Solpugas their precision and therefore partly their speed, and direct their erratic course.

Confined in a room, our Red Men often race round the floor in a circle taking again and again the same route as before. When I was a child, bed-time held for me a brand of fear which few children in softer countries know, for alone in the shadowy nursery I would see spiders in every corner and tear off my clothes and leap into bed before my terrors took form. Often I was not quick enough and as the lights lit up the room, a Red Man would be there. It came like the shadow of a butterfly when the room was dim, and when it was bright like the tip of an orange ostrich feather flowing over the floor, and I would leap upon the nearest chair and bellow. My father, after much experience, knew that note and would appear, weapon in hand, but in those two minutes of time the Red Man would have encircled that room quite twenty times, passing each time beneath the chair on which I trembled.

Many years later I spent a night in a farmhouse in the desert country on the banks of the Orange River. I was very tired and as I sat at the supper-table my eyes began, I thought, to play tricks of fatigue, for as I watched a shadow passed over the table between the plates and seconds later it passed again, and it was only as someone moved the lamp that I saw it was a Red Man playing its old game. But there was not one shadow, there were two and three upon the table, and as I turned my head I saw forms flickering over the floor and up the walls, and I knew the room was alive with spiders, not the Cranemere Red Men but twice as large; as large as the plates, I reckoned, for by then I felt delirious. And in the corner of the room there came a crackling, a Red Man devouring a beetle, or could it be bones?

The farmer and his wife sat eating fat cakes and drinking milk. Presently the farmer's wife scooped a layer of drowned flies out of the jug, gesturing as she did so to the galloping spiders. 'They eat the flies,' she said placidly. 'Then it's easier for us to drink the milk.'

Not many people, Lawrie and the farmer's wife apart, learn to tolerate these spiders. Our servants, who know them very well, swear that at night they get into the hair of sleeping people and snip it off, and this is a very general belief for *haarskeerder*, or hair-clipper is one of their common names. Scientists smile at this, Lawrie for instance, maintaining that their gigantic teeth –

something like those of the sabre-toothed tiger and other carnivores – are fashioned for tearing hunks of meat and not for shearing. Fanny Palmer could have told him it was a debatable point.

My grandmother's great pride was her hair which, when loose, fell below her knees and which she normally wore in coils piled high upon her head. One summer's night, after the household had retired to bed, my father heard her screaming and as never before had he heard a sound of fear from her he concluded that someone was murdering her. Rushing down the dark stoep, falling headlong over every chair, swearing and bellowing, he reached her to find her flying round her room, tearing at her hair, and uttering maniacal shrieks. There in her hair he found two great red spiders, scratching or snipping, who can tell.

Fanny, who had little time for hysterics, sympathized once with an hysterical girl. She gave a dance in the drawing-room at Cranemere and among her guests was a girl in a flowing tangerine-coloured gown. That night eight red spiders ran up her skirts, and she finished the dance in a state of collapse.

Populations wane and blossom. Today we no longer find the hordes of Red Men we once did, or perhaps there are fewer cracks in the floors and below the doors. The hunting spiders, on the other hand, seem to have increased. They all breed in the late spring and are at their peak in the midsummer, and this is the time to know them.

Few people have seen them mating or breeding. Lawrie is the only person in the world to have seen a Solpuga laying eggs in captivity and he counts himself a very fortunate man. She lay on her side, he told us, the eggs appearing regularly and in perfect rhythm for more than four hours until at last a pile of yellow shiny eggs rose higher than her body. He rushed to the telephone to call a friend who arrived with his camera, and together they secured a memorable record.

The eggs were attacked by a fungus, but the mother did well. She appears to have been a lively, pugnacious, courageous creature. Later she and another Solpuga, seemingly drowned in a jar of water, were dried on blotting-paper, to revive completely and fall upon each other fiercely with clapping jaws.

Lawrie hopes to find on Cranemere another such pregnant spider. 'I love the fat ladies,' he told Sita earnestly. 'I want every pregnant lady I can find. I want them to lay eggs for me so that I can hatch them out.'

He had no time while on the farm to hunt for trap-door spiders, and this I lament for they are remarkable. Searching for fossils recently, we saw on the side of a river-bank what we thought was the outline of the round end of a bone. It was the silken lid of a trap-door spider's nest, and we dug out its long, beautiful, tube-like nest with curiosity to find the spider within. It was dark-coloured with reddish lights, and it was smooth, like coloured glass, perfectly motionless, and very pregnant. We were sorry to have disturbed it.

We would have been sorrier still had the plump docile occupant been a baboon spider. This makes a large silk-lined tube, sometimes with a light silken cover, and these are probably everywhere, for Lawrie found them on the koppie near the house and on the flats. Unlike the trap-door spiders, they are very large, very hairy, and very ugly. Their bodies alone are two inches or more in length, and with their hairy legs outstretched they are immense, the biggest spiders in South Africa and among the very big spiders of the world.

They belong to the genus *Harpactira*. With their baboon fur and their padded monkey paws, they are known all over South Africa as baboon or monkey-fingered spiders, and they are commonly believed very poisonous – although not by Lawrie, who finds it difficult to believe anything bad of the spider race. He was enthusiastic about our Cranemere species. 'That fiery carapace and abdomen; those blue-black legs – what contrast, what beauty!' he acclaimed.

Bertram Allan, working in the lands one March, saw something moving in the ploughed field. It was a baboon spider. He slapped it into an empty box – an act of what seemed to me quite desperate bravery – and brought it triumphantly to Sita. She turned it into a two-pound jam-jar and it covered the whole bottom of the bottle.

Its back was covered with grey fur, its paws were deep blue, its chest a golden brown, and it had a fiery red moustache and beard. It reared up on its huge back legs, its front legs raised for attack much like a boxer, its fangs gnashing, its red moustache waving, and Sita found she could not bear to look at it.

I have known people who swear they have heard these spiders, their monkey paws padding softly on the ceiling of a night. I asked Lawrie if this could be true and he said simply, 'Oh yes, it could be so.'

Some time ago a Graaff-Reinetter, sitting on his stoep on an evening of oppressive heat, saw a dark form moving heavily across the stones. It was a great spider eating a mouse. The man leaped up in revulsion, rushed inside, and closed his door; but his curiosity was great and at dawn he went out again to look. There was nothing left of the mouse but a part of the head and a few tiny bones, but the spider was still there, so full, so heavy, it could barely drag itself away.

It is as well, I think, that we see our baboon spiders seldom.

15. Evolution's Darlings

Lawrie finds his Red Men all innocence, and perhaps entomologists think the same of some of the insect hordes that inhabit Cranemere. But I am sure there is not one who would not recognize our cheerful little locust as one of the formidable creatures of the earth.

It has what must be one of the strangest of all stories, and it is one that scientists have learnt to interpret only within the last forty years. Yet at the same time locusts have had more of men's passionate attention for a greater length of time than any other insects.

This is because – until the present century – when men fought the locusts for their food, they invariably lost. The locusts won, hopping or winging their way across a countryside and leaving behind them a land as bare as if it had been swept with a giant broom.

Two thousand years ago nearly a million people in North Africa starved and died after a great flight of locusts. In China they changed history, for the famine they caused forced the emperor to end a war he was waging. We know of them in Palestine and Egypt from the beginning of history. We seldom think of them as a scourge of Europe, yet during the Middle Ages and later they invaded Europe from the east, sweeping west and north and leaving behind them a multitude of starving people. In the late 1740s they reached England and were seen in the streets of London!

They were some of the earliest travellers on our Karoo plains. The Bushmen, who grew no crops and pastured no stock, delighted in them, for they destroyed little they prized and were themselves food. They believed they had been made by a girl throwing up into the sky the peel of a root she was eating, which took the shape of locusts. This was the same girl who made the stars and the Milky Way, and the Bushmen apparently greatly valued her efforts.

Sparrman noted that, when the locusts swarmed, the Hottentots in the space of a few days got visibly fatter.

But for every settler and farmer from the earliest days, particularly those who grew crops and depended on grass for their pasturage, they have been an affliction.

The earliest detailed description that I know of a swarm of locusts in the Karoo was given by Le Vaillant in 1782 when he ate them on the banks of the Little Fish River. Barrow, travelling north of Graaff-Reinet more than a decade later, saw both winged insects and hoppers, the hoppers covering an area ten miles long and their dead bodies choking the river along which he travelled. Not a single field of corn remained standing in the whole countryside. 'In such years the inhabitants eat no bread,' he recorded.

Although the settlers had been free of them for the preceding ten years, he said, they had the liveliest memories of them, for their exit from the Colony a decade before had been singular. A tempestuous north-west wind had blown the great swarms into the sea, and in due course the dead locusts had been cast up on the beach, making a great cemetery three or four feet high for fifty miles along the coast. The wind veered, to blow inland from the ocean, and the stench from the locusts was blown across the land. It reached Cranemere, and even across the barrier of mountains to the north a hundred and fifty miles from the sea.

In 1808 there was a plague of locusts at the Cape, to be followed by sixteen years of peace, and then in 1824 they burst out again to despoil the country for six successive years. Almost a hundred years later, for eight bitter years, they ravaged the Cape and this time we did not depend on books to tell us of them. We saw them ourselves.

I was a very small child but I still remember the gloom that hung over Cranemere for days before the locusts came. My father and Rob talked together. 'They are there, and there, and there,' they would say. 'They can be here in three days.' Then it was two, and then one. Then one afternoon my father, picking me up and pointing to the east, said, 'Look!'

There in the direction of the village was a cloud in the sky. It moved slowly towards us, growing larger and denser and browner, and as it approached us I heard it. The noise was somewhat like that of water pouring down an empty river-bed, until the locusts were above and around us and the roar changed to a rasping and clicking and scratching and pattering.

We put up our hands to shield our faces, for they flew against our cheeks and into our eyes; they tangled in our hair and clothes and they crept into our pockets and down our necks. Every door and window of the house was shut and still the locusts penetrated. We found them in our beds and in our food and drowned in the flower-bowls and in our tea. As I lifted a mug of milk a struggling locust rasped its armoured legs against my lips and I shrieked.

Outside, the world moved and it was a grey world. I remember shielding my eyes and staring upwards, and my feeling of astonishment that the sun I saw was no more than freckles of brightness in the whirring shadow.

At night the locusts settled and we went into the veld to see them. They were now far more horrible than by day, for they covered every bush and our landscape was enveloped in a cloak of shuddering, sighing life. I do not suppose there is anything so monstrous as to see a familiar and beloved thing transformed before one's eyes, and this sight remains with me as a childhood nightmare.

During the years that followed we saw the locusts again and again, always travelling in the same direction for days on end and sometimes, it was said, covering a hundred miles in a single day. Sometimes they flew; sometimes they were in the hopping stage – *voetgangers*, or travellers afoot, as they were known right across South Africa. Farmers may dread them as much as the adult locusts but for me they never held the same terrors, perhaps because they never clicked against my teeth or twined themselves in my hair.

They could be fascinating to watch. Like adult locusts, they clustered in the bushes of a night, and in the morning they descended to the ground to bask in the early sun, lying at an angle to absorb the maximum warmth. They reminded me then irresistibly of animals – tiny meerkats or monkeys warming their bellies – and I could not hate them.

Then they were off, hopping in great columns and armies across the veld, nearly always in a track or path if one were available and at the rate of perhaps a quarter of a mile an hour, tiny dark creatures at first but after successive moults emerging a shining black and orange, the *rooibaadjies*, or red-coats, of the veld.

They ate, of course – usually grass – as they hopped, and they attended to their comforts all the time. When the ground grew too hot for them – and research officers have found that when the air temperature reaches 90 degrees, which it often does, the soil temperature is 145 degrees Fahrenheit – they stopped travelling and climbed up the plants. Here they cooled themselves and rested, descending when the air freshened, marched again, sunned themselves, finally climbing into the bushes for the night.

Men are often unable to deflect them from their chosen path although birds can sometimes halt a marching band. Small birds concentrate on scattered locusts rather than a living mass, and this the locusts appear to know, for at the approach of even a few small birds the insects band themselves into a compact mass. 'Ten men,' wrote a locust research official bitterly, 'cannot do what six or eight small larks succeed in doing.'

When, however, large birds such as storks, appear, the locusts adopt different tactics, for they then disperse madly over the veld! They and the birds are obviously old acquaintances.

Useless as it may be, anyone who sees a locust horde advancing towards his garden or field of wheat enters into battle furiously with them. From ancient times farmers have burnt fires in their path, beaten drums and tins and kettles, waved branches, sacks, clothing, blankets, sheets, before them to divert them; or driven flocks of sheep among the hoppers to trample upon them. I can still see Fanny Palmer as an old woman, her hands and feet deformed with arthritis, a sack clutched between her small crooked fingers, furiously beating at the locusts invading Cranemere rose-garden. There we all were, every child upon the farm of every colour, screaming, howling, waving, bashing, banging, defending that small patch of earth from the locusts, for to defend the lands was beyond our powers. I no longer remember who won.

I do remember that the irrigation furrows did not stop them. They made living bridges across them, hopping and crawling over one another so that the bottom ones soon twisted to the top and none was undermost for long, all surviving to take up their march upon the opposite shore. We children crouched upon the banks to watch them, marvelling.

Years later I was to read of locusts from the Book of the Prophet Joel written some 2,700 years ago:

'They shall run like mighty men: they shall climb the wall like men of war: and they shall march every one on his ways, and they shall not break their ranks.

'They shall run to and fro in the city: they shall run upon the wall: they shall climb upon the houses: they shall enter in at the windows like a thief,' the prophet wrote, and I thought that this could only have been written by one who himself had suffered an invasion.

All the world turns out to devour the voetgangers, but I remember only the white storks which appeared in numbers, and the fowls. When the first voetganger column appeared, our domestic fowls went beserk: with outstretched wings and necks they darted about the yard, gobbling madly. By evening a desultory peck was all they could manage; they were sagging on the ground and only with the greatest difficulty dragged themselves up on their perches.

I have never seen horses eat locusts, but they are reputed to do so. Cattle and pigs devour them, as do jackals, meerkats and other veld animals. A locust migration is a great time for the birds and for such creatures as the hunting spiders and the scorpions. One research officer once told me that during a locust invasion he could hardly walk for the scorpions around his feet

46 *The secretary bird, the most striking bird of the Karoo.*

47 The mountain tortoise – an armour-plated, arrogant giant of the Karoo.

48 The common water tortoise or terrapin. When it rose higher in the water the early colonists believed that rain was near.

49 *The Cape skink shines as if laquered in the Karoo sun.*

50 *A rock leguaan seeks its dinner.*

51 The blinkogie, one of the shy, charming little geckos of the Karoo.

52 The bull-frog has one of the strangest life-stories of Africa.

hunting for the insects; and a naturalist once saw a trap-door spider spring out of its nest to seize a locust and drag it within.

All the native peoples of South Africa at one time or another have prized and eaten them, and once a fine spicy locust paste was manufactured by a French missionary – possibly with a background of exotic cookery – who sent a sample to the Governor, Sir George Grey. With his passion for Africana, Sir George no doubt relished it.

I once asked a locust research officer what he thought fried locusts resembled, and he answered, 'Sardines.' Maurice and I stewed them in the lid of a boot-polish tin. I remember only that they tasted of polish.

Until this century we had no organized protection against the locusts, and the colonists looked to birds for help, particularly the swallow-like pratincoles, swifter on the wing than the locusts, which would suddenly appear when the insects were swarming, darkening the air like a cloud. They devoured the locusts in the air, slicing off their legs and wings which shimmered to the earth 'like a shower of bright sticks and straws', bespattering everything below.

Colonists claimed that the locusts, which seldom flew after dark, would fly by night as well as by day to escape these birds. They knew and understood the danger to them, they said.

They had many tales of the sagacity of locusts. One of the strangest was told by the naturalist Mary Elizabeth Barber, ninety years ago. A vast swarm of hoppers appeared on the southern banks of the Vaal River travelling northward, and they were apparently searching for a ford to cross. But the river was flooded and they travelled upstream. At a bend in the river, where there was an outcrop of rock, they paused 'as if in doubt whether to attempt a passage at this place.' But they passed on, she wrote, 'evidently with the hope of finding a better ford, in which apparently they were disappointed, for three days afterwards they returned to the same bend and there on the morrow plunged into the stream in vast multitudes.' Myriads crossed although myriads perished.

I told this tale with its fine anthropomorphic flavour recently to the chief locust research officer of South Africa, Mr A. Lea.

'What do you think of it?' I asked.

'I think they thought,' he answered succinctly. Then he added sheepishly, 'You know, they do sometimes seem to think.'

'You *like* your locusts,' I said, and he answered: 'Well, yes, I do. Not that that would stop me killing them, of course. But they are such interesting little beggars.' And then he told me the story of their 'phases' that only forty years before had set scientists agog.

In the early 1920s a Russian naturalist, Dr B. P. Uvarov, and a South African scientist, Professor J. C. Faure, working quite independently of each other, made an almost simultaneous discovery which was to turn the recorded life-history of the locusts upside down.

They found that the species of migratory locusts could assume in a matter of several generations two completely different forms, and a transitional form between, so different in appearance and habits that they appeared completely different species. They took on these new forms according to circumstances – and it seemed to me, listening, that they always changed their appearance and character when it most benefited them. It was as if, for example, greyhounds – in a world that favoured dachshunds – changed in four generations into the form of dachshunds, then back into greyhounds when certain circumstances arose. This power to change form, said Mr Lea, was one that all the migratory species of locusts possessed: and my scalp prickled as I listened. Evolution's darlings indeed!

The farmers of South Africa, like those of North Africa, Asia and the Holy Land, watched the great swarms darkening their skies for several plague years in succession, and as suddenly disappearing, perhaps for many years on end. And they asked themselves where they had come from. And where they had gone. For many centuries they wondered, and only forty years ago were their questions answered.

The answer was that – as a race – they never departed at all.

They simply assumed a new form – a disguise so perfect that it had never been questioned by even the most observant naturalist.

Our locust of the Karoo, the brown locust, *Locustana pardalina*, is well known to us as a tiny dark hopper, later becoming black and orange, lively, energetic, disciplined, and loving the company of its fellow hoppers; and as an adult, as a brown winged locust marked with black – and when fully mature with bright yellow on the head and legs, at this stage still a lively gregarious creature, streamlined and strong-winged, formed – and with distinction – as a member of a great invading army. It came and went with its impact of myriads in a great, bright, noisy host. After it had vanished, in the peaceful years that followed, farmers never saw it: and when they noticed grasshoppers in the veld they certainly never connected them with the invading locusts. Why should they?

The little hoppers of these were smaller than those of the migrating locust: they were pale green or brown or speckled – or white or black or blue when they grew up among pebbles of these colours or among blue shale. No brilliant orange and black for them: they were designed to escape notice and they did. They did not congregate and march in columns but separated to live solitary lives, concealing themselves wherever possible, and in their adult form they behaved in much the same way. Farmers sometimes saw the adults as they flew up round their feet, but they never saw them on the wing like migrating locusts. Entomologists noted that they had fewer moults than the locusts, and that the adults were neither so large-winged nor so streamlined, and that – unlike the locusts – they were often active at night.

Scientists and laymen alike knew them as completely different insects from the migratory locusts, until in 1923 science, most improbably, proved them one and the same.

Locusts, claimed Uvarov in Europe and Faure in Africa, existed in three phases: the gregarious form known as phase *gregaria* – and in this form they had invaded continents and frightened half the world; the solitary phase, phase *solitaria*, when they took the form of isolated grasshoppers; and a transitional form, phase *transiens*, showing some of the characteristics of the two extreme forms.

This, they proved, applied to all the migratory locusts, not only to the brown locusts of the Karoo, but to the migratory locusts which had invaded Europe in the past, the desert locust, the red locust: all of them had this singular history.

Locust research and locust control all over the world took a great forward step. Here in South Africa it soon became clear that the crowding or otherwise of the egg packages decided the type of insect to emerge. If the eggs were close together, swarm hoppers would appear; if widely spaced, solitary grasshoppers; and soon scientists learned that the descendants of the grasshoppers, becoming more and more numerous, gradually took on the appearance and habits of the swarming locusts.

Not all locust eggs need the same conditions for hatching. The desert locusts lays its eggs in damp soil only. Our brown Karoo locust lays the finest possible drought-resistant eggs. They can be laid in bone-dry soil and there, in their neat tough pods, they will lie for possibly two years until sufficient rain falls to hatch them out. Once farmers and scientists alike thought they could remain indefinitely in the soil for at least twelve or fifteen years on end, for they could not otherwise account for the hatching of a locust horde after an interval of many years when there had been no sign of them. They did not guess the ingenious role the timid grasshopper played.

A few years ago, close to Cranemere in the Jansenville district, some little swarms of red-coat hoppers appeared to confound the farmers. There had been no locusts for seven years. Where, they demanded, had they come from? Locust research officers went to see, and thanks to two butcher birds, they found the answer.

There, in a clump of thorn trees, they found the larder of the butcher birds – the old dried bodies of a number of grasshoppers speared on the white thorns. They pointed triumphantly to them. 'There,' they told the farmers, 'there are the parents of the red-coats. Grasshoppers, you think! Not at all – locusts. Locusts in the solitary stage.'

By virtue of this solitary stage the brown locust survives. While it is possible to spray a concentrated swarm with poison, it is impossible to rid a country of isolated grasshoppers. Nor, as a grasshopper, is it numerous enough to build up great numbers of enemies – animal, bird, or insect – as do the swarms of locusts after continuous years.

One of the locust's greatest natural enemies is the small fly of the genus *Stomorrhina*, and it is only seen in very great numbers during continuous years of locust plague. This fly lays its eggs in those of the locusts, its larvae completely destroying the eggs. Years ago a locust officer, Jurgen Smith, saw the flies at work on the Graaff-Reinet flats not far from Cranemere and he was one of the first South Africans to guess their importance. It was during the great locust invasion of the Karoo after the First World War and, working on the veld for days on end, he one day noticed the flies, about the same size as houseflies, dull grey and so sluggish that he could catch them by hand. He watched them moving lazily from one locust egg-pocket to another, just as if inspecting the eggs. 'I was a monkey,' he said afterwards. 'I did not know what was happening.'

Soon he did. He dug up the locust eggs to find fly larvae already devouring them. That night in the Graaff-Reinet pub the fly was ardently toasted and re-toasted.

Since then science has learnt a great deal about these little flies. Their lives are linked inseparably with those of the locusts. They have never been noticed when locusts are absent. Nobody has ever seen them travelling or arriving, but when the locusts are swarming, there is the fly. Perhaps they travel with them or after them: it would seem they must. But when the female locusts begin to lay, there the fly is too, hanging persistently around her *before* she lays her eggs, the entomologists swear. As she sticks her tail into the soil to begin laying, the fly follows to lay its eggs on hers. Nobody has ever seen the flies laying their eggs anywhere else but on locust eggs. They spurn manure.

Yet another fly, *Wohlfahrtia*, preys upon the locust and is a frightful enemy, laying not eggs but live maggots, on the body of the locust just below the thorax, and these, wriggling into the locust, eat it steadily until all is consumed within and only the shell remains.

In nature's pattern no creature triumphs consistently, not even these efficient little flies. The termite expert, Dr W. G. H. Coaton, saw on the veld one day a thumbnail drama in which one of these flies and its larva played leading roles.

The flies were trying to deposit their maggots on some very lively locust hoppers but were having the worst of the game, for the hoppers were active and kept knocking off the wings of the flies with their hind legs. A wasp, however, had better luck, for it swooped down, stung and paralysed a hopper, and carried it to its hole near by. As is the habit of such wasps, it laid its victim down at the entrance while it descended first. In a flash a fly, which had been watching, dived smartly down and deposited its live larva on the unattended locust. Soon the wasp returned and dragged the hopper down. Dr Coaton waited. A moment later he heard a furious buzzing and the wasp reappeared at the mouth of its hole dragging the maggot, and with a deft kick it cast it out in a spurt of dust. Here it lay for a moment in the sand until some near-by ants pounced on it and bore it away.

A year ago locusts again invaded the Karoo. Main-line trains and motor-cars on the highways were halted by the hoppers. Men, aeroplanes, helicopters, poison, were all used to halt their march. It was nothing like the invasions of the past, but still it was an invasion. Once again scientists searched for the locusts' place of origin, asking why certain areas were favoured above all others, year after year, decade after decade. These were the *opbouer* – the build-up – areas, the plague spots where the solitary hoppers most often chose to breed and from where the locusts spread. One of the worst opbouer areas lay near Middelburg not far north of Cranemere, and another farther north and west.

Why? What have they got that other areas lack? What makes

a locust select a site – and select it does – one side of a fence and not the other? Lime in the soil? Soil structure? Shelter? Nobody knows for sure and everyone would like to know.

I picked up a solitary brown grasshopper in the veld as it flew up at my feet and looked at it, this tiny fantastic success of evolution, this member of a race two hundred million years old, still living in its magic metamorphic world.

I remembered our friend, Dr Charles Koch, the Viennese entomologist, who lives among the sand-dunes of the Namib Desert with its wonderful insect life, and who sees his landscape as populated not by man but by beetles. He envisages (over the dinner-table, it is true) a time when man has run his race and vanished from the earth, and the world is ruled instead by insects. Through the ancient devious pattern of their lives they would, in this future fantasy, have inherited the earth.

The grasshopper rasped my fingers and I opened my hand and watched it flutter away: and I wondered if its great-grandchildren would be locusts and what the future held for them.

16. 'Masters of Thirst'

When we were children the visitors to Cranemere ran a gauntlet of criticism of which they were happily unaware. If they were interested in certain things they were accepted and welcome at all times, but if they were not they were reckoned transients only, to whom was due courtesy and nothing more.

This attitude has not entirely disappeared. The number of things in which newcomers should – by our standards – be interested has, however, altered with the years, for bones and stones, butterflies, Bushman paintings and many others now swell the score, together with a great new interest: the plants of the Karoo.

These plants are very properly headed by our 'living fossils', relics of a flora which covered the world perhaps 150 million years ago and which still grow on the slopes of Honey Mountain. They are cycads, short, palm-like plants with a crown of long, spiky, blue-grey leaves. Botanists believe they have come down to us in much the same form as their ancestors, but what has fitted them to endure none can say. Perhaps they represent the end of a plant line, an experiment in evolution that went thus far and no further.

Our Cranemere species, *Encephalartos lehmannii*, stand – and they do, man-like, appear to stand – overlooking the valley, the Dig, the hunting grounds of Stone Age Man, the living fossils separated from the 'dead' by a quarter of a mile and a twenty-minute climb.

Their race is, of course, far older than that of man. Perhaps the little lizard that left its bones in the ripple shale below and the ancestors of the cycads existed together. It is certain they have persisted for many million years. I cannot bear to see visitors greet them with a shrug or lift of the eyebrows, for they are worthy of attention and respect. They are our most unusual plants, and in a plant world such as ours this is indeed a distinction, for our Karoo plants are among the most curious and interesting in the world.

As the seasons come and go we are continually reminded of this. Ours is a violent land and all things that live in it must endure and adapt. If this is true of the animals, it is truer still of the plants, which cannot move in search of food and drink and shelter, but are rooted for ever in one place. They endure what animals cannot and prosper in conditions that would kill a man; and they survive because of a number of devices – adaptations to the botanist, tricks of superlative cunning to the layman.

I think of them in a drought – and it is often drought. Plants, botanists tell us, take in moisture at the roots and give it off through the leaves. But in a Karoo drought they cannot afford to part with one drop of moisture, so some of them shed their leaves. We have lived through droughts on Cranemere where plant life seemed to stop, so utterly bare of foliage were the bushes and trees, appearing in the wide arid landscape as a multitude of worn-out brooms, big and small. Sometimes the witgat trees alone bore leaf; the other trees and shrubs were to all appearances dead; yet if we broke a twig, often enough a pale green would show within, the only green visible for many yards around. The thorn trees, the last of all to lose their colour, showed black and white, black trunks, dark branches, in a shroud of long white thorns. At such times we lived in a bright yet ghostly world somewhere between life and death. Some plants did die, but when rains came most of them miraculously returned to life. Blackened stems and twigs burst out in green buds, and not only the plants but we too began abruptly to live.

Other plants reduce evaporation by bearing only the minutest leaves, or leaves with their surfaces protected from evaporation by wax or resin or cork, or thick hairs which make a mat upon the surface, or leaves with deeply depressed stomata. Some fold their leaflets during the hottest time of the day. In others the stems do the work of the leaves. Some – the succulents – make reservoirs of their bodies – of their leaves, their stems, their roots – and looking at them, I am irresistibly reminded of a camel.

Some bury themselves in the soil with a window to let in the light.

Some grow special hairs that can absorb dew or mist, or have leaves arranged in such a way that the young shoots are protected, or shallow roots which absorb the slightest dew. Others have immensely long roots penetrating deeply into the soil, and some have a tremendous capacity to draw water from the earth.

Some, like the burrowing animals, live underground, throwing up leaves and flowers in good seasons and in droughts lying quietly and unguessed beneath our feet. Some, even in good seasons, send up no more than a few fingers, a tiny trail of leaves. Some, with contractile roots, pull themselves annually deeper and deeper into the soil away from the sun and burning soil surface. Others have long thin necks connecting their plump forms with the soil above.

There are a host of annuals. In a drought they are noticeably absent; but when the rain falls their seed germinates in days and they grow and flower at an astonishing rate, finally – as Wells and Huxley put it – retiring into drought-proof safes in the shape of seeds.

One might think that anything as delicate as a seed would have small chance in a desert world. But their delicacy exists only in our eyes and minds: they are immensely tough, and some have been known to survive for decades until, all conditions being satisfactory, they have germinated and grown strongly. My father used to tell the story of a hillside on Cranemere which, after rain, became covered with tall grass of a species he had never seen there before. The seed must have lain dormant there for many years.

The mesembryanthemum's family is a complicated and famous one of our arid areas, and we have many species belonging to it. Their flowers are often spectacular, but they are dear to botanists for other reasons, in particular for their method of seed dispersal. Many of the species are armed from birth against drought, for the seeds are released from the capsules only when these are moistened and so are scattered on earth usually wet and soft and suitable for germination.

244

The German botanist Dr G. Schwantes, in his *Flowering Stones*, taught me something of our mesembryanthemums that I did not know: that when the capsules of some species open, a few seeds 'take refuge' in pockets in the capsule. To him it is as if they are hidden by a special design of nature; and indeed the assumption seems inescapable that our vygies make doubly sure they shall survive – first by withholding their seeds until the rains, and secondly by keeping some in reserve.

In drought two little species of plants appear to take over the veld, for their small prickly forms are everywhere. Satan's bush, Maurice calls them. They belong to the genera *Blepharis* and *Barleria* of the Acanthus family, and their seeds, released in wet weather, are covered with hairs which swell and become slimy and so moisten and protect the developing embryo. The seeds are, in fact, equipped with their own watermaking device!

The genus *Pentzia*, according to the botanist Dr Rudolf Marloth, has the same incredibly efficient arrangement. But then the genus as a whole is a remarkable one. If I were asked which I thought the most important wild plant in South Africa I would not hesitate, as a Karoo-born, to choose *Pentzia incana*. It is a notable drought-resister and, on Cranemere, the principal fodder karoo bush, a low blue-green shrub with greeny-grey stems bearing tufts of tiny leaflets and little round yellow button-like heads of flowers. With its small leaves and its long wandering roots it survives rainless years, and it has in addition two other great virtues: it seeds very freely, and in a good season layers itself vigorously, sending out long thin branches that bend over to take root where they touch the soil. In drought this is a stubby bush perhaps five or six inches across and a few inches tall, perched in solitude on its own little mound of soil; at the end of three good seasons it may be a growth nearly a yard across and a foot high, formed of the original plant and its various offspring, all still firmly united.

In addition, it stands not only drought but considerable grazing, raising the best sheep and mutton in the world, Karoo farmers claim. This is not altogether an empty boast. The karoo bushes in general are aromatic and *Pentzia incana*, the sheep-bush of the farmers, is one of the most fragrant of all. The sheep that feed on it and its relatives have aromatic flesh, a subtle wild herb flavour that mutton from other parts lacks.

Epicures from many parts have sworn to the truth of this. Sir Percy FitzPatrick, that great old South African, used to tell the story of how, long ago on a voyage to England, he found Sir Abe Bailey, the millionaire, on board his ship. Sir Abe invited him to dine in his private dining-room, and he watched with interest the millionaire carving a small leg of lamb.

'Well, Fitz,' Sir Abe asked after a few mouthfuls, 'what do you think of my lamb?'

'There are only two places in the world this could have come from,' answered Sir Percy promptly, 'the Welsh mountains or the Karoo. I guess it is a black-head Persian from the Karoo.'

'You're right,' replied Sir Abe with delight. 'It is Karoo Persian.'

When he travelled he took with him live Persian sheep from the Karoo to be slaughtered when he needed them. He would eat no other mutton.

The bushes that produce such sheep are worth preserving.

Pentzia belongs to the daisy family, Compositae, which botanists today call Asteraceae, which is our most important family in the eastern Karoo. But what we notice most are not daisy flowers, not flowers at all in fact, but fatness – succulence – a characteristic belonging to many species of many families in our veld, including the daisy family, and which makes the Karoo the hunting-ground of botanists and succulent collectors. It has been claimed that in Southern Africa we have the richest assortment of succulent plants in the whole world.

Here on Cranemere, with our annual rainfall of some eleven inches, we have not as many succulents as the drier western Karoo, but we have plenty. Harry Bolus, the famous Cape botanist, who knew our eastern Karoo well, reckoned that nearly a third of all our flowering plants were more or less succulent.

There are the leaf succulents – aloes, cotyledons, crassulas, mesembryanthemums – which make storage reservoirs of their leaves, and many of these are beautiful as well as curious. We have several aloes on Cranemere, among them the tall handsome *Aloe ferox* with its long toothed leaves, and the tiny *Aloe variegata*, or guinea-fowl aloe, with its charming speckled leaves. This is one of the earliest Karoo plants ever cultivated abroad, for it grew in an English garden in 1720. The popular name for it is *kanniedood*, or never die, and die it seldom does except from old age. Marloth suspended one of these in air for four years and then planted it to find that it grew with a will. I once managed to kill one – with water.

Crassulas probably appear in more different forms than any other genus of succulents, and they grow in numbers on Cranemere, from the tall and beautiful *Crassula ovata*, a tree with fleshy silver leaves, to tiny flat species with rosy leaves, often growing in the shelter of other bushes. Those leaves are equipped to give new life, for a leaf shed and buried in the soil will make a new plant.

Sometimes we find them in small colonies, sometimes scattered; and once on the mountainside we collected ten different species in ten minutes. One of them was a gay sight, each fat green leaf outlined in strongest red. I uprooted it and took it to Pretoria, where it promptly lost its brilliant markings, becoming a uniform drab green; and so I learned the hard way that the vivid markings on many of our Karoo plants belong to the Karoo alone.

Many members of the Mesembryanthemum family – *Aizoaceae* – glisten in the sun. In *Mesembryanthemum crystallinum*, one of our common species, the epidermal cells of leaves and stems are swollen water containers, and these sparkle marvellously in sunlight. Very efficient containers they make too. I kept one plant I had uprooted for weeks without water before its water supply dried up and it finally withered.

It is the stem succulents, however, that are the most typical of Cranemere – euphorbias, stapeliads, and other such – all curious and some monstrous in shape, most of them leafless, the work of the leaves being done by the stems and so protected from excessive transpiration; or bearing leaves for a short time only.

This strange array of plants is headed, in numbers at least, by the ferocious euphorbia, *Euphorbia ferox*. It grows in quantity on Cranemere flats in low clumps of large, fleshy, many-angled fingers bristling along the angles with stout and steel-like spines, its form an almost complete safeguard against its enemies: drought and grazing animals.

The noors, as we know it, has need of its spines. Like all euphorbias, it has a milky latex, but unlike the latex of many, this is edible, and were it not for the spines it would never survive a single season. They provide an almost complete protection from animals, only goats and sometimes birds nipping out the tips between the spines; and once we found a tortoise had neatly sliced a stem in two and was eating away steadily at the broken end. The spines are poisonous, laming not only animals but people, and they are very strong. A surgeon operating on a Karoo child with a crippled ankle found a noors spine penetrating the bone and not blunted in the least.

Beneath the spines there is life – life for stock in a drought – and farmers have always known this. Sometimes they burned off the spines with a blow-lamp, but it was cruel, long, back-breaking work. On Cranemere Maurice made a better plan. The men cut long forked sticks, spiked on the fork a candlebush which burns like paraffin, and armed with these they moved quickly from clump to clump, burning off the noors spines in their little fierce blazing fires. After them came the animals, leaping hungrily on to the still smoking plants.

So men cheated the noors and saved lives. We do not know how many head of stock have been saved by the ferocious euphorbia in Cranemere's history, but it must number many thousand. Strangely enough, the euphorbia never seems to grow less. Its spiky form survives triumphantly, to be reviled in the good years and blessed in the bad.

The milk bush grows here, the *Euphorbia mauritanica* of botanists, with its long, smooth, fleshy, yellow-green stems, for ever imprinted on my mind, not by the actual bushes I have seen so often on the barren plains, but by their description in the first paragraph of Olive Schreiner's *Story of an African Farm*, weird and beautiful as they grew in the white light of the moon.

The strangest euphorbia on Cranemere does not belong to the plains but to the mountains, and it has the distinction of being one of the rare succulents of the world. It is the many-headed euphorbia, *Euphorbia polycephala*, locally called the mountain vingerpol.

It grows on the saddle of the high hill, the Rooikop, which stretches into the plains and catches the moist south-easters as they sweep unimpeded of a night over the veld. It is to the cool moisture of these winds that the euphorbia, we think, owes its existence, for it is found nowhere else on the farm. Before we collected it on Cranemere, it was known to botanists only from a small area, not fifteen miles wide, in the Cradock mountains to the north of Cranemere, and nowhere else in the world.

Sita and I climbed up to see the plants one wild day and the height, the far grey plains below, the wind and the clouds, made a memorable setting for these old monsters of the hills. Monsters they are, and many centuries old as we were to discover later.

We battled up the side of the ridge, and on to the top.

'What do you see?' said Sita.

I saw the stony top, the stunted bushes, the bending grass, the lichened rocks.

'Look again,' said Sita, and then: 'Touch it.' I bent and touched a rock and it was living. I must often as a child have ridden past these and thought them rocks and rocks alone.

The plants made great mounds of solid flesh, some six feet across, nearly two and a half feet high, some smaller. Several had grown round and enveloped stones and boulders, taking on their form. Their surface was like knobbly rubber, so hard it could bruise, green with a reddish tinge, and the stems were made up of segments, one on top of the other, like so many small knuckle-bones strung together. One great mound had a hollow centre and we could see the green crust of the euphorbia which seemed to have forced itself up and the white roots growing downwards into the ground.

There was nothing to indicate they were succulent; they seemed more like rock or solid wood, or so we first thought. But presently we saw that they were indeed living and giving life to other plants. On several clumps we found colonies of plants growing, none of them normally parasites – karoo bushes, wild asparagus, a little bulbous plant, and a number of small dark red haworthias not an inch high – and they were growing high on the euphorbias with no contact at all with the earth, their roots apparently absorbing nourishment from their hosts alone.

The euphorbia colony grew in a limited area, perhaps a third of a mile long and a couple of hundred yards wide. We explored it from end to end. Then we set about breaking off a few rooted bits. This proved quite impossible to manage in the big clumps, but finally we loosened a few pieces from the side of a smaller mound, and from a low clump which had been eaten down and was shooting again. We dug and cut with a curious feeling of unease, and finally of horror; and suddenly and at the same moment we knew why – it was like hacking at a body. We watched with distaste the milky juice exude – we who had handled euphorbias all our lives.

That night in bed I dreamed I was struggling with a giant vingerpol that bounced solidly and fleshily upon me. I wrestled with it to fling it finally with triumph on the floor. Next morning I saw it was my hot-water bottle.

Back in Pretoria, I showed the pieces to Dr R. Allen Dyer, the euphorbia expert. He named the species for me, and told me what we had guessed; that the vingerpol had grown upward above the layers of dust of centuries. Our clumps were many hundreds of years old.

The distribution of plants is always a fascinating thing, where some plants occur and why, and why one species should suddenly stop and another species take over. The distribution of our mountain vingerpol seems limited (although not as limited as botanists think), and so is that of species just beyond our borders. The Jansenville noors, with its tall angular stems which make the country south of us a nightmare landscape, stops just short of us, and so too does *Euphorbia obesa*, the living ball, the darling of succulent collectors throughout the world. I always hope to find it on Cranemere but am never likely to.

Among the great plant travellers are the stapeliads of the family Asclepiadaceae: yet strangely, having crossed half the world, they will often stop short and travel no farther. Alain White and Boyd L. Sloane in their great book *The Stapelieae* trace their journeys from 'somewhere in the tropical regions to British India', north, south, east, west – from Burma in the east to southern Spain and the Canary Islands in the west, from Afghanistan in the north southwards to Cape Point in the Cape of Good Hope. Their succulent stems in which they stored sustenance made them free of half the world, adapting them in the words of White and Sloane 'to venture forth into semi-arid lands'; and to set out 'to explore the drier parts of the earth'. There can be few descriptions of a plant race and its adventures more exciting.

As they travelled they changed in form. Those original travellers were carallumas, but as they advanced and explored new forms – new genera – were born. Somewhere in Kenya the first member of the genus *Stapelia* appeared, very like a caralluma but with small botanical distinctions. The genus is now to be found in its full pride in Southern Africa.

In the Transvaal three new genera appeared, but the great burgeoning of the race was in the arid parts of the Great and Little Karoo and Little Namaqualand, and in southern South-West Africa; and the Plains of Camdeboo became part of that Promised Land the stapeliads travelled through three continents to find, on a journey that began how many aeons ago we cannot guess.

In the Karoo often enough the stapeliads journey no longer, and it is surprising that members of this wandering race can settle down in one area, perhaps in one small locality, and go no farther. If one were anthropomorphically minded one could say they were content.

Many new genera of stapeliads are found in the Karoo, as well as those which were born in the north. Botanically they have several unique features, and their appearance, too, is unusual. Not that they look alike – many are completely dissimilar – but they all have angled succulent stems which contain a clear sap, and unusual fleshy flowers – fierce flowers they often are with their colours of liver and red, some spotted like the skin of a leopard, some banded, some knobbed, some hairy, some fringed with hairs. If their colour is often that of carrion, so too is the smell and this is design, unappealing but efficient, for they are pollinated by flies which obviously consider them as pieces of decaying meat. So good is their disguise that such flies sometimes lay their eggs within them, so dooming their maggots to a death of slow starvation. It is a grim little tragedy of the veld with the maggots always the losers. They all, too, have twin seed-pods, often smooth and long and mottled, which give them their common name of *bokhorinkies* – little buck horns.

On Cranemere we have collected stapeliads of seven genera bearing terrible names to the layman: *Caralluma, Duvalia, Huernia, Pectinaria, Piaranthus, Stapelia, Stultitia*. Of these, by far the showiest is the yellow-beaked stapelia, *Stapelia flavirostris*, with dark flowers marked with yellow and ornamented with silver hairs. This was one of the few plants that the Bushmen copied. An engraving of a plant identified as our yellow-beaked stapelia was found near Kimberley many years ago.

There are probably more species here, such as the warty-flowered stapelia, the hodge-podge stapelia, the gem-flowered stapelia, and others, and these wait to be discovered; but only when they flower are they noticeable, at other times being so well hidden among the rocks and bush as to be almost invisible. We come upon stapelias in the veld always with a shock of surprise and pleasure and always pause to examine them. Historically as well as aesthetically they are of interest. A stapelia, *Stapelia variegata* (now *Orbea variegata*), collected by a Dutch missionary, Justus Heurnius, was one of the first South African plants to become known in Europe, and how the seventeenth-century botanists must have rejoiced in its lurid beauty.

Many great names in South African botany are bound up with the genus, in particular that of Francis Masson, the Kew botanist and gardener who in the late eighteenth century collected plants at the Cape, among them thirty-six stapeliads, some of which have never been collected since and are still ardently pursued by botanists. Stapelias and springbuck may seem a world apart, but Masson is a famous link: he was the first great stapelia collector and possibly the first man to write of the springbuck in a book.

All the other stapeliads we have found have been small and nearly all have been hidden and protected by some means or other. The first we found was sheltered by a noors which, apart from its thornlessness, it resembled in miniature, and with which it mingled, deceiving, I am sure, even the goats upon the koppie. It was a little huernia with charming, neat, primrose-yellow flowers looking as if they had been made of wax, and a fine pair of horns.

One day I saw these burst and watched the seeds emerge, all tipped with tufts of silky hairs, which drifted about the plant and settled in a fine cloud around its base. A gentle shower of rain fell that day and two days later when I visited the plant I was astonished to see that every seed had germinated and the parent grew in a carpet of tiny green forms. Why, I asked myself, if the seeds germinated so well and fast was this not a huernia world? I soon knew why. That night a strong wind blew and next morning the little rootless forms had vanished. Only one remained. It had been caught in a crack between two stones and it alone remained of the lusty brood. I covered it with a leaf. A month later it was still there, well-rooted and growing.

Marloth wrote that this seed, which can germinate in twenty-four hours, can remain viable for ten years.

All the stapeliads have those same seeds with their parachutes of silky hairs and all are easily airborne. The seeds float until they rest against a stone, a bush, a clod of earth, and there they germinate; of these, usually only those that grow within a bush survive, for the others are eaten by all manner of stock and wild animals. Years ago we learned that to hunt successfully the little stapeliads on Cranemere we had to move at the pace of a snail, often on all fours, parting the bushes as we moved. There in the centre, often enough, would be the small, thick, angled forms of huernias, or sometimes duvalias, dwarfs that grew in fat, rounded, knobbly segments along the ground with small, solid, claret-coloured flowers. Once we found a plant like a long green worm flat along the ground and half submerged. It was a pectinaria, a genus that had evolved here in our own semi-desert.

One brilliant winter afternoon we were plant-hunting in the hard baked flats towards the mountains and the small boys were finding plant after plant of interest. They see them, I thought, because they are so much nearer the ground than we are, and I promptly set down my basket and knelt at the bush at my feet. I parted its short branches and there within, in its very heart, I saw a curious little plant with several short stubby succulent stems with a downward droop. To my knowledge I had never seen one like it before – and I never had, for that same plant, carefully transported to Pretoria, flowered in time for the botanists, and its flower with its small narrow maroon and yellow tube was new to science. Cranemere had possibly produced a new variety of *Pectinaria*.

We still hunt for some of the dramatic stapeliads, the hoodias with their marvellous rounded flowers, and the many-angled trichocaulons, and I would love to find these fascinating plants and still may, for they range widely. One Karoo hoodia, collected by the botanist Drège about 1830 and named after him, was lost for nearly eighty years until rediscovered by Dr Broom, who was no doubt as thrilled as if he had found a new fossil reptile.

Among the ironstone on the koppie slopes delicate pink and white flowers show after rain. They belong to the thick foot, *Pachypodium succulentum*, and a more deceitful plant it would be hard to find, for its fragile flowers on its few sparse prickly shoots give no indication of the giant stem below the soil. Sometimes in an old plant, or where the soil has washed away, a huge bald base shows from which the shoots emerge. This is a tuberous stem, the underground parts of which sometimes measure a yard across and weigh up to fifty pounds.

One day Reg Doe, who loves plants as well as birds, and I, climbing the koppies to the western boundary, stopped to admire the pachypodiums in bloom, the flowers with their narrow tubes flaring widely, the newly opened and unbleached a deep pink, the older almost white with a claret stripe running down the centre of each petal, and the long slender buds richly coloured. With the clusters of narrow green leaves and the shiny grey swollen stems below, among the rocks covered in orange, green, and smokey lichen, they were very lovely.

Presently we thought we would dig one out. Ten minutes' digging with a trowel, and we guessed for the first time that something unusual lay below the surface. We collected the gardener and a pick. An hour later we had laid bare a great subterranean mass, two and a half feet across, of intertwining stems fitting around and into one another like a giant three-dimensional jigsaw puzzle. They looked like big grey turnips and as we squeezed them the moisture dripped out. We were holding in our hands the most spectacular natural reservoir in the whole Karoo, the more efficient – from the thick foot's point of view – because it contained an acrid principle and was eaten by neither man nor beast. Thunberg saw and first collected this plant in 1794 south of Cranemere and I do not know that it has been much studied since.

Geraniums are to us those fine richly flowered and foliaged plants of our gardens. But some of the Cranemere members of the family are hardy and adaptable desert dwellers. Some have enormously swollen shiny stems bearing incongruously fragile flowers above. Sita and I once collected a little species, *Pelargonium carnosum*, with a gnarled swollen trunk not more than six inches high, and stubby branches carrying minute pink leaves. There can be few things tougher. I dug it out and put it in a note-book with other plants for reference. Months later I noticed a long pink shoot protruding from the book: it was the pelargonium growing vigorously. Planted in a tin, it continued to flourish, as it deserved to do. I once saw one of these succulent pelargoniums from the Namib desert. Water had been withheld from it for two years and it still continued in fine health.

Our most famous member of the family is the candlebush, *Sarcocaulon camdeboense* – fleshy stem – the delight of every child who has ever lived on Cranemere. Its stems and branches are covered by bark containing resin and wax which, besides protecting it from excessive transpiration, are very inflammable and when set alight burst into flame which consumes it fiercely. At one time my father used to have the dead bushes collected regularly and we would gather to watch the wagons return piled high with them; and for weeks our fires would spring into life with a blaze and flourish that not even lighted paper could give. We still collect the dead bush in the veld, but it is now mostly the work of the children, who light it ceremoniously round the fire of an evening.

It grows as a low prickly bush, the swollen stem and branches armed with long thorns, and the small green leaves in the axils of the thorns edged with ruby red. The flowers have five soft crinkled petals in palest yellow; and it is only the long beak-like fruit that shows it to be a member of the geranium family. Even the seeds are something special. They are equipped with twisted 'tails' and when rain falls the seed uncoils itself and digs itself into the soil with a spiralling motion.

The plants that store their water underground are legion, from the cabbage tree with succulent roots that saved many a traveller from death by thirst – and many a baboon too – to the bulbs and corms and tubers by the million. We are seldom conscious of their numbers for most of them are only obvious in bloom, and they may go for decades without flowering if conditions do not suit them. Attempting to dig out a small scilla that stood alone in a bare patch, we once emptied over it a bucket of water, laboriously carried across the veld. When we put in our spade and turned up the soil we found in that one spadeful of earth nineteen bulbs of various kinds, some large, some small, all perfectly healthy and sleeping away in the hot soil until all should be right for them to emerge. Not a leaf above the ground betrayed their presence.

A plant we sometimes try to dig up and replant in our gardens because of its beautiful iris-like flowers is *Moraea polystachya* or the wild tulp. It balks us continually, for in an old plant its corm lies perhaps a foot or more below the surface of the soil, and a foot of cement-hard Karoo soil is a protection indeed. It has what botanists term a contractile root by which the corm is annually pulled deeper and deeper into the earth. Many plants of the semi-desert have this type of root, and a life-saver it proves.

Drought is only one enemy of Karoo plants. The other is grazing animals, and they must always have been a menace for there were the wild animals in great numbers before our sheep and goats.

Their obvious protection is thorns and I am sure that there is no greater variety of these anywhere else in the world than among our Karoo plants. From the pretty little thorn vygie with its purple flowers and thin spikes, to the noors and the numnum with their swords, or the wild asparagus with its delicious fragrance and frightful daggers, they are all armed. Such plants give life to a host of others, and when we look into one we always find some half-dozen other species growing below and through it. Even the little thorn vygie, *Eberlanzia spinosa*, a few inches high, has its small guests growing between its hospitable thorny arms.

Some plants cheat the animals by an unpleasant taste, or poisonous sap or bark, and some by making themselves invisible. The manner in which so many of our Karoo plants merge with their background is still an unfailing source of wonder to me. Many we never see at all as individual plants. As a child, I used to ride over the veld and missed more – in one sense – than I can ever know. Now if I hunt plants I walk, or better still, I sit. It always happens that if I sit in one spot and look, I see things of which I never dreamed. Once I counted seventeen different species of plants within a yard of me. I had guessed at half a dozen.

Some plants are barely recognizable as plants at all, and these are the mimicry plants which are some of the most famous plants in the world. Is their disguise accident or not? Scientists still quarrel, some seeing it as design, others proclaiming that the very idea of disguise is purely anthropomorphic.

Here they are in the Karoo in the form of pebbles and stones and chips and gravel, the 'growing stones and flowering pebbles' of Dr Schwantes, and disguise or not, invisible they often are until they flower. Burchell was one of the first to note this. On a September day in the year 1811 in the solitude of the northern Karoo, in what is now the Prieska district, he found a stone plant and wrote the often quoted passage: 'On picking up from the stony ground what was supposed a curiously shaped pebble, it proved to be a plant, and an additional new species of the numerous tribe of *Mesembryanthemum*, but in colour and appearance bore the closest resemblance to the stones between which it was growing,' and he assumed that this juicy morsel had been so formed to escape the notice of wild animals. He named his find *Mesembryanthemum turbiniforme*, now renamed *Lithops turbiniformis*, and it remains one of our most famous mimicry plants.

The name *Lithops* is from Greek words meaning 'like a stone'. And the fact that they are has been proved over and over again. Stories are told of people, like Burchell, stooping to pick up a pebble and finding they are tugging at a plant. Some reproduce not only the shape of stones, but the weathered surface. Dr Schwantes tells the story of a lithops collector who showed the stone plants in his garden to a neighbouring farmer, asking him if he had similar plants on his farm; to which his neighbour replied tartly that he was trying to trap him: before him lay only stones.

We have never found a lithops on Cranemere, the nearest species that we know of being Burchell's lithops to the north and another species, *Lithops localis* var. *terricolor*, to the west, but we never give up hope.

Another famous mimicry plant grows not many miles west of

us, once known as *Mesembryanthemum bolusii*, now *Pleiospilos bo-lusii*. Its two fat leaves are brownish with a hint of green and have a surface like that of weathered stone, the whole plant appearing like two chunks of stone. It was discovered by Harry Bolus in the 1870s and created a furore among botanists and collectors, who were then prepared to pay a great price for this botanical wonder.

Another member of the genus, *Pleiospilos simulans*, was discovered in the Jansenville district a short way south of Cranemere. Perhaps we have walked over these two species many times on Cranemere and one day when they open their bright flowers we shall see them.

While hunting for them we did find a colony of small stone-like plants that greatly excited us, although we later found they were not classed as mimicry plants at all. They had large fleshy spatulate leaves of a brownish green, marked and pitted like the surface of the stones that lay around them on the koppie, and the likeness was complete. Jenks found the first one: and immediately we fell upon our hands and knees and searched for more. Once I put my hand on one before I saw it: and one with a tiny bud I located and from which I turned my eyes for an instant, vanished. Five of us searched an area two yards square and we never saw it again.

This proved to be *Aloinopsis rubrolineata*, like the lithops a member of the Mesembryanthemum family. In captivity it bloomed generously for us. Its flowers, pale yellow with every petal striped in red, were charming and conspicuous, and for the period of its blooming it, like other stone plants, discarded anonymity, and I find the reason for this mysterious.

As a child I used to look across the Plains of Camdeboo and think it the cleverest land in the world and its animals and plants of a wonderful intelligence. Great men of science have pondered that intelligence and the whys and wherefores of the patterns of plant and animal life in the Karoo – Burchell, Broom, Marloth; White and Sloane wondering at the reasons for plant migrations and the guiding force behind them; and

259

many others. Today one botanist, Dr Schwantes, sees in the marvellous arrangements of our Mesembryanthemum family a design inexplicable by science, and a boundary beyond which lies the realm of speculation, mysticism, and faith. The Karoo breeds few atheists. Perhaps this is accident and its plant and animal world, so bizarre and yet so methodical, plays no part in this at all; or perhaps, unguessed by its people, the pressure of a great plan is about them.

17. The Galgenbosch

Reading the old journals, I am always struck by their fine Swiss Family Robinson flavour. Here on the Karoo were a people marooned, not on an island but on a desert plain, and all they saw, and in particular the plants, they turned to their own uses, like the Bushman and the Hottentot before them; and in so doing made a thousand stories of adventure.

They dug the juicy bulbs on the hills and plains; the roots of the broad-leaved cabbage trees; succulents with dark-red, evil-smelling flowers; and they plucked the fat leaves of the trees – the elephants' food – and of the little vygies on the flats – and quenched their thirst. They devoured the thick oxalis roots; great bulbs as large as melons; little nutty bulbs at the base of slender twiners; like the great bustards, they ate the gum from the thorn trees; they made vinegar from the little fruits of the gwarri trees; they raised their bread with yeast made of a common succulent, and made coffee from the roots of the witgat. The oil from the kernels of the wild plum restored their hair and oiled their guns. The milk of the euphorbia mended their cups; the root of the wild hibiscus polished their floors.

From the commonest plants of the plains and the mountain kloofs they made beer, snuff, powder for their babies, soap, pins, rope, wagons, beams, furniture, coffins, and a hundred medicines.

The most famous plants were naturally those that quenched thirst, the 'water-roots', as the travellers termed them, the kambro of the Hottentots and farmers, and the *Fockea* of the botanists. For centuries they had made life possible for the Bushmen in drought time and had quenched the thirst of baboons and travellers alike. Some hunters, such as Gordon Cumming, swore that a knowledge of them was essential to anyone crossing the Karoo; and they must always have had a special value here on the Plains of Camdeboo, where in times of drought few streams and fountains flowed.

I do not believe that one Karoo farmer in ten today is aware of these plants, so rich in history and story, that grow beneath their feet. We search endlessly on Cranemere for them, but it is pure luck when we find them for they are some eight inches below the surface of the soil, the only clue to their presence being a few delicate shoots, and (as Le Vaillant noted) even these are often absent.

There are in all some eight or nine species of kambro. Our local species, *Fockea angustifolia*, was once used as both food and drink; and in parts it is still made into preserves by country folk, who use the scrapings as soap for it makes a splendid lather. Water is extracted by simply squeezing the pulp.

Perhaps we have as well *Fockea edulis* which has been collected close by. Its tuber can weigh fifty pounds and more!

The most famous species is *Fockea crispa*. Marloth records that a plant of this, found in the late eighteenth century, probably by two Viennese who were collecting at the Cape at this time, was sent to the famous garden of Schönbrunn near Vienna and described in 1800. It was of great interest to botanists, for they thought it the only survivor of an extinct species, until one hundred and six years later it was rediscovered in the Great Karoo near Prince Albert. Some news travels slowly. Many years later the Viennese water-root was still being described as the only existing specimen and the rarest plant in the world. 'Myths,' wrote Marloth, 'have a tough life.'

Many of the stapeliads are thirst-quenching, containing a cool, rather liquorice-flavoured juice. Among these are the ngaaps, species of *Trichocaulon* or hairy stem, found widely in the Karoo. Like many other stapeliads, they are of an astonishing appearance, succulent, ribbed and knobbed, and surprising things are claimed for them. If eaten before smoking, it is said, the coarsest tobacco becomes ambrosial – and how the early farmers must have loved them.

Marloth, plant-hunting in the Karoo, was once driven by hunger and thirst to follow the example of his Hottentot guide and eat a *Trichocaulon piliferum*. It removed the pangs of hunger most efficiently, he stated dryly: for a full day after he could eat nothing at all.

Growing all over the flats on Cranemere is a little twining autumn-blooming creeper with pretty flowers from palest pink to wine red. It is the baroe, one of the famous food plants of the Bushmen and early settlers, who relished its smallish bulbs. These smell like potatoes and have a good nutty flavour, and even today are hunted by all the children of the farm. Our species is *Cyphia undulata* and is widespread. I wonder what stories have been made around its slender form.

One October day we were hunting fossils near the Mountain Dig when we discovered one of the old Bushman plants, almost forgotten on the farm. We walked slowly, admiring the blue shale underfoot and the bare grey and white roots of the trees, often suspended in air where the bank had washed away. Presently among these we saw a strange sight, a round rock the size of a football *hanging* against the face of the bank; and as we gazed we saw there were not one but several. We crowded round curiously and only then did we see our rocks were tubers suspended from an underground vine two feet below the surface of the soil, and only visible because the outer layer of the bank had fallen away. The vine stretched for twenty feet and was well decorated at intervals with the tubers.

We pulled two down and took them to the farmhouse. The native women shook their heads over them. They had never seen them before, they said. Only Angelina, turning them over in her hands, remembered something of them. Once, she said, she was sure she had seen these used as food; and the fruit above the soil was a kind of grape.

She was right. I took the tubers to the Botanical Research Institute in Pretoria, and the botanists regarded them with astonishment, finally – with the help of a leafy shoot – identifying them as *Rhoicissus tridentata* of the grape family. It is closely related to a Transvaal species even now used by the blacks as a food for their infants.

A week later we visited an exhibition of rock art in Johannesburg, and taking up an entire wall was a great and miscellaneous Bushman painting. There before us, lifesize, was a painting of our subterranean tubers. The Bushmen had known and surely treasured them; and I have no doubt they once fed Bushman babies here on Cranemere.

The Bushmen used the seeds of a Karoo plant in the springbuck rattles they wore upon their feet when they danced. They called them kerri berries, and described the plant as like a pumpkin with red flowers and the seed as black and small. I longed to know what species of plant this was and once asked Dr Inez Verdoorn of the Botanical Research Institute, whose gentle exterior disguises a top-ranking plant detective. It was a problem after her own heart. With my slender clues she went to work, point by point, finally tracking down the plant and identifying it as our *Radyera urens*. But did the seeds really rattle as well as the Bushmen described? It was a final test. From a seed capsule in the Herbarium files she extracted the seeds, boiled and dried them, put them in a little box, and shook them. They rattled royally.

We do not know if the cycads on Honey Mountain ever fed the peoples of the Plains, but it is possible, for cycads were the bread trees of the Hottentots. Thunberg saw them growing 'in dry sterile places between stones', and described how the Hottentots scooped out the pith, buried this for two months in the earth, and then kneaded and formed it into cakes, which they baked in the embers.

The seeds, growing in a large, splendid, pineapple-like fruit, contain a highly toxic liver poison. Perhaps the Bushmen once used these.

On the southern slope of the Rooikop we once came on an elephant's foot. It is one of the most curious plants in the world, belonging to the yam family and, like it, edible. It grows about our hills like a squat grey elephant's foot covered not with hide but with the shell of a tortoise. Its woody body may be three feet or more high and two broad, and from the top of this spring a few slender twining stems. Burchell saw this on the hills round

Graaff-Reinet and described how the Hottentots ate the flesh below the 'shell', baking it in the embers of their fires.

One great elephant's foot, five feet high, planted on the grave of Sir Percy FitzPatrick in the Sundays River Valley of the Eastern Province, was destroyed by the Africans who over the years gouged out piece after piece as medicine. This was unusual, for it does not seem to have been generally used as medicine by the primitive peoples. But it is by modern scientists. Our elephant's foot is *Dioscorea elephantipes* (*Testudinaria elephantipes*), and its genus has recently leaped to fame for certain of its members – among them our elephant's foot – contain diosgenin from which cortisone is manufactured. This makes it one of the life-givers of the world.

It is very slow-growing indeed. A famous old Cape gardener, Auge, brought a specimen of the elephant's foot to the Municipal Gardens at Cape Town over two hundred years ago. Marloth, who over periods had checked the increase in diameter of a baby plant the size of an apple, reckoned by comparison that in Auge's day the plant must already have been several hundred years old. By such reckoning the old plant that stood on Sir Percy's grave must have been alive before William the Conqueror came to Britain; and the plant on Cranemere hill may have been a youngster when Jan van Riebeeck landed at the Cape.

The age of Karoo plants fascinated Marloth. The age of a big *gifbol* or poison bulb, *Boophane disticha*, was, he reckoned, greater than that of the oldest oaks in South Africa. It is not for longevity, however, that this plant is most famous, but as a bearer of life and death, and in these twin capacities it has been sought perhaps since Early Stone Age Man. Its bulb contains a virulent poison with effects similar to those of hyoscine poisoning, yet the dry scaly outside covering has a healing power that is unparalleled in all the salves of the Karoo.

Bushmen used the dried juice of the bulb mixed with the venom of snakes, and this, in a gummy state, they spread upon the heads of their arrows. It was a notable poison described again and again in the early journals, Thunberg maintaining that the strongest poison was found in the plants growing in the shade.

Modern science bears out the fact that this plant was used in Bushman poisons. When Lichtenstein – the same traveller who crossed Cranemere and thought it a desert – returned to Europe in 1806 he took with him some Bushman arrow poison. A century later the poison was analysed, giving a reaction similar to that of the poison of the boophane.

Who, I wonder, was the first person to find that the outer covering of this deadly bulb could heal, and how was this amazing piece of knowledge learnt? All the early colonists knew it. When I was a child Hannie Rafferty, our old housekeeper, kept a bottle in the pantry filled with thick papery scales with which she, and Fanny Palmer before her, treated all manner of boils and wounds. No cut, my grandmother affirmed, *ever* turned septic if bound with these, and she had incredible stories to tell of their efficiency. I never knew their name, and by the time I wished to learn it, nobody on the farm even remembered the healing bottle. Not for many years did I realize that the scales on the gifbol and my grandmother's cure-all were the same. And perhaps they heal the troubles of the mind. Watt and Brandwijk, authors of *The Medicinal and Poisonous Plants of Southern and Eastern Africa*, say that a Karoo remedy for the relief of hysteria and sleeplessness is to lie on a mattres filled with the bulb, and they add, 'It is thought that such a mattress should be used with caution!'

The boophane grows throughout South Africa but nowhere is it more spectacular than here, with its big fan of blue-green leaves and its single head of rosy flowers incongruous and lovely on the stony veld. Beautiful the flower-head may be but not innocent, for there are stories of people admiring the blooms too closely and for too long who have been mildly poisoned, suffering drowsiness and violent headaches.

The boophane has a slightly comic name. It is the only comic thing about it; even its spelling is unnerving, having changed

53 *For six generations Cape cobras have lived under Cranemere homestead.*

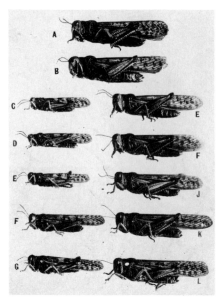

54 *The brown locust of the Karoo. A and B are the parents of the brood shown in part above, but the offspring differ. C and D were raised singly and became, to all appearances, grasshoppers. E and F grew up together and became typical swarming locusts. They also differed in colour.*

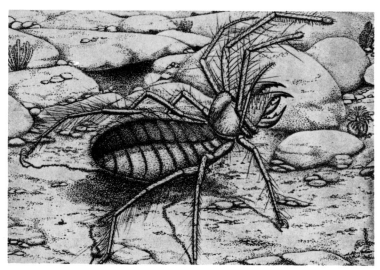

55 *A Solpuga female prepares to attack her enemy. From a drawing by Dr R. F. Lawrence.*

several times in the past, depending on whether the botanists at the time judged the name to be derived from the Greek word for a toad (*Bupho*) or from words for ox and murder (*Bòùs* and *oun*) – and whether signifying 'poisonous as a toad' or 'the killer of the ox'.

There was almost no disease or pain that the early settlers did not treat with local plants, and if today we look with astonishment at their cures for cancer or snake-bite or their like, they were nevertheless often clever and successful herbalists. They used plants of the Mesembryanthemum family for dysentery, gargles, and burns; the pretty little *Sutherlandia humilis* – the cancer bush – not only for cancer but for flu; the root of the gwarri for toothache; the cotyledons to remove their warts; the bitter karoo bush that poisoned their lambs to cure their gout; the sweet karoo for stomach-aches and to give them appetite; and the prickly *Blepharis capensis* for snake- and insect-bites; the malva to bathe sore eyes; tea made of the leaves of the rhenoster or rhinoceros bush to cure their indigestion. This low grey bush which sprawls over many of our Karoo mountains is famous in our family for easing dyspepsia which no drug can relieve. My mother used to keep a supply in bottles on her pantry shelf.

Species of the genus *Sceletium*, with leaves which when dead resemble skeletons, are still regarded as medicinal plants of the first order. The juice of *Sceletium strictum* is used today, as it was a century ago, for teething troubles in babies. *Sceletium anitomicum* of the Karoo was once the most famous member of the genus for the Hottentots, who pounded the plant and twisted it up like pig-tail tobacco, hawked it over the countryside, using it in place of money, and buying with it even cattle. It was much prized for very good reasons – when fermented it both quenched thirst and intoxicated.

One of the ngaaps, *Trichocaulon officinale*, is still a cure-all in the north-western Karoo. Cut into discs and dried, it is used for a variety of ills.

Medicine of the dried sap of the aloe must be almost as ancient as man. In the Karoo it is still used to cure many things, including toothache. It is a famous purgative. Once on Crane-mere we made rheumatism pills of the sap of the fierce aloe, *Aloe ferox*. Its fleshy spiked leaves were stacked in containers all about the stoep for many days. I no longer remember if they cured anyone, but I recollect they tasted as bitter as gall.

Once the Hottentots used the ash from the burnt leaves to give a kick to their snuff, and they probably still do.

All the children and baboons on Cranemere love this aloe when in bloom for the flowers hold a sweet liquid. Often near the mountain we find the flowers stripped and torn and lying about the plants and know the baboons have been sipping. I do not know if they have ever doped themselves but it can be done. The authors of *The Medicinal and Poisonous Plants* say the nectar is narcotic and tell the story of two African boys in the Eastern Cape who were admitted to hospital partly paralysed after suck-ing the juice. Their condition, said the doctor, was suggestive of curare poisoning!

The 'old people' were a tough breed and nowhere is this shown more clearly than in their medicines. I still treasure an old Cape remedy for dysentery I once found, not a plant remedy but of the Karoo. It read: 'Nothing is better than to drink old pontac – a wineglassful about three times a day: and to prevent the destruction of the coating of the stomach, the manure of a goat, strained through a rag, and a wineglassful of this taken several times.'

Like all the Karoo, Cranemere has its poisonous plants. Our most notorious poisoner is also our most charming, the wild iris or tulp, a slender plant some two or three feet tall with narrow ribbed leaves and six-petalled flowers of clear soft mauve touched with yellow at the base. In years of drought the plants do not bloom, but after good summer and autumn rains they stretch across Cranemere flats and across great areas of the Ka-roo – a sea of flowers, mauve or blue or silver as they move in the wind. They are then one of the great flower sights of the world, all the more remarkable for their arid setting.

Thunberg collected the tulp nearly two hundred years ago and named it *Iris polystachya*, later renamed *Moraea polystachya*, but it was not until many years later that its deadliness was known to scientists. It has killed thousands of head of stock, yet still the nature of the poison eludes scientists. At least four institutions in South Africa have studied the plant chemically, but the active principle remains a mystery.

On Cranemere the stock – cattle, sheep, and goats – know the plant well and avoid it, and there is seldom a fatality; or perhaps they become somewhat immune to the poison. One animal is said to eat it with perfect impunity and this is the porcupine. Oddly enough, it seldom chooses the plants growing in the thickest masses and this, say the people of the farm, shows the cleverness of the animal – it feeds only on the tulp plants standing isolated for then it knows no enemy can shelter near to catch it as it eats.

Most people who travel our Karoo remember the drought, the sand, the stunted karoo bush, the empty river-beds, a muted landscape of black and grey and dun bushes, red and cinnamon earth, and a white hot sky above. It was Lichtenstein who described the Karoo in such a drought as monstrous. And it was he who wrote of it a few days after rain as a country enamelled with glowing flowers of a wonderful fragrance, particularly delightful 'when after a calm day the sun declines, and the warm breath of the flowers rests quietly on the plain'.

All deserts have their blooming, but nowhere is it finer than on the Karoo. Now is the time we tramp the veld for days on end. It is true there are no times, even in the worst drought, when plants of interest are not found here, and we have had memorable finds in unexpected places. At such times we are continually struck by the 'little climates' in the veld and mountains, one existing in the coolness of a rock, another on the southern face of a hill, one in the lee of a fallen log, one in the overhang of a stream-bed, or in the heart of a bushy clump, and every one giving life to some plant that a foot away would find life insupportable.

But after rain the *whole* veld blooms. The common karoo bushes flower in yellow, strawberry pink and blue, the thorn vygies in purple, and the other vygies in every shade. Many grow in communities together so that there are not pinheads of colour but great bright stretches merging into one another, not the flaring oranges and yellows of the desert flowers of Namaqualand but richer and softer. Airmen flying over the Karoo compare it then with a giant Persian carpet, and from the air the Plains of Camdeboo must indeed have an Eastern richness.

Now plant-hunting becomes a heady joy. There are the big blue daisies, *Felicia ovata*, and their charming small relations, *Felicia muricata*; low bushes with flowers in red, orange, brick, smoke blue, and yellow, which hang their bell-like heads and these, lifted, reveal petals curled like half opened roses. These are all species of *Hermannia* and as far as I know they are never grown in gardens. There are the little suteras with pink flowers and the karoo violets, *Aptosimum procumbens*, which grow in mats upon the ground and are covered in blue flowers. This is one of the very lovely flowers of the Karoo. Gardeners have found seed difficult to germinate and the plants with their long drought proof tap-roots impossible to transplant. They often grow next to the pentzias with their bright yellow flowers and the two together, blue and yellow, are wonderful.

On the koppies grow the wild pinks, true *Dianthus*, flesh pink, deep pink, and white, deliciously fragile among the rocks and with a true pink scent. And among them all, on the koppies and the flats, are the bloubekkies, four-petalled flowers of bright blue-mauve on long whippy stems, that grow up through other bushes. They are a species of *Heliophila*, and are as distinctive in seed as in flower, for their slender seed-pods shine bright silver in early or late sunlight. There are nemesias and gazanias, and scores of other species, most of them bright and beautiful, and plants like the limeum with minute white flowers striped in green, exquisite but too small to be seen with ease. The springbuck find and strip them.

There are vygies by the score, and all the great succulent race, with brilliant flowers. The little kanniedood, or guineafowl aloe, with its speckled leaves and shortish spikes of salmon-pink flowers tipped with green, is one of the earliest Karoo plants ever cultivated abroad for it grew in an English garden in 1720. On the flats grows a pretty little aloe with greenish-yellow and orange flowers, *Aloe longistyla*; and right across Cranemere grows the tall *Aloe ferox* with big spikes of bright honeyed bloom that the children and baboons love. History records that these plants, so human in form, were often taken for Xhosas by the colonial troops in the Frontier Wars, causing much dismay. They still march splendidly across the veld.

Here and there are pelargoniums – wild geraniums to us – always interesting and sometimes beautiful. Among the mountain scrub we once found a scrambler with finest heads of mauve flowers, and along the cool rocky southern side of the hills pelargoniums with tiny scented leaves and thin pale flowers. On the flats, in a hard patch of burning soil, we found the most dramatic of all, a stocky little plant with a swollen, shiny, leafless stem bearing the most unlikely flowers – bright yellow and red, the calyx striped brown and yellow, and the long thin seed heads, borne together with the flowers, a lively purple. It was incredibly gay and gaudy.

In such a season we fill our cushions with kapok. This is the fluffy cotton-wool-like fruit of several small bushes of the genus *Eriocephalus*. They usually flower in profusion after good autumn rains, looking as if they are covered in tiniest snowflakes. They are a wonderful excuse for wandering over the veld for hours on end in the bright winter sun, armed with bags, and plucking the heads which come off in the fingers with a pleasant rasp. They are pungently and exquisitely scented, and so at the end of the day are we, and slightly sticky as well. I think then of James Kitching who, after searching the Karoo for fossils and tramping through the aromatic bushes, cannot – back in Johannesburg – bear to clean his boots and polish away the scent.

One spring Sita found, growing on the side of an ironstone koppie, some of the most unusual flowers she had ever seen, and

271

she talked of them for months. I knew why when I saw them, for they sprang out of the hardest ground like folds of blood-red velvet, and at first glance I doubted that they were plants at all. They were *Hyobanche sanguinea*, exotic parasites; and when crushed, the sap of those velvet spikes once made the ink of the early colonists. They christened it the ink plant.

One plant has drawn botanists from as far away as Cape Town, the ground orchid, *Eulophia hereroensis* (*E. pillansii*). In the beginning we were greatly surprised to find that an orchid grew on Cranemere at all, for to us orchids were exotic plants of the lush green places of the world, not of Karoo hill slopes. Many years ago Reg Doe and his wife, who were then collecting the orchids of the softer country to the east, spend a weekend on Cranemere and quite by chance, a couple of miles from the farmhouse, came upon a clump of eulophias. Reg did not find them again for twenty years. Nobody did. We quartered the section of the veld where they had been found, and we spent hours, as did visiting botanists and Reg himself, on the koppie slope, parting the bushes and searching between the stones, but in true Karoo fashion an individual plant not marked with a good beacon or stake is gone, often for ever.

It was Reg, properly enough, who rediscovered the eulophia. Three years ago he came to Cranemere again and wandered into the camp where he had found the eulophia so long before. He walked up the slope of the little hill and on the top sat down and prayed, 'O Lord, lead me to eulophia.' Then he got up, walked slowly over the crest down a little kloof, parted the thorny branches of a little bush in his path, and there in its heart was the eulophia!

Sita went up that afternoon to see his find. Reg was confident he had marked the bush clearly but it was nearly an hour before he located it. Like so many plant treasures on Cranemere, it was part of a greater clump, its ribbed leaves hardly showing in the wild asparagus, the kruisbessie, and the thick foot that enveloped it.

For two years we haunted the eulophia to see it bloom. Last

November it did: and in triumph Sita sent the flower to Anthony Hall of the Bolus Herbarium in Cape Town, who had himself hunted it in vain on Cranemere. It was only then that we knew for sure the identity of our orchid.

The flower is pale with bright yellow markings, and is not particularly beautiful. But the plant fascinates botanists because its distribution is the most extraordinary of any South African orchid known. It was first found – in our eastern Karoo – at Cookhouse, sixty miles east of Cranemere, and named *Eulophia pillansii* after Pillans who collected it. Later Anthony Hall concluded that it was a synonym of the older name, *Eulophia hereroensis*, based on a plant discovered previously just south of Windhoek in South West Africa, a thousand miles away. But so too, botanists learned, did it grow in the northern Transvaal, in Lourenço Marques in the east, in Bulawayo and Salisbury and north Bechuanaland, in climates ranging from near desert to tropical, and – and this titillated them still further – it did not apparently stretch in a sweep or band across the country but hopped across the continent leaving gaps of hundreds of miles between its various homes.

A few other plants of the Eastern Cape have this strange distribution, this way of apparently leaping across a countryside, and they are a continual puzzle and interest to scientists.

Three years ago heavy autumn rains were followed by a very mild winter instead of the usual heavy frosts and bitter cold. We revelled in the mildness, little thinking that the bulbous plants of the veld were too; but in late winter and spring we were startled to see the veld beginning to flower as we had never seen it before, and a host of things appearing that were completely new, not only to us but even to the shepherds in the veld.

First came the babianas, not the tallish ones of the gardens but little tufts of ribbed leaves bearing their sweet-scented mauve and white and purple flowers almost at ground level. On the koppies and flats we found slender plants with thin, grass-like leaves and greeny-white or yellow flowers veined with purple, the lower petals a gentle blue; and these smelt strongly, even by day, of lemon blossom. They were the wild gladiolus, *G. permeabilis* subsp. *edulis*, and very lovely. As fragrant, even when dried, were the little cyanellas. There were the green-lilies, the *Dipcadi*; and all the other green or green and white flowers of the veld, such as the eucomis, whose name means 'beautiful hair' and which bears a great tuft of leaves above its greenish inflorescence. Ours is *Eucomis autumnalis* subsp. *autumnalis* (*E. undulata*), delicately and beautifully formed, with wavy leaves, and it has been famous in horticulture for more than two hundred years, for about 1760 the plant was growing in England in the Chelsea Gardens. Those early plants were grown from seed probably collected not very far from Cranemere.

The albucas are much neglected green and white beauties, for some of them are beautiful in a strange, pale, rigid way. We collected many species that wonderful spring, but of these many have remained unnamed by the botanists. Some were giants, some dwarfs a couple of inches high, and one we found among the babianas on a koppie was a surprise. We found it in tiny clumps of hair-like, blue-green leaves, every leaf with a frivolous twist at the top, and two of these we dug up because of their curious leaves, not even guessing at their genus. We put them in a tin and forgot them, but two weeks later were surprised to see they had thrown up slender flowering stalks, laden with buds, and these opened into flowers of green and yellow, like snowflakes in shape, and sweetly scented. We thought how lovely these would look massed on some garden slope, and perhaps the gardeners of the future will know them.

Most albucas have the three inner petals closed and the three outer ones widely open, the inner ones forming a neat box which the bees sometimes force open. Children know them generally as Sentry-in-a-Box; and Africans use them still in parts to ward off evil spirits, and charming, humble, little good luck tokens they make.

We found lachenalias with greenish flowers streaked with red; and a little scilla with tiny insignificant blooms, its only interest purely snobbish for it is a relation of the famous English bluebells. Milk-white ornithogalums of various species grew here and there, chinkerinchees to us all; and I thought how Thunberg had known them as Tintirinties from the sound the stalks made when rubbed together.

Near the mountain we passed drifts of hesperantha, tall flowers, a dazzling white with yellow centres, the outside of the petals marked with a wine colour, so that in bud they were claret-coloured. They had a fine sweet fragrance and shone among the grass and bush. Harry Bolus, talking of the years that may pass while the monocotyledons of the Karoo remain in a dormant state, noted that a man might live seven years near a mountainside before seeing it covered with hesperantha in bloom.

Between Honey Mountain and the Rooikop grew a field of tritonias some eighteen inches tall, a bright clear orange and most deliciously scented. The botanists could not name this species definitely for me. A scented tritonia in itself is unusual, so it was with special interest that I read that Burchell, travelling north-west of Cranemere towards the Zak River, picked on a rocky hill a beautiful tritonia 'with orange-coloured flowers of a most delicate odour', and I like to think it was the same as ours.

Sita and Alex climbed the Rooikop that spring to find the top covered in fire lilies, *Cyrtanthus contractus*, tall plants with heads of glowing tubular flowers, the most dramatic and unexpected thing they had seen all that brilliant spring. Nobody remembered a field of fire lilies there before – although the bulbs were bigger than cricket balls and obviously very old – and nobody has seen them in numbers since.

On the plains and low hills around the farmhouse we found the little-men-in-a-boat, or the baboon-shoes of children, *Androcymbium melanthioides*. Stemless, they hugged the ground, the little flower-heads hidden in the great papery bracts of white striped with green or purple. It was Mary, smelling one of these, who was the first to find it scented, for none was generous with its scent: to find it, we had to bend our noses to the ground.

Often growing in company with the men-in-a-boat is a singular little plant of the genus *Massonia* of the lily family, and this we call Abraham's Book, presumably because of its two leaves like an open book which lie flat along the ground. We often see these here and there in the veld, but that spring they grew in many thousands and we stopped continually to admire them. They were very decorative with their leaves striped in a purple-brown, the rosette of tight green buds between the leaves opening into greenish-white flowers so flecked with pink that they appeared a rosy colour, the stamens loaded with pollen, and the whole cup filled with a thick sweet liquid.

In the sun this gleamed and the leaves glistened with myriads of tiny points of light so that often our eyes were drawn to them not by colour but by the glistening. Later the plants aged with considerable elegance, the leaves turning red and the flowers drying to silver-pink papery cups filled with shining brilliant black seed.

I dug up one of these massonias and took it back to the botanists in Pretoria, who identified it as *Massonia jasminiflora*, or possibly *Massonia grandiflora*, and for a year I thought no more of it. Then one day a botanist bearing a potted plant called upon me. Did I, she asked, recognize the plant? I did not. Two enormous dull green leaves hung flaccidly over the sides of the pot, and between them rose a small pineapple-like cone of flowers of a sickly green. I was certain that I had never before seen it, and definite that I had not collected it. But I had! It was my charming little Abraham's Book of the year before; and this was how it had reacted to potted life in a Transvaal city.

I was revolted, but the botanists were not, for this potted monster was now showing characteristics not only of a massonia but of another genus, *Whiteheadia*. Half a century ago a whiteheadia from an unspecified locality had been described in the Eastern Cape; and the plant had never been seen since. Perhaps this was it, and the whiteheadia had been no more than a cultivated massonia.

I look at the massonias on Cranemere now with added interest. I always knew they had character, but now they have mystery too. They are a very fitting link with Francis Masson, who never reached the Plains of Camdeboo but who left us records of our plant life on which we – and the world – still build.

Above all on Cranemere there are the trees, few on the plains and greatly treasured. They grow thickly at the base of the mountain, however, incomparable tough little trees – bloubos, gwarri, wild olive, spekboom, wild plum, and the like – and these once made a roof that the early trekkers who camped beneath them swore was watertight. Along the river-beds across the plains are thorn trees and karees, and on the plains and koppies grow the boerboons and the witgat trees.

The early farmers of our Plains trekked to the Boschberg for timber for their houses, but they used these local woods in many ways. They used the thorn tree, *Acacia karoo*, for almost everything. It is the tree of the Karoo, crowding along every river, stream, dam and pool, our most loved, most common tree, giving food to all manner of browsing animals and shade and shelter to men and animals alike. Travellers usually delighted in it. One traveller across the Plains did not: he lost an ox here which dashed into a thorn tree and was impaled upon its thorns. These can be up to six inches long and we have had visitors who collected them as the most exotic things they had seen in Africa. Le Vaillant, for one, used them instead of pins in his scientific collections.

The trees flower in midsummer at the hottest time of the year and are covered in mimosa-like flowers of a pure deep gold, which often so envelop the trees that they turn them into glowing mounds which scent the air far around, and attract insects by the million. 'The honey will be fat,' the Hottentots used to say, looking at the thorn trees in flower.

One thorn tree became a piece of family history. It was a big tree that stood in the deep soil of the cultivated lands below the farmhouse. Known as 'Oupapa's Tree', its spreading leafy crown gave shelter for half a century or more to men and animals. When Fanny Palmer was still active she used to take my elder sister, Iris, to the tree, and tell and retell its story.

Here, in the days of the Boer War, George Palmer had hidden for two days with a Boer commando on his trail, for he was of some local importance and the Boers had set a price upon his head. Here, under cover of darkness, Fanny had brought him food which he had hauled up the tree with a rope; and here the third night she had brought his horse on which he escaped in mist and blackness to Graaff-Reinet.

It was a splendid story with a famous finish, for in the mist George had blundered into a neighbour's yard, his horse's hoofs had rung upon the cobbles, the light had streamed upon his face, and Briton and Boer had come face to face. The Boer had laughed a great laugh from the belly and grasped his rein and said, 'Come in, come in, my old friend; by night my guest, by daylight my enemy.' But by day George was galloping to Graaff-Reinet.

The karee trees, with their round crowns of yellow-green drooping foliage, were a welcome sight to the travellers who camped under them, and men named their farms after them right across the Karoo. The Bushmen used their wood to make their bows, and they had gentler uses too, for the last crook-maker in our countryside uses their wood to make his shepherds' crooks.

I have often wondered what it was that made Fanny Palmer, crossing the Plains with her cart and horses, know so instantly that she wanted Cranemere for her home, and sometimes I think the spekbooms must have been in bloom, for the old high-way ran for a short distance through these low trees. For most of the year they are drab with small fat leaves, their greatest beauty being in the often ruby-coloured trunks and roots; but after rain they burst into bloom, their small scented flowers massed on the trees and turning the bush for a short space a lilac rose. In the old maps the Rooikop was marked as Spekboom Kop and many travellers must have passed here with great pleasure when the trees were in flower.

Sometimes they must have stopped to pick the klapper – travellers still do although the tree is now protected – for the fruits, like inflated paper lanterns, are rose and mauve and apple-green and parchment-coloured, and a little tree blazing with its lanterns is enchanting.

Many plants on the Karoo give the feeling of great age, but none more so than the boerboons. They grow, sometimes singly on the slopes of the low koppies, or in denser bush at the foot of the mountains and along the mountain streams, low stubby trees with big crowns of dark leathery foliage, their trunks and branches covered in lichen, suggesting an antiquity that can impress and sometimes frighten. In late spring, after rain, a most extraordinary thing happens to them: their branches burst into fierce red, and the trees bloom with a splendour and abandon, each red cup of a flower, facing upwards in its cluster, filled with nectar, and drawing birds from far around. I am constantly surprised, spring after spring, that anything so old and sombre can show such life and ardent beauty; and I think every spring how some myth of death and life, Bushman or pre-Bushman, might once have been made about this tree. Botanists know our boerboon as *Schotia afra*, and Burchell collected it on the Plains of Camdeboo a century and a half ago.

It was Burchell who described one of the most typical of all the plants of the Karoo – of all the desert regions of South Africa – the witgat trees. These stand, sometimes with a single trunk, sometimes branched, and neat browsed crowns, and the stems, as Burchell noted, appear to have been newly whitewashed. Our species is *Boscia oleoides*, a close relation of Burchell's tree. It never grows very tall – none of the wild trees of our plains do – but several of these trees on Cranemere give, like the boerboons, an impression of great age with their thick, twisted, white trunks and crowns of thickly woven shining branches. It was one of these that gave Cranemere its old name of Galgenbosch, and as a gallows tree it was known to every traveller and to all the Plains of Camdeboo.

This tree, which stood beside the old highway, gave rise to a strange story. Having gradually become more and more decrepit and ghostlike as the years passed, it died a few years ago. I kept a piece of the dead wood, grey and ribbed and of an unusual shape, upon my bookshelf, until one day, hearing of a psychometrist in Johannesburg, I took my piece of wood to her and asked her what she could tell me of its history.

Psychometry is the power of divining something of the history or nature of people, or things, that have been in contact with some object. Psychometrists usually 'divine' by holding the object in their hands and waiting quietly until impressions fill their minds, and these are sometimes from long ago. It is a most remarkable power and one that most people, even those deeply suspicious of the supernatural, credit and respect, perhaps because most of us can on occasions sense atmosphere, and psychometry seems to be this power greatly developed.

My psychometrist was an old Irish lady, very gentle and kind. I told her nothing whatsoever but put the wood in her hands. For a moment she said nothing, then exclaimed, 'Oh, my dear, someone died here and the passing was not easy.'

I told her then of the reputation of the tree. No, she said vehemently, nobody had been hanged on the tree: it was surrounded not with evil but with tragedy. I recounted the even older story of the traveller who had taken refuge in the witgat from a lion and here been killed: and she nodded. This, she said, could be so.

She held the wood again for some minutes and then, very quietly and naturally, began to describe to me the familiar plains, Honey Mountain to the north, and below the land sweeping away to the horizons, the space and loneliness and air of peace.

'Animals, animals, animals of all kinds; I can't count them all, thousands and thousands of them,' she said in a tone of wonder, and I thought of the great company of beasts that once were here and had gone.

'Do you know there is a grave near here?' she asked.

I thought of the graves we sometimes still find on Cranemere, piled high with stones and white and grey with lichen, but I could not remember one near the Galgenbosch. I shook my head.

'I think I am right,' the old lady said, and then more slowly, 'Yes, I am right. It *is* there.'

A few months later Maurice found it.

Maurice has now fenced off and enclosed the Galgenbosch, gaunter than of old but still upright. Whatever its past, it is the most famous landmark in all the Plains.

18. The Greatest of All

In midwinter we drove down to Cranemere, and as we climbed the mountains near Graaff-Reinet we saw a startling sight. Snow, which had fallen weeks before, was still lying in drifts, like brilliant streams, beside the road, and the mountain slopes were white.

At Cranemere a log fire greeted us and, crowded round it – feeding it candlebush and laughing and exchanging the latest news – we all began to talk about the snow. It was the heaviest fall in living memory and the biggest news of the year. Listening, it seemed that I had heard this hundreds of times before, this talk of the weather, of snow or hail or floods or drought or dust-storms, these things that had shaped our lives on Cranemere, and sitting there I began to think of the great stories of the weather we had heard from Fanny, and from my father and mother, and all that we had experienced ourselves, stories not of comfort and discomfort but of life and death.

On Cranemere the weather has been recorded in detail for over seventy years.* The first rainfall entry was made on January 2, 1891, and the records have been kept continually ever since in the long, flat, faded, official books which tell so much so briefly of the farm's history. Paging through the books is an experience for every Palmer of every generation, for a single entry can recall a drama, a childhood story, forgotten for many years. Sometimes the handwriting in itself gives a hint of the story of the farm. In September 1940 a new handwriting replaced for a while that of my father and Maurice. It was Sita's, for she and Maurice had just been married. In 1942 my father's entries stopped: in that year he died. In April 1945 there is Maurice's handwriting again – the Second World War was over and he was back from a prisoner-of-war camp.

*In 1986 for 95 years

The first rainfall register was started too late to record the fearful drought of 1877 and 1878. In Beaufort West a hundred miles west of Cranemere there was less than one inch of rain, and when my father was a boy men still talked of this drought and the suffering it brought to men and animals; and of the countless larks and other little birds it killed. It was too late to record the Big Snow of June 11 and 12, 1886, when the Plains were blanketed, the children on Cranemere fought with snowballs round the stables, and built a snowman that became legend. The farmers in the mountains, still talking of the snowstorm of 1869 when great flocks of sheep were buried, faced another catastrophe. Once again they walked over the backs of their sheep hunting for the little tell-tale lines of steam, the breath of the sheep, snaking up through the snow.

The year of the first records must have been a glorious one. Nearly twenty inches of rain fell, almost double the normal amount. What a year to start a rain record in a semi-desert!

The weather in the 1890s was on the whole good to Cranemere, and my father later remembered the fruitful decade with nostalgia, when as a boy and youth he began to discover the plants and animals and all the joys of the Karoo. But from 1903 to 1905 there was drought. A few inches of rain in a year on the Karoo can mean the difference between drought and plenty. In these years the rainfall averaged eight inches, some three inches less than usual, but for lack of those inches birds and animals died by the thousand. The blue cranes died. Decades later we knew Cranemere as a world of cranes, but my father used to say we knew nothing of cranes, we who had not seen them before 1903.

Up to this time nobody had ever seen Cranemere dam dry, and as the water sank Fanny watched it with terror, until it was no more than a pool. One evening when George was away she heard thunder to the north and watched the lightning, but not a drop of rain fell on her upturned hands. Sick at heart, she went to bed and fell into a sleep of exhaustion. At daybreak she got up and walked up alone to the dam wall, and there before her amazed eyes stretched a great sheet of water. The storm had fallen in the mountains and all through the night the water had swept down into the dam. She fell upon her knees and wept.

The year 1918 was another drought year. It was also the last year of the First World War. What the world needed was food. Wheat, wheat, the South African government pleaded, wheat and more wheat. What could Cranemere do? My father looked at the water in the dam. It was very low and every drop of this would be needed if a wheat crop were to be harvested, leaving none for other needs. Should they use it and plant wheat? Or hoard the water? It was a terrible choice. In the end they planted. All the farm prayed for rain but none fell. In time the last water was led. At least, said my father, looking at the green waving harvest, there would be a superb wheat crop. Once he had got a hundred bags from one bag of seed and this crop, with luck, would be as good.

Three weeks later rust struck the wheat and he reaped not one healthy ear.

This was the forerunner to 1919. The dam was bone dry. The rainfall for the year was 3.61 inches; for six months not one drop of rain fell, and the Karoo and Cranemere with it sweated, thirsted, and starved. It was a terrible period in the history of the farm. For years afterwards my father used that year as something by which to mark time. 'Before 1919' or 'after 1919', he used to say. He was not alone in this. His father's generation had spoken like him of the 1877 drought. Years later Maurice and Sita were to speak of the drought of 1947 as just such a mark in the life of Cranemere.

In 1926 the dam dried up again and the family was frightened. This was no longer a calamity to mark a century but something that could happen twice in a decade. Now there was talk of the dam silting, which was to echo down the years. This time there was a new horror. After 1919 my father had stocked the dam with fish which had increased enormously. Week by week the water sank until there was only one small muddy pool in the centre of the dam and into this were crowded the fish in a solid, living mass. The whole countryside turned out to catch fish. Men, women and children came in cars, carts, on bicycles, on horseback and on foot, with tin baths, buckets, jugs, sheets and bags, and they caught fish with their hands and bore them away by the thousand. For years afterwards the Pearston district lived on pickled carp from Palmer's dam.

When the pool finally dried up nobody could believe that any fish had ever been removed, for they lay in their tens of thousands, rotting and bleaching. And always the hot north wind blew over the empty dam towards the house. The stench was terrible. I was a child and I remember that my mother made me smoke. It was all she could think of as a disinfectant. For years afterwards the smell of cigarette smoke appalled me.

When a man lives through a drought he feels it can never end. On Cranemere we felt it would never rain again and that the veld would never know anything but dust and bones. I was one of the company of children on the farm who could not remember real rain; white or black, we knew only the menace of rainless years. In March 1928 the drought broke with nearly five inches of rain, a soft steady warm rain, and we were all a little crazed. We did not remember what it was to be wetted by steady rain and we ran out and stood with our faces and hands upturned and our tongues out and soaked up the rain in our hair and our clothes, and rushed into the puddles, and rolled and stamped and laughed and howled.

Would the dam be filled? During the first day of the rains it was all we asked. Would the dam overflow? Would it hold? Would it burst? My father was away, pacing the floor with at least four swollen rivers between him and the farm. Rob Rafferty was out all day and half the night patching a weak spot in the wall. All night long my mother and I, alone in the house, listened to the rain drumming on the roof and the roar of the distant water as it rushed into the dam.

I woke early in the morning and lay listening. Surely the roar was different, louder and nearer? I remembered nothing like it in volume or power. Then as I lay there came the pounding of heavy feet in the passage outside: the door flew open, and in burst Hannie Rafferty, her blue kappie askew, her round face red, and tears streaming down her cheeks. Her hands were clasped in front of her as if in prayer and she rocked backwards and forwards in a gale of sobs.

'What, what?' I squealed in my bed.

She threw up a hand. 'Listen, listen. It's the dam. Dear God! It's running over.'

Then I knew that the new roar was the sound of the water pouring over the spillway a few hundred yards away. The dam was overflowing and the drought was over.

All that day Rob and a gang of men worked patching and strengthening the wall. It was a splendid excitement for the children but not as wonderful as the water itself. We ran into the dam up to our knees and waists, wild with delight to feel the water slapping against our bodies. That night my mother and I slept with our coats and slippers under our hands ready to leap out of bed and dash up the koppie at the side of the house should the dam wall burst and the water rush down upon us: but it held as it has always done. ·

It was a wonderful year. Spring rains are rare in the Karoo but that year 2.30 inches fell in September. 'Warm steady rain,' my father wrote in the records. The veld bloomed. My father and I alone of the family were on the farm and we walked through the veld, at every footstep crushing a score of flowers. There was no bare space on the ground for every inch was covered; nor was there much green, for the leaves were smothered with minute petals of purple, magenta, wine, mauve, blue, yellow. The Plains were aglow with colour and saturated with scent. Such springs are rare. My father said he had only seen one like it and that when he was a child. I have never seen another as good.

Good and average years followed. In the autumn of 1940 it rained heavily. The blow-fly, the eggs of which hatch into maggots that eat the living sheep, revelled in the heat and moisture. 'A hundred cases a day and this is only the beginning,' wrote my father of the afflicted sheep.

Maurice could not get the poles and thatching grass for his first home and Sita's, close to the big farmhouse. The mountains were sodden and not even a truck could get up or down.

In 1941 the dam overflowed again with a great rush of water. In December, almost midsummer, a tremendous gale blew up, followed by showers of rain and intense cold, and the swallows died by the score. So did the Persian sheep. My father saw them dying in the veld and tore back to the house shouting for brandy. He could find only liqueur brandy, and with this and black coffee he and Sita rushed back and dosed the sheep – to thaw the fat round their kidneys, my father said. They saved many of them.

The day before Christmas that same year there was a snow-storm in the mountains and the wind which blew from them was ice-laden. The swallows died by the hundred. This was the Christmas that my father scooped them up by the basketful and spread them over the kitchen to warm.

We have had several cyclones in the history of Cranemere. One plucked a fine stallion out of the stable, dashed it upon the cobbles, and killed it. In 1942 a memorable cyclone swept across the farm close to the native houses. A little girl was playing in its path. Her father seized her and hurled her out of its track; it passed a few feet away leaving her unharmed. It tore past the big house, plucking up and crumpling the steel windmill on the hill, and across the dam. A native girl standing on the wall was paralysed with terror when she saw a tall brown funnel of water sweeping across the surface.

In May 1944 the dam overflowed again. It was the last time for a long while. Next year there were only seven inches of rain. 'Dam nearly dry – veld burnt black,' were laconic entries. In 1946 Maurice wrote: 'Drought conditions acute, losing stock daily,' and in February, 'Up to the middle of this month lost 33 per cent of weaned lambs, some ewes heavy in lamb, and several head of cattle.' In one small camp thirty-six springbuck – those tough, resilient, almost drought-proof buck – died. The veld was littered with corpses. When Sita went out on the veld it seemed to her that wherever she looked she saw only sheep that tottered and died. A hot wind came from the north and north-west and the dam dried up overnight. Sita remembers that twenty-four ostriches did a bizarre dance in the swirls of dust in the dam as the desert wind blew around them. Dust enveloped the world. Maurice and Sita could not even see where the lands had been.

In 1947 there were only eight inches of rain and the dam had been dry for a year, the longest time in the history of Cranemere. In May Maurice wrote in the records, 'Weaned all lambs to save the ewes. Veld absolutely black.' In August the sheep start-ed to die as soon as shorn. All lambing ewes strong enough to travel were sent to a farm in the Colesberg district where con-ditions were better. South of Cranemere a farmer lost 500 sheep in one day. 'Sell, man, sell,' his friends urged him, but he would not. 'It will rain tomorrow,' he replied. But it did not.

The drought broke in March 1948 and the Karoo lived again, but at a price, for the tremendous flow of water did great dam-age all over the country. The water made a hole in the shale bank under the wall of Cranemere dam but the wall fell in and filled it. The Palmers breathed again.

In the winter of 1953 snow fell on Cranemere itself and the koppies were white. The children on the farm had never seen snowflakes. 'Feathers, feathers,' cried Mary and Alex, and they danced with the piccanins. But the snow brought its own prob-lems. The goats, hysterical mothers always, rushed to high ground, abandoning their kids. A neighbour lost 500 sheep and the African and coloured people came out from Pearston with sacks and carted them away.

In October there were floods.

Hail can be the most frightening of all things. In November the heaviest hailstorm in living memory, with hailstones like cricket balls with jagged edges, stunned the farm. It fell for twenty-five minutes and at the end of it two and a half feet of hail lay packed along the walls of the house, every window on the side of the storm was shattered, and the wire gauze stripped off. Not a leaf was left on the trees; of a grove of mimosas on a neighbouring farm only burnt stumps were left and no trace of fences. The storm came out of a black sky in a great forked cloud stretching down to the earth, and where a prong touched nothing was left.

The animals sensed it and ran for shelter, but on the farm below Cranemere thirty-six Persian sheep were too slow and nothing was left of them but a mound of mangled bodies. Two natives who had crept into bushes for protection were later found stunned but alive. A neighbour was caught in his lorry. He crept underneath it but was forced out by the hail piling high around him and slowly enclosing him in a frozen box. His wife, waiting for him at home, had a heart attack.

In 1957, 1958 and 1959 there were no more than nine inches of rain a year. An old man in Pearston, sitting in the Magistrate's Court with closed eyes, was reprimanded sharply. 'I am not sleeping,' he replied with dignity. 'I am praying for rain.' What could any Karoo official reply to that!

In 1961 the rains did come and Maurice found the stock in the veld were dying. The bulbous plants, so many of which are poisonous, had grown tremendously and were killing sheep and goats.

In the years that followed the pattern repeated itself – drought, floods, disaster, drowned animals, wind, hail. In December 1962 a young neighbour riding on the veld was caught in a violent hailstorm. Friends found him tottering home, battered and terribly shocked. He had saved his life, as so many men of the Karoo had done in the past, by crouching on the bare veld with his saddle over his head.

In January 1963 four inches of rain fell and the grass on Cranemere, which had started to grow with the late spring rains the year before, stood like a field of corn.

Almost a year later rain fell again, the fierce heat of midsummer turning to icy cold, and frantic farmers across the Karoo fought to save their sheep and newly shorn goats from death by exposure. The animals died by the tens of thousands. So did the little birds that had taken refuge from the cold upon the ground and were drowned by the storm waters.

It grew warm again and the veld was filled with juicy food while the water lay in pools about the countryside. But the sheep still died. They were suffering the worst attack of internal parasites that Maurice remembered, and for days on end he stopped all other work to dose them.

'Pray for a drought,' said the veterinary officer sourly.

Then came the snow. It began to fall in June, not on the flats but in the mountains. It was the heaviest snowfall anyone remembered, and in the farms above us men and women were marooned for weeks and horses plunged belly deep through the snow to bring them food. Three of the Hottentot gipsies froze to death upon the road. A train in the mountains near Graaff-Reinet was lost for days.

Three sheep made headlines. Trapped in a mountain snowdrift for weeks, they yet survived. The warmth from their bodies melted the snow immediately around them and they moved backwards and forwards, in their little tunnel deep under the snow, for three foodless weeks. When they were rescued I am sure that the whole farm gathered round them to marvel that any living things could be so tough.

In August it snowed again, and this time Cranemere itself was white. It was a dazzling world. Maurice remembers it, however, for other reasons besides beauty. His goats had just been shorn and he and his men were out in bitter sleet and snow not only herding them into the sheds, but building their stone walls higher. Hysterical and silly, but nimble as always, the young goats climbed the stone walls of the shed and kraal to leap back into the snow.

In October it snowed again. As we came back from the mountains, huddled in the back of an open lorry, the flakes floated down upon us. Two days later on Cranemere stoep the thermometer registered 94 degrees in the shade!

Reading these records it is easy enough to believe – as the early farmers did – that it is the weather that brings all the good and bad things we know on the Karoo. Not everyone today believes

56 *David measuring the tuberous stem of a* Pachypodium succulentum. *It was nearly a yard across.*

57 *Sita examines a boulder-like specimen of the many-headed euphorbia, one of the rarest plants in the world.*

58 *The Galgenbosch.*

this. John Acocks, Karoo botanist, sees men more than weather as the makers of deserts in South Africa. He sees the karoo bushes on their little mounds of soil with the cinnamon-red earth between them too often shining like a bald head, and he trumpets that this was once grassland, and that its deterioration is the work of man. He points the march of the true desert into the Karoo and of the Karoo eastward and northward across the country, claiming that if nothing halts this march, in a hundred years time the Cape Province will be desert or near desert.

Men, he says, have done this, not drought but men with their sheep. The millions of wild animals of the past, the hordes of migrating springbuck, never, he claims, harmed the veld as do the sheep; rather, they ate the veld flat and moved on, leaving it to rest and revive. But not the sheep. He sees them, and in particular in the last century, nibbling their way across the farms of the Karoo, choosing the foods they liked best. They did not move on, as had the game. They grazed the same area year after year. At the best, the most palatable plants were destroyed, the grasses first of all; at the worst, the whole plant cover disappeared, and when this happened, he says, desert or semi-desert had arrived.

Gerrit Lodewyk Coetzee, who built Cranemere dam, was the first man on the Plains to live constantly on the spot with his flock. It was a great achievement – but if Acocks is right, he had set the Plains a new problem. I am certain he never guessed the possibility of it. Perhaps my grandfather never did. But my father did. He would, I think, have accepted the basic truth of Acock's theory even if he had not believed in this perpetual grassy paradise of several hundred years ago.

He knew our Plains well. He watched the bare places growing barer, the winds whipping away the surface soil between the bushes, the dust-storms like red fogs, the dust-devils spiralling across the veld, the rain-water swishing through the veld, bearing away surface soil and ripping gullies, the bitter karoo bush spreading. He knew the danger and he prepared to fight. But how to fight? What to do?

George Palmer had built the first fence in our countryside, which he had had to guard day and night from travellers and farmers who felt it a curtailment of their liberty and cut it when they could. My father built more. Long before our agricultural services stressed the importance of fencing, every spare penny on Cranemere went into hundreds of miles of fencing, to make camps and more camps; and into dams, water-troughs, silt traps, walls across the veld to hold flood waters and soil; into rooting out the weeds and burning the prickly pear. He worked for a life-time with commonsense and passion, and when he died I believe he had got to the point where he counted the new sweet karoo bushes yard by yard in the veld.

Conservation in a semi-desert needs both technical knowledge and money, and after the war there were both on a scale my father never knew. In the 1930s he had sold his wool for 6d. per pound. In 1952 Maurice was selling his for 125d. per pound, and there were farmers who sold theirs pound for pound. The Karoo was flooded with money; and if there were those who squandered it, there were many who returned it to their land.

One year long after the boom had finished I went back to Cranemere.

'Maurice,' I said the first evening, 'tell me, what is happening in the veld?'

He went away and fetched a pile of papers. They were details of the conservation scheme drawn up for Cranemere under the Soil Conservation Act, something my father had envisaged but never seen, and on which Maurice had been working. We read them soberly.

'Are they the answer?' I asked, and he replied. 'They are very good. But you know quite well in a big drought there *isn't* a fool-proof grazing scheme here. There isn't a fool-proof system for anything when there isn't any rain. Then we just try to stay alive any way we can;' and these were words I seemed to have heard all my life.

Sita said, 'Let's go and see what he's done in the veld. It's exciting. Let's show you where the money's gone.'

We went first to the Os Dam. It is a dam that my father built in 1924 just below the old highway, and in its forty years of life it has never once been dry. It is small and very deep, with knotty wild willow trees upon the bank, for ever, it seems, streaming in the wind. My father had made it and Maurice had converted the stream that filled it into a shallow vlei. Here had been the road the old travellers had reviled nearly two hundred years ago as waterless; and here for the last forty years water had lain through every drought!

We went north, and now my eyes searched continually for grass, not only the steekgras which sheep farmers dislike, but the softer and more palatable species. It had been a wonderful season. The grass waved across the Plains and in Pearston it had become an evening's jaunt for the people to drive to Galbosnek and see Maurice's North Devon cattle – the Devon rubies – belly and sometimes shoulder deep in grass. We climbed towards Honey Mountain. The rooigras, one of the great grasses of South Africa, grew in a red vivid cloud.

Had my father even known such grass? How did it compare with the grass that Van Plettenberg had noted? We did not know – and can never know for sure. But as I crossed the Koppie Camp I did see something new.

I remembered this as a hard-worked little camp with not a great deal of interest in its veld. Maurice had grazed it hard, then spared it for eighteen months during which time rain had fallen. There between the bushes was a mat of grass, and – I was fascinated to note – a little stapeliad in the heart of one bush in twenty.

We turned north-west to Koens Camp. I remembered it as a great, shiny, empty plate, one of my father's perennial head (and heart) aches. On the edge of this pan I had sometimes sat as a child watching the only living things upon it, the termites working along the edges, cutting the poor fringe of vegetation and helping the plate to spread. I looked now on a new scene, row upon row of American aloes, the great spiky desert plants seen right across the Karoo, with pointed fleshy leaves of fine blue-grey – dear to all manner of stock – fenced and self-contained upon the plain and flourishing.

'I remember,' said Sita, 'the day the men started work here. Maurice broke up the soil with a sub-soiler. It had a long tooth and in half an hour it was red hot. He put in a new blade. Then another, and another. I don't know how many he used that day. But I remember we ate red dust all day long.'

We walked through the aloes. They had held both soil and water, and between them were all the new things to which they had given life: the pioneer plants – the salt-bush and rush-and-tumble weed, and ganna – and then the karoo bushes, and finally the grass.

'Last time Maurice and I walked here,' said Sita, 'a quail flew up under our feet.'

I looked north towards the mountains. This land, beyond Cranemere's boundaries, had in my childhood been a jungle of prickly pears, imported nobody knows for sure how or when, which had invaded our countryside. It was a monstrous weed, for its fruits and flat green 'leaves' were covered in tiny, fine, blond thorns that most horribly killed the animals that hungered after succulence. I remembered that they had never spread across Cranemere boundary, and how my father had ranged up and down the farm, burning every invading leaf.

I turned and there, in orderly plantations across the veld, stood their spineless brothers, their large, succulent, leaf-like stems now as common a Karoo sight as the aloes and, like them, food, and soil protectors.

We walked south. I stopped to look at the wire-netting across the empty stream-beds to hold the silt, at the earth walls across the veld, and at the plants growing in the soil and moisture they had held. Many were grasses.

It was not only Maurice, I knew, who was doing these things. So were many of our neighbours, and of this we had very obvious proof. No longer did Cranemere dam fill so easily; more and more the rain in our catchment area was, by one means or another, being held where it fell.

We struck out towards the Maalgat, the Whirlpool, which in our childhood had been a great eroded hole in the bed of a donga that ran through the western end of the farm, and which I had not seen for fifteen years. I remembered it as the eeriest place I had ever known, with a deep rocky bottom into which twisted the pale roots of the trees that still clung about the rim. We used to talk in whispers, and at times we crossed our fingers when we crept under the thorny branches and looked down on to the stones and slime below.

I raced up and down the old stream-bed, and my astonishment grew. Fencing, and a caterpillar tractor throwing great earthen walls across the gully, had changed its face. The Maalgat had vanished. I could see no trace of where it had once been. Instead there lay a string of pools, ringed with karee trees, bloubos with the berries the birds and monkeys love, kruisbessie, sweet-thorns.

There were the sounds of bees and woodpeckers. There was the twittering of innumerable small birds. Half a dozen yellowbill duck and a pair of Egyptian geese flew up noisily as we called, and two large well-fed mountain tortoises ambled down to the river bank, hissing as we touched them, flopped into the water, and swam away. Man versus the weather, Maurice against the desert, had their rewards after all.

To the east lay Honey Mountain, and at its base our reptiles of so many million years ago; the Dig with its bones; and everywhere lay stones of men of Early, Middle, Late Stone Age – history, all of them. To the north stretched the remains of the historic highway. I stood in the bright light in the heart of the antique landscape and I thought that perhaps the greatest story of all was now in the making.

References

ACOCKS, J. P. H.: 'Veld Types of South Africa', *Bot. Survey of S.A. Memoir*, No. 28, Pretoria, 1953

ALEXANDER, ANNE, J.: 'A Survey of the Biology of Scorpions of South Africa', *African Wild Life*, Vol. 13, No. 2, 1959

ARCHER, W. H.: 'South African Tortoises', *African Wild Life*, Vol. 14, No. 2, June 1960

ARDREY, ROBERT: *African Genesis*, London, 1961

ASTLEY MABERLY, C. T.: 'The Extinct Cape Lion', *African Wild Life*, Vol. 8, No. 1, March 1954

ATHERSTONE, W. G.: 'From Graham's Town to the Gouph', *Cape Monthly Magazine*, July 1871

AUSTIN, OLIVER L.: *Birds of the World*, London, 1961

BACKHOUSE, JAMES: *A Narrative of a Visit to the Mauritius and South Africa*, London, 1844

BARBER, M. E.: 'Locusts and Locust Birds', *Trans. S.A. Phil. Soc.*, Vol. 1, 1879

BARNARD, P. J.: 'Phenomenon of Game Migration in the Kalahari Gemsbok National Park', *Koedoe*, No. 4, Pretoria, 1961

BARROW, JOHN: *Travels into the Interior of Southern Africa in the Years 1797 and 1798*, London, 1801

BATEMAN, JAMES A.: 'The Discovery of Elephant Remains in the Aberdeen District, C.P.', *Annals Cape Prov. Museums*, Vol. 1, March 1961

BATTISS, WALTER W.: *The Amazing Bushman*, Pretoria, 1939

BIGALKE, R.: *Animals and Zoos Today*, London 1939; 'Early History of the Cape Mountain Zebra', *African Wild Life*, Vol. 6, No. 2, June 1952

BLEEK, W. H. I.: *Reynard the Fox in South Africa*, London, 1864; *A Brief Account of Bushman Folk Lore*, Cape Town, 1875

BLEEK, W. H. I. and LLOYD, L. C.: *Bushman Folklore*, London, 1911

BOLUS, HARRY: *The Flora of South Africa*, Cape Town, 1893

BOONSTRA, L. D.: 'The Karoo Fauna and the Origin of Mammals', from 'Africa's Place in the Human Story', S.A.B.C., Johannesburg, 1953

BREUIL, HENRI: *Beyond the Bounds of History*, London, 1949

BROOM, ROBERT: 'On the Early Development of the Appendicular Skeleton of the Ostrich, with Remarks on the Origin of Birds', *Trans. S.A. Phil. Soc.*, Vol. XVI, Part 4, 1906; 'Fossil Hunting in the South African Karoo', *Nat. Hist.*, Vol. XXVII, New York 1927; *The Mammal-like Reptiles of South Africa*, London, 1932; *The Coming of Man*, London, 1933; 'A Few More new Fossil Reptiles from the Karoo', *Annals Tvl. Museum*, Vol. XIX, Part 1, 1937; 'On a New Type of Primitive Fossil Reptile from the Upper Permian of South Africa', *Proc. Zoo. Soc., London*, Vol. 108, Part 3, 1939; 'On some New Genera and Species of Fossil Reptiles from the Karoo Beds of Graaff-Reinet', *Annals Tvl. Museum*, Vol. XX, Part 2, 1940; 'Animals which Lived in South Africa Millions of Years Ago', *Outspan*, Feb. 26, 1943

BROWN, JOHN CROUMBIE: *Water Supply of South Africa*, Edinburgh, 1877

BROWN, J. R.; WHITE, ALAIN; SLOANE, BOYD; REYNOLDS, G.W.: *Succulents for the Amateur*. Pasadena, N.D.

BRYDEN, H. ANDERSON: *Nature and Sport in South Africa*, London, 1897; (ed.): *Great and Small Game of Africa*, London, 1899; *Kloof and Karoo*, London, 1889

BUFFON, G. L.: *Oeuvres Complètes de Buffon, Mammifères* Tome IV, Brussels, 1830

BURCHELL, WILLIAM: *Travels in the Interior of Southern Africa*, Vols. 1, 2, London, 1953

CAMPBELL, JOHN: *Travels in South Africa*, Vol. I, London, 1815

CATTRICK, ALAN: *Spoor of Blood*, Cape Town, 1959

CLARK, J. DESMOND: *The Prehistory of Southern Africa*, London, 1959

CLOETE, PIETER: *Reizen in Zuid Afrika*, 1776-1805, Vol. 4, The Hague, 1932

COMPTON, R. H.: 'The Flora of the Karoo', *S.A. Jnl. Science*, Vol. XXVI, 1929

CODD, L. E.: 'Drugs from Wild Yams', *African Wild Life*, Vol. 14, No. 3, Sept. 1960

COOKE, H. B. S.: 'Primitive Mammals and Primates of Africa', from 'Africa's Place in the Human Story', S.A.B.C. Johannesburg, 1953

CORY, G. E.: *The Rise of South Africa*, Vol. I, London, 1910

COURTNEY-LATIMER, M.: 'The Black Springbuck', *African Wild Life*, Vol. 15, No. I, March 1961

CRONWRIGHT-SCHREINER, S. C: *The Migratory Springbucks of South Africa*, London, 1925

CUMMING, ROYALEYN GORDON: *Five Years of a Hunter's Life in the Far Interior of South Africa*, London, 1850

CUTHBERTSON, MARGARET B.: 'African Game 400 Years Ago', *African Wild Life*, Vol. 3, No. 2, June 1950

DART, RAYMOND: 'The Proto-Human Inhabitants of Southern Africa', from 'Africa's Place in the Human Story', S.A.B.C., Johannesburg, 1953; Introduction to 'Africa's Place in the Human Story', S.A.B.C., Johannesburg, 1953; 'Africa's Place in the Emergence of Civilization', S.A.B.C., Johannesburg, N.D.; *Adventures with the Missing Link*, London, 1959

DE MIST, AUGUSTA UITENHAGE: *Dairy of a Journey to the Cape of Good Hope and the Interior of Africa in 1802, 1803*, Amsterdam, 1954

DE WET, W. J. AND VAN V. WEBB, D.: 'Behaviour of Hopper Swarms of the Brown Locust', *Farming in S.A.*, May 1952

DRENNAN, M. R.: 'The Prehistoric Inhabitants of the Cape', from 'Africa's Place in the Human Story', S.A.B.C., Johannesburg, 1953

DREYER, T. F.: 'The Prehistory of South Africa', from 'Africa's Place in the Human Story', S.A.B.C., Johannesburg, 1953

DUNCAN, F. MARTIN: *Wonders of Migration*, London, 1946

DYER, R. A.: 'The Vegetation of the Divisions of Albany and Bathurst', *Bot. Survey of S.A. Memoir*, No. 17, Pretoria, 1937

ELOFF, F. C.: 'Observations on the Migration and Habits of the Antelopes of the Kalahari Gemsbok Park', *Koedoe*, No. 2, 1959

FITZSIMONS, F. W.: *The Natural History of South Africa*, Vols. 1, 2, London, 1919

298

FITZSIMONS, VIVIAN F. M.: *Snakes of Southern Africa*, Cape Town, Jbg, 1962

FORBES, VERNON: *Pioneer Travellers in South Africa*, Cape Town, 1965

GILL, LEONARD: *A First Guide to South African Birds*, Cape Town, 1936

GODFREY, ROBERT: *Bird-Lore of the Eastern Cape Province*, Johannesburg, 1941

GRANT, C. H. B.: 'Levaillant's Travels in South Africa', *The Ostrich*, April 1957

GUGGISBERG, C. A. W.: *Simba*, Cape Town, 1961

HALLEMA, A.: Introduction to *The Cape in 1776-1777*, The Hague, 1951

HARRIS, W. C.: *Narrative of an Expedition into Southern Africa*, Bombay, 1838

HAWKES, JACQUETTA: *Prehistory*, London, 1963

HENRICI, M.: 'Fodder Plants of the Broken Veld', *Science Bulletin*, No. 142, 1935

HORSBRUGH, BOYD: *The Game Birds and Water-fowls of South Africa*, London, 1912

JACKSON, ALFRED DE JAGER: *Manna in the Desert*, Johannesburg, N.D.

JACOBSEN, H.: *Succulent Plants*, London, 1935

KING, L. C.: *South African Scenery*, London, 1942

KLINTWORTH, H.: 'Desert Encroachment over the Karoo', *Farming in S.A.*, Nov. 1948

KOKOT, D. F.: 'An Investigation into the Evidence bearing on Recent Climatic Changes over Sn. Africa', *Irrigation Dept. Memoir*, 1950

KOLBEN, PETER: *The Present State of the Cape of Good Hope*, Vols. I, II, London, 1731

LATROBE, CHARLES J.: *Journal of a Visit to South Africa*, 1815, 1816, London, 1818

LAWRENCE, R. F.: 'Observations on the Habits of a Female Solifuge', *Annals Tvl. Museum*, Vol. XXI, Part 2, 1949: *Die Spinnekoppe, Jagspinnekoppe, en Skerpioene van ons land*, Johannesburg,

1943; 'Dr. R. F. Lawrence Unravels the Spider's Web', *African Wild Life*, Vol. I, No. 3, 1947

LEA, A.: 'The Continuing Challenge of the Brown Locust', *Journal Ent. Soc. S.A.*, Vol. 21, No. 1; 'African Locusts and Their Control', Dept. Agric. Tech. Services, Pretoria.

LESLIE, T. N.: 'Rare Karoo Plants and their Cultivation', *S.A. Jnl. of Nat. Hist.*, Vol. VI, 1927

LETTY, CYTHNA: *Wild Flowers of the Transvaal*, Johannesburg, 1962

LE VAILLANT, F.: *Travels into the Interior Parts of Africa in the years 1780-1785*. Translated from the French. Dublin, 1790; *Histoire Naturelle des Oiseaux d'Afrique*, 6 vols., Paris, 1799-1808

LICHTENSTEIN, H: *Travels in Sn. Africa 1803-1806*, 2 vols., Dublin, 1812 and 1815

LIVERSIDGE, R.: 'The Wattled Starling', *Annals Cape Prov. Museums*, Vol. 1, March 1961

LIVINGSTONE, DAVID: *Missionary Travels and Researches in South Africa*, London, 1857

LUNDHOLM, B.: 'A Skull of a Cape Lioness', *Annals Tvl. Museum*, Vol. XXII, Part 1, 1952

MACOWAN, PETER: 'Colonial Stock Food-Plants', *Cape Monthly Mag.*, Aug. 1877

MCLACHLAN, G. R.: 'Birds of Prey', Dept. Nature Conservation, Report 12, 1955

MARAIS, EUGENE: *The Soul of the White Ant*, London, 1937; *My Friends the Baboons*, London, 1939

MARLOTH, R.: 'Mimicry among Plants', *Trans. S.A. Phil. Soc.*, Vol. XV, 1904; 'Further Observation of Mimicry among Plants', *Trans. S.A. Phil. Soc.*, Vol. XVI, 1905; 'Mesembrianthemum calcareum – a new Mimicry Plant', *Trans. S.A. Phil. Soc.*, Vol. XVIII, 1907; 'Notes on the Absorption of Water by Aerial Organs of Plants', *Trans. Roy. Soc. S.A.*, Vol. I, 1909; 'Some Adaptions of S.A. Plants to the Climate', *Trans. S.A. Phil. Soc.*, Vol. VI, 1889; *The Flora of South Africa*, Vols. 1-4, London, 1913-32

MARTIN, ANNIE: *Home Life on an Ostrich Farm*, London, 1890

MASON, REVIL: *Prehistory of the Transvaal*, Johannesburg, 1962

MASSON, F.: 'An Account of three Journeys from the Cape into the Southern Parts of Africa', *Phil. Trans. Roy. Soc.*, London, 1776; *Stapeliae Novae*, London, 1796

MENDELSSOHN, SYDNEY: *South African Bibliography*, Vols 1, 2, London, 1910

MERRIMAN, N. J.: *The Cape Journals of Archdeacon N. J. Merriman* 1848-1855, Cape Town, 1957

MOFFAT, ROBERT: *Missionary Labours in Southern Africa*, London, 1942

MOFFAT, JOHN S.: *The Lives of Robert and Mary Moffat*, London, 1885

MOORE, RUTH: *Man, Time, and Fossils*, London, 1954

MUSIKER, R.: 'Great South African Naturalists', *African Wild Life*, Vol. II, No. 1, March 1957

NEL, G. C.: *Lithops*, Stellenbosch, 1947

PALMER, E. M.: 'The Extinct Cape Lion', *African Wild Life*, Vol. 4, No. 1, June 1950

PAPPE, LUDWIG: *Florae Capensis Medicae Prodromus*, Cape Town, 1857

PETTMAN, CHARLES: *South African Place Names*, Queenstown, 1931

PLACE, ROBIN: *Finding Fossil Man*, London, 1957

POYNTON, J. C.: 'Bullfrog Guardians', *African Wild Life*, Vol II, No. 1, March 1957

PRINGLE, THOMAS: *Narrative of a Residence in South Africa*, London, 1835

PURCHELL, W. F.: 'New Arachnida collected by Mr S. C. Cronwright-Schreiner at Hanover', *Annals S.A. Museum*, Vol. 3, 1905

REYNOLDS, G. W.: *The Aloes of South Africa*, Johannesburg, 1950

ROBERTS, AUSTIN: *The Birds of South Africa*, London, 1940; *The Mammals of South Africa*, Johannesburg, 1951

ROBINSON, J.: 'The Trekbok', *African Wild Life*, Vol. 5, No. 1, March 1951

ROSE, WALTER: *Reptiles and Amphibians*, Cape Town, 1950

ROSENTHAL, ERIC: Introduction to *Cave Artists in South Africa*, Cape Town, 1953

RUBIDGE, SIDNEY: 'The Origin of the Rubidge Collection of Karroo Fossils', *S.A.M.A.B.*, March 1956

SARGENT, J. U.: 'Place Names and the Fauna of the Cape before 1800 A.D.'. Dept. Nature Conservation, Report II, 1954

SCHAPERA, I.: *The Khoisan Peoples of South Africa*, London, 1930; *The Bantu Speaking Tribes of South Africa*, London, 1937

SCHUMACHER, JOHANNES: *The Cape in* 1776-1777, The Hague, 1951

SCHWANTES, G.: *Flowering Stones and Mid-day Flowers*, London, 1957

SCLATER, P. L. and THOMAS OLDFIELD: *The Book of Antelopes*, Vol. III, London, 1897-8

SCLATER, W. L.: *The Fauna of South Africa*, London, 1900; 'Land Vertebrates of South Africa', *Science in S.A.*, Cape Town, 1905

SCULLY, WILLIAM C.: *Between Sun and Sand*, Cape Town, N.D.

SEELEY, H. G.: 'Some Scientific Results of a Mission to South Africa', *Trans. S.A. Phil. Soc.*, Vol. VI, 1889

SHORTRIDGE, G. C.: *The Mammals of S.W. Africa*, Vols. 1, 2, London, 1934

SKAIFE, S. H.: *African Insect Life*, London, Cape Town, 1953

SKEAD, C. J.: 'Mammals of the Uitenhage, Cradock, C. P. districts in Recent Times', *Koedoe*, No. 1, Pretoria, 1958

SMIT, BERNARD: *Insects in South Africa*, Cape Town, 1964

SMITH, ANDREW: *Illustrations of the Zoology of S.A. Mammalia*, London, 1849

SOGA, J. H.: *The South-Eastern Bantu*, Johannesburg, 1930

SPARRMAN, ANDREW: *A Voyage to the Cape of Good Hope from the year* 1772-1776, Vols. 1, 2, Dublin, 1785

STARK, ARTHUR C.: *The Birds of South Africa*, London, 1900

STEBBENS, ROBERT C. and EAKIN, RICHARD M.: 'The Role of the Third Eye in Reptilian Behavior', No. 1870, *American Museum Novitiates*, Amer. Mus. Nat. Hist. New York, Feb. 26, 1958

STEEDMAN, ANDREW: *Wanderings and Adventures in the Interior of Southern Africa*, Vols. 1, 2, London, 1935

STEVENSON-HAMILTON, J.: *Wild Life in South Africa*, London, 1947; 'Specimen of the Extinct Cape Lion', *African Wild Life*, Vol. 8, No. 3, Sept, 1954

STOCKENSTROM, ANDRIES: *The Autobiography of the late Sir Andries Stockenstrom*, Cape Town, 1887

STOW, GEORGE WILLIAM: *Rock paintings in South Africa*, London, 1930

SWANEPOEL, D. A.: *Butterflies of South Africa*, Cape Town, 1953

TEILHARD DE CHARDIN, P.: *The Appearance of Man*, London, 1965

TERRY, ROY W.: 'Man in Africa' (Institute for the Study of Man in Africa), Johannesburg, 1963

THEAL, GEORGE MCCALL: *History of South Africa*, 1795-1834, London, 1889

THUNBERG, CARL: *Travels in Europe, Africa, and Asia*, Vols. 1, 2, London 1794, 1795

TOBIAS, P. V.: 'The Very Ancient Human Inhabitants of Africa', from 'Africa's Place in the Human Story', S.A.B.C., Jbg., 1953

TOOKE, W. HAMMOND: 'The Star Lore of the South African Natives', *Trans. S.A. Phil. Soc.*, Vol. v, Part II, 1886-9

VAN BRUGGEN, A. C.: 'The Last Quagga', *African Wild Life*, Vol. 13, No. 4, Dec. 1959; 'More Cape Lions Discovered', *African Wild Life*, Vol. 15, No. 2, June 1961

VAN PLETTENBERG, JOACHIM: *Reizen in Zuid Afrika*, Vol. IV, The Hague, 1932

WATT, J. M. and BREYER BRANDWIJK, M. G.: *The Medicinal and Poisonous Plants of Southern Africa*, Edinburgh, 1932

WHITE, ALAIN AND SLOANE, BOYD L.: *The Stapeliea*, Pasadena, 1937

WHITE, A., DYER, R. A. AND SLOANE, B.: *The Succulent Euphorbieae*, Pasadena, 1941

WILLCOX, A. R.: *The Rock Art of South Africa*, London, 1963

WILLIAMS, C. B.: *Insect Migration*, London, 1958

Miscellaneous – *Eeufees Gedenkboek*, Pearston, 1859-1959

A Guide to the Vertebrate Fauna of the Eastern Cape Prov. – Albany Museum, Grahamstown, 1931

Palaeontologia Africana, Annals of Bernard Price Institute for Palaeontological Research, Vols. 1, 2, 1953, 1954

Flowering Plants, Vols. 1, 4, 6, 9, 11, 14

Files, Botanical Research Institute, Pretoria
A History of Scientific Endeavour in South Africa (ed. Brown, A. C.)
Cape Town, 1977
Original Title Deeds of Cranemere

Index

Aardwolf (maanhaarjakkals, *Proteles c. cristatus*), 168, 170
Aberdeen, 18, 123, 130
Abraham's Book, 276
Abraham's Kraal, 87
Acacia karroo, see Thorn trees
Acinonyx jubatus, see Cheetah
Acocks, John, 291
Agama atra, see Koggelmander
Aizoaceae, 247
Albany Museum, 75, 166
Albucas (*Albuca spiralis* etc), 274
Alcelaphus busephalus, see Red hartebeest
Almond stone, 116
Aloe
   ferox, 247, 268, 271
   longistyla, 271
   variegata, 247
Aloinopsis rubrolineata, 259
Alopochen aegyptiacus, see Egyptian goose
American aloe, 293
Anas undulata, see Yellow-bill duck
Anglo-Boer War, 36, 176
Angora goats, xv, 11, 290
Anomodonts, 92, 93
Ant-bear (aardvark, *Orycteropus afer afer*), 1, 167, 169, 173, 174, 180
Antidorcas marsupialis marsupialis, see Springbuck
Aonyx capensis, see Otter
Ape-man, 105, 115
Aptosimum procumbens (*A. depressum*), see Karoo violet
Arachnids, 222
Ardea cinerea, see Herons
Ardeotis Kori, see Kori bustard

Arrow-heads, 1, 63, 109
Asclepiadaceae, 251
Atherstone, Dr William Guybon, xv, 85, 86
Atilax paludinosus, see Mongoose
Australia, 46, 87
Australopithecines, 104
Australopithecus, 81, 103, 105
   afarensis, 104
   africanus, 104, 105
   boeisei, 104
Avocet (bont-elsie, *Recurvirostra avosetta*), 182, 183

Babianas (*Babiana patersoniae*), 273
Baboon (*Papio ursinus*), 158-67, 261, 268
Baboon spider, 228, 229
Baggage, travellers', 43-51, 53, 54, 56, 60
Bain, Andrew Geddes, 82, 83, 85
Bain, Thomas, 83-5
Bantu, 25, 26, 32, 35, 173, 215
Barber, Mary Elizabeth, 203, 235
Baroe (*Cyphia undulata*), 263
Barrow, John, 50, 64-6, 125, 127, 128, 130, 132, 155, 188, 202, 205, 231
Barry, Dr James, 55
Bat-eared fox (Delande's fox, desert fox, bakoorjakkals, *Otocyon m. megalotis*), 169
Battiss, Walter, 78, 79
Beaufort series, 93
Beaufort West, 87, 130, 148, 197, 283
Bernard Price Institute of Palaeontology, xvii, 113, 139
Bitis arietans arietans, see Puff-adder

Bitter karoo (*Chrysocoma tenuifolia*), 267, 291

Black-backed jackal (red jackal, *Canis mesomelas*), 169, 170

Black rhinoceros (*Diceros b. bicornis*), 45, 49, 129

Black wildebeest (white-tailed wildebeest, *Connochaetes gnou*), 122, 123

Bleek, Dorothea, 67-9, 72, 74, 177

Bleek, Wilhelm, 67-9, 177

Blepharis capensis, see Satan's bush

Blinkwater monster, 83

Bloubekkies (*Heliophila suavissima*), 270

Bloubos (*Diospyros lycioides*, subsp. *lycioides*), 277, 295

Blue crane (*Tetrapteryx paradisea*), 16, 29, 175-79, 195

Blyrivier, 7, 41

Boerboon (*Schotia afra*), 75, 187, 277, 279

Bokhorinkies, 252

Bokmakierie, see Shrikes

Bolleurs, John, 10, 11

Bolus, Harry, 43, 246, 259, 275

Bone artefacts, 110, 114-16

Boomslang (green tree snake, *Dispholidus typus*), 211

Boophane disticha, see Poison bulb

Border Cave, 107

Bore-holes, 18-20

Boschberg, 41, 45, 54, 55, 277

Boscia
  albitrunca, see Witgat
  oleoides, 42, 62, 243, 261, 277, 279

Boskop skull, 107

Botanists, 14, 42, 43, 53-5, 258, 262, 264, 272, 273

Bowker, Thomas Holden, 109

Brain, Dr C. K., xvii, 104

Bread trees, 264

British Museum, xv, 83-6, 139

Broken Hill Man, 106

Broom, Dr Robert, 43, 81-3, 87-101, 103, 104, 138, 168, 214, 222, 254, 259

Brown, Alfred 'Gogga', 87

Brown, John Croumbie, 11

Brown locust (*Locustana pardalina*), 237-41

Brown-hooded kingfisher (*Halcyon albiventris*), 186

Bruintjeshoogte, 1, 7, 8, 13, 28, 41, 43, 48, 51, 52, 54, 59, 90, 172

Buddleja (*Buddleia glomerata*), 167

Buffalo (*Syncerus caffer*), 45, 48, 113, 114, 118, 122

Bull-frogs (*Pyxicephalus* species), 219, 220

Burchell, William, 35, 41, 53-5, 71, 72, 125, 126, 128, 138, 258, 259, 264, 275, 279

Burchell's zebra (*Equus burchelli*), 130

Bushmen, 5, 9, 25, 48, 49, 52, 62-80, 102, 109, 125, 128, 140, 145, 175, 177, 179, 185, 195, 217, 230, 252, 261; affinity with animals, 69, 70, 145; arrows, 64, 65, 70; artefacts, 62, 63; beliefs, 71-4, 78; bows, 70, 145, 278; burial, 73; clothing, 64, 74, 145; folklore, 68, 72, 73, 175, 195, 217, 230; food, 63, 70-2, 75, 125, 145, 230, 261, 263, 264; houses, 62; origin, 63; paintings, 62, 68, 76-9, 139, 140, 264; poison, 64, 70, 265, 266

Butcher bird, see Shrikes

Buys, Coenraad, 42

Cabbage tree (kiepersol, *Cussonia spicata*), 256, 261

Calidris minuta, see Stint

Camdeboo, Plains of, 1, 2, 8-10, 14, 25, 27, 28, 40-55, 57-62, 81, 90, 117, 127, 134, 146, 147, 151, 155, 164, 173, 188, 251, 259, 261, 264, 270, 277, 279, 291

Camdeboo Mountains, 2

Campbell, Rev John, 52-4

Cancer bush (*Sutherlandia humilis*), 267

Candlebush (kersbossie, *Sarcocaulon camdeboense*), 248, 256, 282

Canis mesomelas, see Black-backed jackal

Cape lion (*Leo leo melanochaitus*), 37, 122, 132-40

Cape Town, 1, 26, 47, 53, 55, 56, 58, 61, 84, 123, 265, 272, 273

Cape vulture (Kolbe's vulture, gewone aasvoël, *Gyps coprotheres*), 197

Caracal c. caracal, see Lynx

Caralluma, 252

Carallumas, 251

Carfax, Patrick, xii, 78

Carissa bispinosa, see Numnum

Cave of Hearths, 106

Cercomela familiaris, see Familiar chat

Cercopithecus aethiops pygerythrus, see Vervet monkey

Chameleon (*Microsaura ventralis*), 215

Cheetah (jagluiperd, *Acinonyx jubatus*), 124

Cheek-lizard, 84, 91, 93, 98

Chelles-Acheul culture, 116

Chinkerinchees, 275

Chrysococcyx caprius, *C. klaas*, see Cuckoos

Chrysocoma tenuifolia, see Bitter karoo

Ciconia ciconia, see Stork

Circumcision, 33, 34

Cistecephalus zone, 93

Clark, Desmond, 109

Cloete, Pieter, 45, 122, 124

Coaton, Dr W. G. H., 240

Cobra (Cape cobra, yellow cobra, geelkapel, *Naja nivea*), xv, 1, 70, 154, 163, 207-10

Coetzee, Gerrit Lodewyk, 9, 10, 16, 24, 61, 291

Coetzeeberg, 7, 48, 65

Colesberg, 148, 182

Colonists, 3, 7-9, 44, 64, 65, 125, 128, 129, 131, 132, 138, 147, 150, 212, 235, 261

Compositae, 246

Connochaetes gnou, see Black wildebeest

Conservation, 292-95

Coot (African coot, red-knobbed coot, bleshoender, *Fulica cristata*), 183

Cope, Edward, 83, 87

Copland-Crawford, General, 139

Cormorant, 183

Cortisone, 265

Cotyledons, 246, 267

Cradock, 123, 131, 148, 182, 249

Crane (blue crane, Stanley crane, *Tetrapteryx paradisea*), 16, 28, 155, 167, 175-79, 283

dancing, 178, 179

Cranemere, 2, 5, 9, 16, 49, 61, 62, 76, 78, 102, 110, 117, 121-23, 125, 130, 131, 133, 140, 141, 144-46, 154, 167-70, 172, 175, 176, 178-88, 191, 192-97, 199, 202, 205, 207-10, 212-17, 219, 221-24, 227, 230, 231, 234, 238-40, 242-49, 254-59, 262-66, 268, 269, 271-79; dam, 10, 11, 14, 16, 17, 62, 176, 179, 180-84, 219, 284, 285-88, 291; dig, 112-19; house, 14, 15, 19, 207; museum, xii, 79, 150

Cranemere's sailors, xiv, xv

Crassula ovata (*C. argentea*), 247

Creatophora cinerea, see Starlings

Crithagra albigularis, see Seed-eaters

Crocuta crocuta, see Hyena

Cronwright-Schreiner, S. C., 144, 149, 152, 193, 224

Cuckoos

Didrik (diedrikkie, *Chrysococcyx caprius*), 189, 205

Klaas's (meitjie, *Chrysococcyx klaas*), 205

red-chested (Piet-my-vrou, *Cuculus solitarius*), 189, 205, 206

Cumming, Royaleyn Gordon, 5, 66, 125, 127, 128, 148, 150, 261

Curlew (wulp, *Numenius arquata*), 184

Cussonia spicata, see Cabbage tree

Cyanellas (*Cyanella lutea* var. *rosea*), 274

Cycads (*Encephalartos lehmannii*), 242, 264

Cynictis penicillata, see Meerkats

Cynodonts, 93

Cyphia undulata, see Baroe

Cyrtanthus contractus, see Fire lilies

Daisy family, 246

Dams, xvi, 10, 11, 13, 16, 17, 175-85, 219, 284-88, 291

Danaus, 152

Dart, Prof Raymond, 74, 103, 104, 115

Darwin, Charles, 82

Dassie (rock rabbit, *Procavia capensis*), 157, 198

David Konos, xii, 30, 61

David Pretoria, 30, 61, 208, 222

De Mist, J. A. U., 51

De Mist, Julie Philippe Augusta Uitenhage, 51

De Perthes, Boucher, 109, 116

De Stefano, Amelia, xii

Deacon, Hilary, xvii, 75, 120, 129

Deacon, Janette, xvii, 75, 120, 129

Dear Boy, 104

Dianthus, see Wild pink

Diceros b. bicornis, see Black rhinoceros

Dicynodonts, 92

Dig, 112-19, 121, 122, 123, 129, 141, 195, 201, 263, 295

Dinogorgon rubidgei, 96

Dinosaurs, 93, 190

Dioscorea elephantipes, see Elephant's foot

Diospyros lycioides, see Bloubos

Dipcadi, see Green lilies

Dispholidus typus, see Boomslang

Doe, Rev Reg, 186, 255, 272

Dog-tooths, 93

Doves, 186, 187

Drège, J. F., 42, 254

Droogerivier (Droge River), 9, 10

Drought, xvi, 3, 4, 6, 7, 8, 11, 13, 17, 41, 42, 243, 257, 261, 269, 283, 287, 288

Dubois, Eugene, 105

Duiker (*Sylvicapra grimmia*), 1, 156, 167

Dutch oven, 21

Duvalia, 252

Dyer, Dr Allen, xviii, 250

Eagles
  black eagle (dassievanger, witkruis-arend, *Aquila verreauxi*), 198, 199
  lammergeier (bearded vulture, *Gypaëtus barbartus*), 198
  martial eagle (lammervanger, breëkop-arend, *Polemaëtus bellicosus*), 198
  tawny eagle (kouvoël, *Aquila rapax*), 198

Early Stone Age, 108, 109, 115, 120, 265, 295

Eberlanzia spinosa, see Thorn vygie

Egret (little egret, klein witreier, *Egretta garzetta*), 186

Egyptian goose (Nile goose, kolgans, *Alopochen aegyptiacus*), 179, 180, 295

Eland (*Taurotragus oryx*), 41, 49, 122, 125-27

Elephant (*Loxodonta africana africana*), 48, 117, 123

Elephant shrew, 168

Elephant's foot (*Dioscorea elephan-tipes*), 75, 264, 265

Encephalartos lehmannii, see Cycads

Endothiodon, 93

Equus capensis, 130; *quagga quagga*, see Quagga; *zebra zebra*, see Mountain zebra

Erect ape-man, 105

Erinaceus frontalis, see Hedgehog

Eriocephalus, see Kapok

Euclea crispa, *E. undulata*, see Gwarri

Eucomis autumnalis subsp. *autumnalis* (*E. undulata*), 274

Eudinosuchus vorsteri, 92

Eulophia
    hereroensis, 272
    pillansii, 272

Euphorbia, 167
    ferox, see Noors
    mauritanica, 248
    obesa, 251
    polycephala, see Many-headed euphorbia

Euplectes orix, see Red bishop bird

Evolution, 82-101, 102-121

Explorers, 3, 43-56

Falco naumanni, see Lesser kestrel

Familiar chat (dagbreker, spek-vreter, *Cercomela familiaris*), 201

Faure, Prof J. C., 236, 237

Felicia
    muricata, 270
    ovata, 270

Ffrancolinus africanus, see Grey-wing partridge

Findlay, Dick, 76-9, 119, 139, 140, 171, 179

Fire lilies (*Cyrtanthus contractus*), 275

Fish, 284, 285

Fish Hoek, 107

FitzPatrick, Sir Percy, 246, 265

FitzSimons, Dr Vivian, xvii, 212, 219, 220

FitzSimons, F. W., 164, 169

Flamingo (greater flamingo, *Phaeni-copterus ruber*), 183

Fleas, 5, 44

Flies, 5

Floods, 4, 288, 289, 292

Florisbad Man, 107, 114, 117

Flowers, 269-77, 286

Fockea
    angustifolia, 262
    crispa, 262
    edulis, 262

Food, 20, 21, 70, 71, 125, 126, 131, 149, 194, 200, 235, 245, 246, 261, 262, 265

Fossils, xv, 68, 80-101, 102-08, 110, 111

Fountains (springs), 4, 65, 118

Frontier Wars, 11, 27, 28, 271

Frontiersmen, 8, 9, 42

Fulica cristata, see Coot

Galgenbosch (Gallows tree), 9-13, 42, 43, 49, 52, 54, 55, 58, 61, 133, 279, 281

Gazanias (botterblom, *Gazania kreb-siana* subsp. *krebsiana*), 270

Geckos, 214, 215

Gemsbok (*Oryx gazella*), 4, 122, 124, 127-29

Genet, small-spotted (*Genetta genetta felina*), 168

Gifbol, see Poison bulb

Gill, Dr Leonard, 196

Gladiolus permeabilis subsp. *edulis* (*G. edulis*), see Wild gladiolus

Golden mole (kruipmolle, family Chrysochloridae), 168

Gompou, see Kori bustard

Gordon, Col Robert, 45-7, 76, 128, 142

Gorgonopsians, 92, 93
Graaff-Reinet, xi, xv, 2, 7, 8, 13, 17, 22, 23, 38, 40-2, 52-4, 57, 58, 66, 80, 87, 127, 133, 134, 146, 147, 166, 231, 239, 265, 290
Graaff-Reinet Buck-hound Club, 125
Grahamstown, 41, 52, 55, 57, 59
Grass, 41, 47, 76, 233, 289, 293, 294
Grasshoppers, 237-39, 241
Great Fish River, 26, 48, 123
Great Karoo, 1, 2, 54, 84, 85, 251, 262
Green lilies (kurtrekker, *Dipcadi* species), 274
Greenshank (groenpoot-ruiter, *Tringa nebularia*), 184
Grewia robusta, see Kruisbessie
Grey, Sir George, 67, 235
Grey-wing partridge (grey-wing francolin, bergpatrys, *Ffrancolinus africanus*), 200
Grinding stones, 62, 63, 120
Ground squirrel (waaierstertmeerkat, *Xerus inauris*), 1, 154, 155
Guineafowl (crowned guineafowl, tarentaal, *Numidea meleagris*), 167, 200
Gwarri (*Euclea crispa, E. undulata*), 70, 261, 267, 277
Gyps coprotheres, see Cape vulture

Haarskeerder, 226
Hail, 288, 289
Halcyon albiventris, see Brown-hooded kingfisher
Hall, Anthony, 273
Hamerkop (paddavanger, *Scopus umbretta*), 184, 185
Hand-axe, 116, 117, 120
Hares, 156
Harpactira (baboon spiders), 228

Harris, Capt William Cornwallis, 59, 60, 125, 127, 136, 143
Hartebeest, 122
Hawks, 199
Hedgehog (krimpvarkie, *Erinaceus frontalis*), 168
Heliophila suavissima, see Bloubekkies
Hermannia, 270
Herons,
grey heron (*Ardea cinerea*), 181, 182
Hesperantha (*Hesperantha longituba*), 275
Heurnius, Justus, 252
Higgins, Albert, 87
Hippos (seekoei, *Hippopotamus amphibius*), 122, 123
Hobson, Edgar, 73
Homo
erectus, 105, 106
habilis, 105
sapiens, 62, 106, 107
sapiens neanderthalensis, 106
sapiens rhodesiensis, 106
sapiens soloensis, 106
Honey Mountain, xiii, 110, 111, 114, 117, 132, 179, 197, 199, 242, 264, 275, 280, 295
Honey-badger (ratel, *Mellivora capensis*), 171, 172, 204, 213
Honey-guide (greater honey-guide, *Indicator indicator*), 172, 204, 205
Hoodias, 254
Hopefield Skull, 106
Hospitality, 21-4
Hottentots, 25, 26, 35, 44, 45, 47, 48, 62, 63, 65, 66, 123, 138, 145, 158, 173, 194, 204, 231, 261, 264, 265, 267, 268, 277, 290
Huernia, 252
Hughes, Alun R., 104
Hunting, 70, 124-31, 173
Hunting spiders (diurnal *Solpuga* species), 1, 223-25, 227, 234

Hyena (spotted hyena, *Crocuta cro-cuta*), 122, 124
Hyobanche sanguinea, 272
Hystrix africae-australis, see Porcupine

Ictidosaurians, 93, 94
Ictonyx striatus striatus, see Muishond
Indicator indicator, see Honey-guide
Ink plant, 272
Iris polystachya, see Tulp

Jack (the baboon), 164-67
Jackals, 124, 168, 234
Jagspinnekop (*Solpuga* species), 223
Jansenville, 238, 259
Jansenville noors, 251
Java Man, 105, 106
Jenkins, David, xii, 30, 61, 208, 222
Jenkins, Denise, xii
Jenkins, Dylan, xii
Jenkins, Hayley, xii
Jenkins, Taryn, xii
Jenks (Geoffrey Jenkins), xiv, 30, 112, 113, 117, 120, 171, 259
Johanson, D. C., 104
Jubb, Prof Rex, xv

Kabwe Man, 106
Kambro (*Fockea* species), 162, 261, 262
Kannemeyer, Dr D. R., 87
Kannemeyeria, 93
Kanniedood (*Aloe variegata*), 247, 271
Kapok (*Eriocephalus aspalathoides, E. pubescens*), 271
Karee (*Rhus lancea*), 70, 277, 278, 295
Karoo, 1-14, 18, 25, 41, 48, 49, 58-61, 109, 110, 122-27, 131-35, 141-45, 147-49, 154, 158-62, 174-76, 179, 184, 189-91, 201, 222, 231, 237, 240, 242, 247, 257-62, 265-75, 277, 279, 283-93; bush, 2, 11, 47, 246,

270, 291, 294; fossil reptiles, 80-102, 111; geology, 81, 82, 89; violet (*Aptosimum procumbens*), 270
Kees (the baboon), 161-63
Kitching, C. J. M., 89, 90, 95
Kitching, Dr James, xv, xvii, 90, 91, 95, 96, 102, 104, 113-15, 118, 130, 139, 271
Kitching, James, 89
Klapper (*Nymania capensis*), 167, 279
Klasies River Mouth, 107
Klipspringer (*Oreotragus oreotragus*), 156
Knight, Cyril, xii
Knight, Iris, xii
Koggelmander (Cape rock agama, bloukop, *Agama atra*), 215
Kolben, Peter, 129, 158, 177
Kommadagga, 41, 54
Konos, xii, 30
Korhaans, 200
Kori bustard (gompou, *Ardeotis kori*), 199, 200
Kromme River, 181
Kruisbessie (*Grewia robusta*), 186, 295
Kudu (*Strepsiceros strepsiceros*), 41, 113, 117, 167, 168
Kuruman, 52, 57, 58
Kwane, 27

Lachenalias, 274
Landman (carpenter), 23, 160, 161, 174
Larks, 1, 154, 201
clapper lark (klappertjie, *Mirafra apiata*), 201
Late Stone Age, 62, 74, 75, 108, 109, 115, 120, 295
Lawrence, Dr R. F., xvii, 222-28
Le Vaillant, Francois, 47-50, 61, 65, 123, 125, 134, 147, 151, 161, 162, 196, 200, 201, 205, 231, 262, 277

311

Lea, A., xvii, 236
Leakey, Mary, 104
Leakey family, 106
Leavachia duvenhagei, 97, 99
Leguaans (rock leguaan, monitor, *Veranus albigularis*; water leguaan, monitor, *Veranus niloticus*), 216
Leo leo melanochaitus, see Cape lion
Leopard (*Panthera pardus*), 49, 124
Lesser kestrel (*Falco naumanni*), 199
Lichtenstein, Henry, 50-3, 64, 134, 266, 269
Limeum (*Limeum aethiopicum* subsp. *aethiopicum* var. *aethiopicum*), 270
Lions, 4, 41, 48, 49, 51, 56, 79, 113, 114, 124, 163, 280
Litakun, 52, 54, 55
Lithops, 258
  localis var. *terricolor* (*L. terricolor*), 258
  turbiniformis, 258
Little Fish River, 41, 48, 138, 231
Little Karoo, 1, 251
Little-men-in-a-boat (baboon shoes, *Androcymbium melanthioides*), 275
Little Woolly Sister (*Solpuga* species), 224
Livingstone, David, 56, 58
Livingstone, Mary, 58
Lizards, 154, 213
Lloyd, Lucy, 67, 74
Locustana pardalina, see Brown locust
Locusts, 5, 203, 230-41
London, 131, 138, 230
London Missionary Society, 52, 56, 58
Loxodonta africana africana, see Elephant
Lucy, 104, 105
Lundholm, Dr B., 137, 138
Lycaon pictus, see Wild dogs
Lynx (rooikat, *Caracal c. caracal*), 124, 170

Lystrosaurus, 92, 93

Maanhaarjakkals, see Aardwolf
MacOwan, Dr Peter, 43
Maggie, 30, 32
Malachite sunbird (jangroentjie, *Nectarinia famosa*), 187
Malva (kissieblaar, *Malva parviflora*), 267
Mammal-like reptiles, 82-5, 87, 92-5, 100, 102
Mantis, 1, 72, 145
Many-headed euphorbia (*Euphorbia polycephala*), 249, 250
Marais, Eugene, 158, 159, 161, 164, 221
Marloth, Rudolph, 42, 245, 247, 253, 259, 262, 265
Mason, Dr Revil, 108, 119
Masson, Francis, 253, 277
Massonia, 276
  grandiflora, 276
  jasminiflora (*M. bowkeri*), 276
Matjies River, 107
Mawby, Fanny, 12, 13
Medicinal and Poisonous Plants of South Africa, The, 266, 268
Meerkats, 154, 155, 212, 213, 234
  grey (slender tailed meerkat, graatjiemeerkat, *Suricata suricata*), 155, 156
  red (yellow mongoose, locally known as the hunting meerkat, *Cynictis penicillata*), 156
Melkrivier, 7, 22, 31, 41, 123
Mellivora capensis, see Honey-badger
Merino sheep, 11, 46
Merriman, Archdeacon Nathaniel James, 60
Mesembryanthemum, 258
  bolusii, 259
  crystallinum, 247
  family, 244, 247, 259, 260, 267

turbiniforme, 258
Mesozoic Era, 94
Microsaura ventralis, see Chameleon
Middle Stone Age, 107, 108, 109, 113-15, 195, 295
Milk bush, 248
Milleretta rubidgei, 95, 97, 100
Millerina rubidgei, 95
Mimicry plants, 258
Mirafra apiata, see Larks
Missing link, 103, 104, 105, 168
Missionaries, 52, 55-8, 252
Modern man, 62, 106, 107
Moffat, Mary, 55-8
Moffat, Robert, 55-8
Mole snake (*Pseudaspis cana*), 210
Mongoose, 156, 171, 212, 213
    large grey (Ichneumon, *Herpestes ichneuman cafer*), 171
    water (water muishond, kommetjiegat muishond, *Atilax paludinosus*), 171
Moraea polystachya, see Wild iris
Moselekatse, 57, 59, 60
Motacilla capensis, see Wagtail
Mountain vingerpol, see Many-headed euphorbia
Mountain zebra (*Equus zebra zebra*), 131, 132
Mousebirds, 186
Mrs Ples, 104
Muishond (stinkmuishond, Cape polecat, *Ictonyx striatus striatus*), 157
Mules, 35-7
Murray, Andrew, 57
Murraysburg, 98, 137, 138, 146

Naja nivea, see Cobra
Namaichthys digitata, xv
Namaqua sandgrouse (Namaqua partridge, kelkiewyn, *Pterocles namaqua*), 200

Namaqualand, 56, 88, 147, 150, 151, 251
Names (Xhosa), 30, 31
National suicide of the AmaXhosa, 28
Naturalists, 3, 41, 53, 59
Neanderthal Man, 106
Nectarinia famosa, see Malachite sunbird
Nemesias (*Nemesia* species), 270
New Bethesda, 89, 98
Ngaaps (*Trichocaulon* species), 262, 267
Nojoli, 26
Noors (*Euphorbia ferox*), 248, 253, 257
Numenius arquata, see Curlew
Numidea meleagris, see Guineafowl
Numnum (*Carissa bispinosa*), 257
Nymania capensis, see Klapper

Oil drilling, xii, xiii
Oil Rig, xii, xiii
Old highway, 40, 61, 134, 278, 279, 293, 295
Olea europaea subsp. *africana* (*O. africana*), see Wild olive
Olifant, 35-8
Opisthophthalmus karrooensis, see Scorpions
Orbea variegata (*Stapelia variegata*), 252
Orchid, 272, 273
Oreotragus oreotragus, see Klipspringer
Origin of mammals, 82, 88, 94, 95
Origin of man, 91, 94
Ornithogalum (*O. thyrsoides*), 275
Orpen, Joseph, 86
Orycteropus afer afer, see Ant-bear
Oryx, 129
Oryx gazella, see Gemsbok
Ostrich (*Struthio camelus*), 125, 130, 189, 190-96
Ostrich feathers, 16, 190, 191
Otocyon m. megalotis, see Bat-eared fox

Otter (Cape otter, clawless otter, groototter, *Aonyx capensis*), 171, 172
Owen, Sir Richard, 83, 87
Owls, 179, 201
Oxalis, 261

Pachypodium succulentum, see Thick foot
Palaeontology, 81-121
Palmer, Alex, xii, 115, 116, 208, 275, 288
Palmer, Bernadette, xii
Palmer, Clifford, 13, 14, 29, 189, 191, 197, 210, 219, 231, 244, 282, 283, 286, 287, 291-93
Palmer, Elizabeth Sita, xii
Palmer, Eve, xiv
Palmer, Fanny, 12, 13, 14, 15, 16, 20, 21, 22, 29, 31, 81, 88, 109, 119, 146, 170, 175, 176, 191, 227, 233, 266, 267, 278, 283
Palmer, George, 12, 13, 14, 16, 17, 20-2, 29, 109, 168, 176, 181, 191, 210, 278, 292
Palmer, Iris, xii, 16, 31, 278
Palmer, John, 12
Palmer, Katinka (Kate), 21, 23, 29, 192, 193, 208, 224, 267, 285
Palmer, Lindelize, xii, xvi
Palmer, Marianne, xi, xii, xv
Palmer, Mary, xii, 78, 275, 288
Palmer, Maurice, xi, xii, xiii, 15, 16, 29, 78, 112, 121, 140, 168, 169, 170, 180, 183, 197, 199, 202, 209, 210, 211, 214, 217, 222, 235, 245, 248, 281, 282, 287, 288, 290, 292-4
Palmer, Sita, xi, xii, xiii, xiv, xv, xvii, 21, 23, 29, 33, 78, 79, 111, 115, 116, 121, 123, 146, 169, 170, 171, 176, 180, 181, 182, 183, 187, 188, 202, 209, 214, 217, 218, 222, 228, 255, 271-73, 275, 282, 287, 288, 292
Palmer, Thomas, 12, 212

Panthera pardus, see Leopard
Papio ursinus, see Baboon
Pareiasaurus, 83, 93
  rubidgei, 98
Parietal eye, 214
Pearston, xiii, 2, 8, 13, 17, 35, 37, 40, 41, 65, 81, 82, 88, 89, 133, 174, 199, 222, 224, 289
Pectinaria, 252, 254
Pedetes capensis, see Springhare
Pelargonium carnosum, 255
Pelargoniums, 167, 271
Pelican (white pelican, rosy pelican, *Pelecanus onocrotalus*), 179, 182
Pentzia, 145, 245, 256, 270
  incana, see Sweet karoo
'People of an Earlier Race', 32, 140, 175
Persian sheep, 246, 287, 289
Phacochoerus aethiopicus, see Warthog
Phalacrocorax carbo, see White-breasted cormorant
Phoenicopterus ruber, see Flamingo
Piaranthus, 252
Pied barbet (bont houtkapper, *Tricholaema leucomelas*), 186
Piet-my-vrou, see Cuckoos
Pigeons, 187
Pipits (*Anthus* species), 201
Pithecanthropus erectus, 105
Platalea alba, see Spoonbill
Platrivier, 7, 9, 49, 205
Platycyclops crassus, 98
Pleiospilos bolusii, 259
  simulans, 259
Plesianthropus, 104
Ploceus velatus, see Weaver birds
Plovers, 184
  three-banded sandplover (drie-band-strandlopertjie, *Charadrius tricollaris*), 186
Poison bulb (gifbol, *Boophane disticha*), 34, 70, 265

Polecat, see Muishond

Porcupine (*Hystrix africae-australis*), 168, 269

Port Elizabeth, 16, 37, 41, 59, 134, 135, 137, 158, 164, 166, 181

Portulacaria afra, see Spekboom

Pratincoles (black-winged pratincole, *Glareola nordmanni*), 235

Prehistory, 80-121

Prickly pear (*Opuntia* species), 157, 158, 159, 294

Prince Albert, 84, 87, 90, 262

Pringle, Thomas, 55, 139, 147, 151

Procavia capensis, see Dassie

Pronking, 144

Protasparagus (*Asparagus*), 257

Proteles c. cristatus, see Aardwolf

Psychometry, 280

Pterochelidon spilodera, see Swallows

Pterocles namaqua, see Namaqua sandgrouse

Ptynoprogne fuligula, see Rock martin

Puff-adder (*Bitis arietans arietans*), 5, 154, 210, 211

Putterhill, Arthur, 87

Quagga (*Equus quagga quagga*), 41, 45, 119, 122, 124, 130, 131

Quail (Cape quail, African quail, kwartel, *Coturnix coturnix*), 200, 294

Radyera urens (*Hibiscus urens*), 264

Rafferty, Hannie, xvii, 23, 266, 286

Rafferty, Rob, xvii, 16, 155, 156, 180, 285

Rain, 4, 5, 6, 49, 74, 151, 185, 270, 285, 286

Rainfall records, 282

Ransom, Wilfred (Bunny), xiv

Raphicerus campestris, see Steenbok

Ratel, see Honey-badger

Recurvirostra avosetta, see Avocet

Red bishop bird (rooi kaffervink, *Euplectes orix*), 187

Red cat, 170

Red hartebeest (*Alcelaphus busephalus*), 123

Red jackal, see Black-backed jackal

Red men (rooimans, nocturnal *Solpuga* species), 223, 225-27

Redunca fulvorufula, see Ribbok

Religion, 72, 73

Rhinoceros, 123, 129

black, 45, 49, 123

white, 54

Rhodes, Cecil, 22, 24, 200

Rhodesian Man, 106, 107

Rhoicissus tridentata, 263

Rhus lancea, see Karee

Ribbok (mountain reedbuck, rooiribbok, *Redunca fulvorufula*), 113

Roberts, Deborah, xii

Roberts, Dr Austin, 136, 137

Roberts, Jacqueline, xii

Roberts, John, xii

Roberts, Linda, xii

Roberts, Mary, xii

Robinson, Dr John, xvii, 104

Rock martin (winterswael, kransswael, *Ptynoprogne fuligula*), 188

Rock rabbit, see Dassie

Rooigras (*Themeda triandra*), 293

Rooikat, see Lynx

Rooikop, 42, 62, 110, 117, 155, 249, 264, 275, 278

Rubidge, Bruce, xv

Rubidge, Dr Richard, 68, 96

Rubidge, Peggy, 95, 96

Rubidge, Richard, xv, 97

Rubidge, Robert, xv

Rubidge, Sidney, xv, xvii, 80, 82, 95-101, 102, 123, 214

Rubidge Museum, 80, 93, 95, 97-101

Rubidgea atrox, 97

315

Rush-and-tumble weed (*Salsola kali*), 294

Sable antelope, 59
Sacred ibis (*Threskiornis aethiopicus*), 182
Sagittarius serpentarius, see Secretary bird
Saldanha Bay, 106, 117
Salsola kali, see Rush-and-tumble weed
Salt bush (*Atriplex* species), 294
Sarcocaulon camdeboense, see Candlebush
Satan's bush (*Blepharis capensis, Barleria irritans*), 245
Sceletium
    anitomicum, 267
    strictum, 267
Schotia afra, see Boerboon
Schreiner, Olive, 1, 144, 240
Schumacher, Johannes, 45
Schwantes, Dr G., 245, 258, 260
Scilla, 256, 274
Scopus umbretta, see Hamerkop
Scorpions (*Opisthophthalmus karrooensis* – and many additional species of several genera), 1, 5, 167, 221, 222, 234
Scott, Sir Walter, 139
Scully, W. C., 151
Secretary bird (*Sagittarius serpentarius*), 196
Seed-eaters (white-throated seed-eater, sitkeel-sysie, *Crithagra albigularis*), 187
Seeley, Prof H. G., 83, 84, 87, 90, 93
Selous, Frederick Courtenay, 138
Sentry-in-a-box, 274
Shelduck (African shelduck, bergeend, *Tadorna cana*), 180
Shrikes,
    bokmakierie (kokkewiet, Janpierewiet, *Telophorus zeylonus*), 187

fiscal shrike (butcher bird, Jacky hangman, laksman, Janfiskaal, *Lanius collaris*), 187
Silver jackal (silver fox, draaijakkals, *Vulpes chama*), 169
Sissiewolle (*Solpuga* species), 224
Skead, C. J., xvii, 181
Skinks, 216
Smilesaurus ferox, 98
Smith, Dr Andrew, 151
Smith, Pauline, 1
Snakes, 5, 70, 163, 184, 196, 207-13
Sneeuberg (Snow Mountains), 7, 48, 52, 64, 76
Snow, 282, 283, 287, 288, 290
Snow Mountains, see Sneeuberg
Soga, Rev John, 26, 27, 34
Solpuga, 222-27
Somerset East, 2, 8, 13, 26, 27, 41, 42, 59, 128, 133, 136, 147, 212
Somerset, Lord Charles, 55
Southern Ape, 81, 103
Sparrman, Andrew, 42-5, 47, 128, 136, 138, 147, 150, 172, 196, 204, 231
Sparrows
    Cape (mossie, *Passer melanurus*), 186
    house (English sparrow, *Passer domesticus*), 186
Spekboom (*Portulacaria afra*), 167, 277, 278
Spekboomkop, 42, 278
Spiders, 189, 221-29
Spoonbill (*Platalea alba*), 182
Springbuck (*Antidorcas marsupialis marsupialis*), 1, 41, 45, 113, 122, 125, 141-53, 167, 253, 270
    migrations, 147
Springhare (*Pedetes capensis*), 168
St Acheul, 109, 116
Stanley crane, see Blue crane
Stapelia, 251, 252

flavirostris, see Yellow-beaked stapelia

Starlings, 186

wattled (locust bird, vaal-spreeu, *Creatophora cinerea*), 202-04

Steenbok (*Raphiceros campestris*), 1, 41, 122, 156, 167

Sterkfontein, 103, 104, 105, 106

Stevenson-Hamilton, Col J., 136, 168, 172

Stiletto, 115, 121

Stint (little stint, klein strandloper, *Calidris minuta*), 184

Stockenstrom, Andries, 147, 151

Stomorrhina, 239

Stone Age Man, 62, 93, 106, 108, 110, 113, 115, 119, 120, 122, 179, 242, 265

Stone artefacts, 108-10, 116, 117, 119, 120, 167

Stone plant, 258

Stork (white stork, groot wit sprinkaanvoël, *Ciconia ciconia*), 182, 233, 234

Stormberg series, 93

Story of an African Farm, 249

Story-telling, 37-9

Stow, George, 67, 68, 76, 96

Strepsiceros strepsiceros, see Kudu

Struthio camelus, see Ostrich

Stultitia, 252

Succulents, 246-55

Sunbirds, 187-89

Sundays River, 41, 48, 265

Sun spiders (solpugas), 222-28

Supernatural, 31-3

Suricata suricata, see Meerkats

Suteras (*Sutera pinnatifida*), 270

Sutherlandia humilis, see Cancer bush

Swaershoek, 7, 48, 131

Swallows, 188, 199, 287

cliff (familieswael, *Petrochelidon spilodera*), 188, 189, 287

Swan, 181

Swartberg, 2, 86

Swartkops salt-pan, 135

Swartkrans, 106

Sweet karoo (*Pentzia incana*), 267

Swellengrebel, Hendrik, 42, 45

Sylvicapra grimmia, see Duiker

Syncerus caffer, see Buffalo

Tadorna cana, see Shelduck

Tandjiesberg (Mountain of Teeth), 7

Taung, 103

Taungs Baby, 103, 104

Taurotragus oryx, see Eland

Terrible Eyes, 92, 93

Testudinaria elephantipes, see Elephant's foot

Tetrapteryx paradisea, see Blue crane

Theal, George McCall, 8, 35, 67

Themeda triandra, see Rooigras

Therapsids, 82

Therocephalians, 93, 94

Thick foot (*Pachypodium succulentum*), 254, 255

Third eye, 214

Thorn trees (*Acacia karroo*), 261, 277

Thorn vygie (*Eberlanzia spinosa*), 257, 270

Threskiornis aethiopicus, see Sacred ibis

Thunberg, Carl, 14, 42, 43, 136, 147, 152, 255, 264, 269, 275

Tingy, xii

Tobias, Prof P. V., 104

Tokoloshes, 32

Tortoises, 154, 216

geometric (tent tortoise, *Psammabates tentoria*), 216

mountain (leopard tortoise, *Testudo pardalis*), 217, 218, 295

padloper (*Homopus femoralis*), 216

water (marsh terrapin, *Pelomedusa subrufa*), 218

Transvaal Museum, xvii, 91, 222

Trapdoor spiders (*Strasimopus* species), 214, 228, 235

Travellers, 2-5, 8, 13, 21-5, 31, 40-61, 122, 134, 143, 261, 277, 278

Trees, 42, 117, 180, 277-81

Trek routes, 9, 40-2, 52, 54

Trekboers, 9, 10, 11, 122, 127

Trekbokke, 147-53

Trichardt, Louis, 42

Trichocaulon
  officinale, 267
  piliferum, 262

Trichocaulons, 254, 262

Tricholaema leucomelas, see Pied barbet

Tringa nebularia, see Greenshank

Tritonias (*Tritonia laxifolia* etc), 275

Tshiwo, 27

Tulp (wild iris, *Iris polystachya*, *Moraea polystachya*), 257, 268, 269

Turtle doves, 187

Uitenhage, 12, 41, 58, 164, 165, 166

Unicorn, 127, 128, 129

Uvarov, Dr B. P., 236, 237

Van der Byl, W., 87

Van der Post, Sir Laurens, 67, 123

Van Plettenberg, Baron Joachim, 46, 47·

Van Riebeeck, Jan, 26, 123, 132, 135, 190

Van Riet Lowe, C., 76

Veld deterioration, 291

Verdoorn, Inez, xviii, 264

Vermin, 199

Vervet monkey (*Cercopithecus aethiops pygerythrus*), 157, 158

Voëlrivier, 7

Voetgangers, 232, 234

Vogelsrivier, 7, 9, 41, 42, 48, 52, 62

Vulpes chama, see Silver jackal

Vultures, 1, 134, 197

Vygies, 270

Wagon road, 40, 42, 45

Wagtail (Cape wagtail, kwikkie, *Motacilla capensis*), 186

Wapad, 40

Warthog (vlakvark, *Phacochoerus aethiopicus*), 122, 212

Water, 4, 9, 11, 16, 17, 18

Water-divining, 18-20

Water-roots, 261

Weather, xvi, 3-5, 8, 49, 151, 189, 243, 273, 282-90

Weaver birds (masked weaver, swartkeel-geelvink, rietvink, *Ploceus velatus*), 187, 189

Wells, Michael, xvii, 75

Wellwood, xv, 80, 95, 96, 97

Wessels, Hans, 98

Whaits, Rev John, 87

White, Alain, and Sloane, Boyd L., 251, 259

White-breasted cormorants (*Phalacrocorax carbo*), 183

Whiteheadia genus, 276

Wide, James, 165, 166

Wild asparagus (katdoring, *Protasparagus* species), 1, 257

Wild Beast Heads, 93

Wild cat, 113, 124, 168, 213

Wild dogs (Cape hunting dogs, *Lycaon pictus*), 122, 124

Wild duck, 180

Wild geese, 16, 167, 179, 180

Wild gladiolus (aandblom, *Gladiolus permeabilis* subsp. *edulis*), 1, 274

Wild hibiscus, 261

Wild iris, see Tulp

Wild olive (*Olea europaea* subsp. *africora*), 71, 76, 277

Wild pigs, 45

Wild pinks (angelier, *Dianthus micropetalus*, *D. namaensis*), 270

Wild plum (*Pappea capensis*), 167, 261, 277

Wild pomegranate, 145
Wildebeest, 41, 113, 114, 124
Willcox, A. R., 78
Witch-doctor, 31
Witgat (Cranemere species, *Boscia oleoides* – Burchell's species, *Boscia albitrunca*), 279
Wohlfahrtia, 240
Worked stones, 108-10, 116, 117

Xerophytes, 243-58
Xerus inauris, see Ground squirrel
Xhosa (chief), 26

Xhosa affinity with animals, 35-7
Xhosa people, 25-31, 178, 184, 187, 201

Yellow-beaked stapelia (*S. flavirostris*), 252
Yellow-bill duck (*Anas undulata*), 295
Yellow cobra, 207-10

Zebra, 132
Zeyher, Karl, 42
Zwartberg (Swartberg), 2, 86
Zulus, 26